Supporting Paraeducators in Special Education and Inclusive Settings

Series Editor
Dee Berlinghoff, PhD

Supporting Paraeducators in Special Education and Inclusive Settings

Emily E. Sobeck, PhD
Franciscan University
Steubenville, Ohio

Sarah N. Douglas, PhD
Michigan State University
East Lansing, Michigan

Denise J. Uitto, EdD
(Retired)
Wayne College
The University of Akron
Orville, Ohio

Routledge
Taylor & Francis Group
NEW YORK AND LONDON

Instructors: *Supporting Paraeducators in Special Education and Inclusive Settings* includes ancillary materials specifically available for faculty use. Included are an *Instructor's Manual* and PowerPoint slides. Please visit www.routledge.com/9781630918071 to obtain access.

First published 2023 by SLACK Incorporated

Published 2024 by Routledge
605 Third Avenue, New York, NY 10158

and by Routledge
4 Park Square, Milton Park, Abingdon, Oxon OX14 4RN

Routledge is an imprint of the Taylor & Francis Group, an informa business

Copyright © 2023 Taylor & Francis Group.

Drs. Emily E. Sobeck, Sarah N. Douglas, *and* Denise J. Uitto *reported no financial or proprietary interest in the materials presented herein.*

All rights reserved. No part of this book may be reprinted or reproduced or utilised in any form or by any electronic, mechanical, or other means, now known or hereafter invented, including photocopying and recording, or in any information storage or retrieval system, without permission in writing from the publishers.

Trademark notice: Product or corporate names may be trademarks or registered trademarks, and are used only for identification and explanation without intent to infringe.

Cover: Tinhouse Design

Library of Congress Control Number: 2023938576

ISBN: 9781630918071 (pbk)
ISBN: 9781003526636 (ebk)

DOI: 10.4324/9781003526636

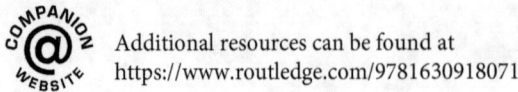

Additional resources can be found at
https://www.routledge.com/9781630918071

Dedication

To my husband and parents who have given me endless support and encouragement throughout all of my academic journeys; my children Levi, Tensley, Charlie, and Crew for their unending patience and love; and to God for His love, grace, and calling me to serve individuals with disabilities.
—*Emily E. Sobeck, PhD*

To my parents for instilling in me a love of education, and to John and my children, Harrison, Claire, and Ella, for their patience and support in all my scholarly endeavors.
—*Sarah N. Douglas, PhD*

To my husband, family, and professional colleagues who have supported my quest to continually serve future special educators.
—*Denise J. Uitto, EdD*

Contents

Dedication . . . . *v*
Acknowledgments . . . . *viii*
About the Authors . . . . *ix*
Preface . . . . *xi*
Introduction . . . . *xiii*

Chapter 1	Roles and Responsibilities of Team Members in Relation to Paraeducators. . . .	1
Chapter 2	Establishing Effective Communication and Collaboration With Paraeducators	17
Chapter 3	Introduction to Paraeducator Supervision.	37
Chapter 4	Supervision Responsibilities of Team Members.	55
Chapter 5	Paraeducator Training	77
Chapter 6	Common Challenges and Areas for Growth.	93
Appendix A	*Initial Practice-Based Professional Preparation Standards for Special Educators (K-12)*	*107*
Appendix B	*Initial Practice-Based Professional Preparation Standards for Early Interventionists/Early Childhood Special Educators*	*113*
Appendix C	*Standards for Professional Practice*	*119*
Appendix D	*Core Competencies for Special Education Paraeducators*	*125*

Glossary *135*
Index *139*

Instructors: *Supporting Paraeducators in Special Education and Inclusive Settings* includes ancillary materials specifically available for faculty use. Included are an *Instructor's Manual* and PowerPoint slides. Please visit www.routledge.com/9781630918071 to obtain access.

Acknowledgments

We have more than 40 years of combined classroom experience working with paraeducators and 33 years of combined experience in higher education conducting research, developing interventions, and providing training and professional development support to teachers, paraeducators, and educational teams. Our collective experience and expertise have provided important insights that have been incorporated into this text in an effort to bridge the research to practice gap as related to paraeducator support for students with disabilities.

This book is dedicated to the hard working, but often underappreciated, educators and educational teams (including paraeducators, teachers, and administrators) who work tirelessly to instruct students with disabilities. We hope you know how important you are—you are changing lives each day! Our aim is that the content within this text will help guide educational teams in their work with paraeducators and ultimately support the work of collaborative teacher–paraeducator teams as they improve services for all students with disabilities.

About the Authors

Emily E. Sobeck, PhD earned a bachelor's degree in Special Education and Elementary Education from California University of Pennsylvania in the fall of 2007 and began working as a special education teacher in the spring of 2008 in a public school district in Pittsburgh, Pennsylvania. She first served as a special education teacher for students in 9th to 11th grades, and then transitioned to a K to 1st special education position. With many of her students diagnosed with autism and a desire to learn more ways to support her students, Dr. Sobeck went back to California University of Pennsylvania to earn both a master's degree in Special Education and an Autism Specialist Certification. While completing graduate school, Dr. Sobeck also worked closely with the Watson Institute receiving additional training, consultation, and support for her students.

In 2012 Dr. Sobeck was selected for an Office of Special Education Programs (OSEP) grant-funded position as a doctoral student in Special Education at the University of Pittsburgh. With the support of the grant funds, Dr. Sobeck was able to transition out of the classroom and into a full-time doctoral fellowship. It was during this time that she began her research related to paraeducators. In 2015, she was selected as a Doctoral Student Scholar within the Division for Research within the Council for Exceptional Children (CEC) where she participated in training and coaching from top researchers in the field of special education.

Upon graduating with a PhD in Special Education in 2016, her dissertation study, *The Effects of Didactic Instruction and Performance Feedback on Paraeducator Implementation of Behavior Support Strategies in Inclusive Settings,* was selected for the Outstanding Dissertation award through the Teacher Education Division (TED) within CEC in 2017. Dr. Sobeck has served as a faculty member at Franciscan University since 2016 where she is currently an Associate Professor of Special Education. She also has served as the membership chair for the Paraeducator Special Interest Group (part of the Teacher Education Division of CEC) since 2016. Within this role she has assisted in developing position papers, conducting research relative to paraeducators, creating webinar trainings, and supporting advancements in professional standards for paraeducators and teachers who work with paraeducators.

Since working in higher education, Dr. Sobeck has obtained several grants, published more than 15 items, maintained an editorial position for several special education journals, and given more than 60 presentations and trainings, many of which had a primary focus on paraeducators. The Division for Research within CEC featured one of Dr. Sobeck's manuscripts in 2019, and she was awarded Franciscan University's Excellence in Scholarship in 2020. Much of her work has focused on paraeducator training, equipping paraeducators to manage challenging behavior, teacher and paraeducator relationships, and supporting paraeducators who implement Behavior Intervention Plans. Dr. Sobeck wholeheartedly believes this area of special education is crucial to the educational service delivery for students with disabilities and is excited to be able to share the information within this text.

Sarah N. Douglas, PhD started her career in 2003 as a special education teacher in Flagstaff, Arizona, after earning a degree in Elementary and Special Education from Northern Arizona University. In her time in the classroom, she supported students with a variety of disabilities in resource, inclusive, and self-contained classroom settings. Dr. Douglas worked with a variety of paraeducators in her role as a teacher, and learned first hand about some of the benefits and challenges of their utilization in school settings. During her time teaching, she obtained a master's degree in 2007 in Special Education with an emphasis in Low Incidence Disabilities and obtained a graduate certificate in Assistive Technology.

The time Dr. Douglas spent in the classroom inspired her to go on to obtain a PhD in Special Education from Penn State University in 2011, where she began her research related to paraeducators and explored interventions to support students with complex communication needs. Since that time Dr. Douglas has served as faculty at Penn State University (2012 to 2014) and Michigan State

University (2014 to current), where she now is an Associate Professor and Director of the RADD (Research in Autism and Developmental Disabilities) lab. Dr. Douglas has served as the secretary for the Paraeducator Special Interest Group (part of the Teacher Education Division of CEC) in 2013. In this role she has developed position papers, webinar trainings, shared recent research, and worked to move forward professional standards for paraeducators and teachers in their roles with paraeducators.

During her career in academia, Dr. Douglas has obtained various funding to conduct research related to paraeducators, including a large-scale federal grant. She has published more than 60 items, with a large portion of her work focused on paraeducators. This has included the development and testing of interventions for paraeducators, exploratory work to understand paraeducator roles and experiences, literature reviews, reviews of training materials, and practitioner articles to bridge the research to practice gap. Dr. Douglas's vast experience as a leader in the paraeducator literature and professionally related to paraeducators (as a teacher and researcher) makes her well qualified as an author of this text.

Denise J. Uitto, EdD began her career as a speech-language pathologist after earning her degree at Bowling Green State University. She served one year in a county school system providing speech therapy services to students in multiple buildings. In the next few years, the field of special education changed rapidly with the implementation of new federal laws. Students previously denied an education were enrolled in public schools, including students with multiple disabilities. Dr. Uitto entered her teaching career serving as a teacher for students living in a long-term residential facility.

Following the birth of her son, she returned to the school district as a paraprofessional in a resource room for students with cognitive disabilities. She performed multiple roles within the resource room such as clerical work, playground supervision, reinforcement of academic skills, and assisted students joining their peers in general education classrooms. Continuing her career as a teacher for students with multiple disabilities, her team supervised paraprofessionals as they performed health-related tasks and reinforced vocational and daily living skills. With encouragement and support from colleagues and administrators, she pursued a master's degree in Special Education to earn a supervisory degree and an administrator certificate. Her administrator career began as a Supervisor of Special Education Programs, Preschool Special Education Administrator, then moved into two elementary principalships. Throughout her administrative career, the motivation to improve services for students with disabilities and special education programming continued. She wrote grants and utilized local funding to provide professional development for both teachers and paraprofessionals to support students with disabilities.

Dr. Uitto earned a doctoral degree in Organizational Leadership with a cognate in professional development. With her background in teaching and administration, she became the administrator of an associate degree program for paraprofessionals at the University of Akron, Wayne College. She joined colleagues from across the United States in promoting the supervision and training of paraprofessionals. Joining the Paraeducator Special Interest Group with the Teacher Education Division of the CEC, she served as co-chairperson and developed position papers and the current *Core Competencies for Special Education Paraeducators*. She has co-authored book chapters and articles throughout her career and consulted with regional special education centers to provide professional development opportunities for both teachers and paraprofessionals. As an advocate for all students with disabilities, she continues to serve special education programming by co-writing research articles and projects involving paraprofessionals in special education.

PREFACE

Supporting Paraeducators in Special Education and Inclusive Settings is designed for both pre-service and in-service special education and general education teachers who direct, or will direct, the work of paraeducators. Incorporating research and evidence-based practices, our text provides teachers with a clear understanding of their role and responsibilities as supervisors of paraeducators within inclusive and special education settings. This text also offers recommendations and tips for managing and supporting paraeducators in their roles. Additionally, we discuss current challenges within the field (e.g., lack of training, turnover) and their implications for teachers, administrators, and paraeducators. Our text gives teachers a practical guide to assist in supervising nearly half a million paraeducators serving students with disabilities in the United States (U.S. Department of Education, 2021).

Within this comprehensive text, personnel at all levels can use and apply the information and practices shared. Specifically, educator preparation faculty and pre-service teacher candidates will find the content to supplement current coursework on the essential role teachers are expected to fulfill in both special education and inclusive settings. Novice in-service teachers will find the content and tools relevant for effective supervisory practice with practical implementation guidance. School administrators can use this text to better understand their specific roles and responsibilities and the ways they can best support teacher–paraeducator teams.

Our text also incorporates the standards provided by the Council for Exceptional Children (CEC) as well as the *High-Leverage Practices* as they pertain to paraeducators. Additionally the *Core Competencies for Special Education Paraeducators* are also addressed within the text. These standards, practices, and competencies are described, explained, and provided as a resource within the appendices.

Our user-friendly format is designed to address the challenges instructors within institutions of higher education (IHE) have noted in research (see Sobeck et al., 2020) and support them in preparing pre-service teacher candidates to develop the skills to work with, manage, and supervise paraeducators. Additionally, school leaders or professional development providers can use our text to support in-service teachers as they improve their practices through professional growth and reflection. Each chapter includes: (a) a set of objectives; (b) a list of key terms; (c) case studies; (d) tools to implement practices; (e) questions for discussion; and (f) resources for further study. Case studies and vignettes provide realistic examples of the application of these topics within school settings. Questions are also provided to support group discussion, individual reflection, prompt educators to think about supervisory practices, or discuss how to incorporate new knowledge into their role as supervisors to paraeducators. Within each chapter resources are provided to equip educators with the tools needed to successfully apply the content discussed and implement the recommended practices. Definitions of key terms and a glossary are included in the book.

Our text will aid in preparing teachers and administrators to supervise, manage, and support paraeducators through addressing these critical questions:

- What are the roles and responsibilities of teachers and paraeducators in our schools? (Chapter 1)
- How do teachers and paraeducators collaborate and communicate as team members to support the needs of students with disabilities? (Chapter 2)
- What does the supervision of paraeducators mean? (Chapter 3)
- What does supervision of paraeducators look like in the special education and inclusive general education classroom? (Chapter 4)
- How do school districts prepare paraeducators to work with students with disabilities? (Chapter 5)
- What are the current challenges schools face when utilizing paraeducators? (Chapter 6)

A complementary *Instructor's Manual* is also provided to assist faculty, school leaders, and professional development providers in their preparation of pre-service and in-service teachers. The *Instructor's Manual* provides answers to the case studies and review questions in each chapter, presentation slides with content consistent with the text to accompany each chapter, and suggestions for learning activities related to the focus of each chapter. It is our hope that the content covered within these chapters will equip teachers, school leaders, IHE faculty, and professional development providers with the information and resources they need to support paraeducators in meaningful and effective ways.

References

Sobeck, E., Douglas, S. N., Chopra, R., & Morano, S. (2020). Paraeducator supervision in pre-service teacher preparation programs: Results of a national survey. *Psychology in the Schools, 58*(4), 669-685. https://doi.org/10.1002/pits.22383

U.S. Department of Education, Office of Special Education and Rehabilitative Services, Office of Special Education Programs. (2021). *42nd Annual Report to Congress on the Implementation of the Individuals with Disabilities Education Act, 2020, Washington, D.C.* https://sites.ed.gov/idea/files/42nd-arc-for-idea.pdf

Introduction

Understanding the history of paraeducator utilization can help educators in their support and supervision of paraeducators. This introduction provides a brief history of key historical changes related to the employment and roles of paraeducators and teacher supervision of paraeducators. Relevant teacher preparation standards related to paraeducators and paraeducator competencies to guide the training of paraeducators are also introduced. The introduction is concluded with highlights for each chapter in this text.

The Employment and Roles of Paraeducators

Paraeducators began their employment in the 1950s supporting teachers with clerical and nonprofessional tasks. Gradually, paraeducators transitioned from clerical and nonprofessional tasks to primarily instructional support roles. As schools faced the challenge of supporting individual students with complex medical needs, challenging behaviors, or significant educational needs, paraeducators were also hired for one-on-one roles attending to these needs (Fisher & Pleasants, 2012). Currently approximately half a million paraeducators are employed to serve students with disabilities in the United States (U.S. Department of Education, 2021).

The Education for All Handicapped Children Act (ESEA) of 1975 ensured the provision of special education and related services to students with disabilities. This federal act renamed and amended to the Individuals with Disabilities Education Act (IDEA) of 1997 mandated paraeducators be appropriately trained and supervised to assist in the provision of services for students with disabilities. The Individuals with Disabilities Education Improvement Act (IDEIA) of 2004 reinforced these training and supervision responsibilities.

Federal guidance clarified for state and local education agencies that it is the teacher's responsibility to plan direct instruction and introduce new skills, concepts, or academic content to students, and declared these responsibilities inappropriate for paraeducators (U.S. Department of Education, 2004). The No Child Left Behind Act (NCLB) of 2001, reauthorized as The Every Student Succeeds Act of 2015, defined the role for paraeducators for the first time in federal legislation. The U.S. Department of Education defined special education paraeducators as:

Employees who provide *instructional support,* including those who:
- Provide one-on-one tutoring if such tutoring is scheduled at a time when a student would not otherwise receive instruction from a teacher
- Assist with classroom management, such as organizing instructional and other materials
- Provide instructional assistance in a computer laboratory
- Conduct parental involvement activities
- Provide support in a library or media center
- Act as a translator
- Provide instructional support services under the direct supervision of a teacher (U.S. Department of Education, 2022, p. 37)

Teacher Supervision of Paraeducators

From the early days of paraeducator employment, teachers acknowledged their responsibility to provide supervision by delegating appropriate tasks and training them for their responsibilities. Paraeducators were first mentioned in federal legislation with the passage of IDEA of 1997. This law mandated they be appropriately trained and supervised to assist in the provision of services for students with disabilities. Although the special educator's role consistently focused on the instruction of students with disabilities, more recently their role has shifted to being a supervisor of paraeducators, directing their work to effectively monitor student progress and utilizing evidence-based instructional practices (Dukes et al., 2014).

Teacher Standards Related to Paraeducators

The Council for Exceptional Children (CEC) is recognized as an international professional organization focused on the education of students with disabilities. The organization creates standards and guidelines for the preparation and certification of special educators. CEC guidelines and standards are utilized by teacher preparation programs, accreditation organizations, and credentialing/licensing agencies. Specific to the supervision of paraeducators, the *Standards for Professional Practice* (Appendix C) prompts pre-service teachers to: (a) provide training for the tasks they will be assigned; (b) only assign tasks for which they are prepared; (c) give feedback on their performance of assigned tasks; (d) share timely, supportive, and collegial communications for tasks and expectations; and (e) intervene when a paraeducator's behavior is illegal, unethical, or detrimental to students (CEC, 2015).

These actions are consistent with Standard 7.4 in the *Initial Practice-Based Professional Preparation Standards for Special Educators* (*K-12*; Appendix A), which states, "Candidates work with and mentor paraprofessionals in the paraprofessionals' role of supporting the education of individuals with exceptionalities and their families" (Berlinghoff & McLaughlin, 2022, p. 64). Continued reference to these standards is *Initial K-12 Practice-Based Standards*. In addition, the *Initial Practice-Based Professional Preparation Standards for Early Interventionists/Early Childhood Special Educators* (Appendix B) emphasizes collaboration and teaming with professionals, including paraeducators, through the "use of communication and group facilitation strategies to enhance team functioning and interpersonal relationships with and among team members" (Berlinghoff & McLaughlin, 2022, p. 89). Further reference to these early education standards is *Initial Practice-Based Professional Preparation Standards for EI/ECSE*.

Often college and university-based personnel—including faculty, instructors, and field supervisors—serve as the entry point for pre-service preparation where teachers learn to direct the work and collaborate effectively with paraeducators. Preferably prior to their first teaching experience, special educators and general educators need to develop competencies to work with paraeducators (Biggs et al., 2019). Using the *Initial K-12 Practice-Based Standards* and/or *Initial Practice-Based Professional Preparation Standards for EI/ECSE*, pre-service special educators can document their proficiencies demonstrated through their program completion. Two specific proficiencies include: "understand the importance of working with paraprofessionals and the potential roles of the paraprofessional based on the needs of individual learners and the educational setting" and "the various roles that they must assume in order to work effectively with paraprofessionals" (Berlinghoff & McLaughlin, 2022, p. 50).

Although special and general education teachers need to develop competencies to work with paraeducators (Biggs et al., 2019), many special educators do not acquire essential competencies prior to their employment (Douglas et al., 2016). School leaders cannot presume that novice or experienced special education teachers will understand their role or have acquired competencies to supervise the work of paraeducators. In-service teachers often express the need to work effectively with paraeducators as part of their ongoing professional development and informal learning experiences (Biggs et al., 2019). These special educators need support from administrators and experienced mentor teachers, as well as professional learning activities to develop competencies to effectively direct the work of paraeducators.

Special educators can use standards and guidelines to guide their continuous improvement and help evaluate their professional practices, develop a professional development plan, and renew credentials. The *Standards for Professional Practice* (Appendix C; 2015), *Initial K-12 Practice-Based Standards,* and/or *Initial Practice-Based Professional Preparation Standards for EI/ECSE* (Berlinghoff & McLaughlin, 2022) are excellent resources for in-service teachers and can help guide their development of skills to become competent in directing the work of paraeducators.

The CEC standards also align with the InTASC standards. For example, one of the categories "Collaborating with Team Members" states "Candidates apply team processes and communication strategies to collaborate in a culturally responsive manner with families, paraprofessionals, and other professionals within the school, other educational settings, and the community to lead meetings, plan programs, and access services for individuals with exceptionalities and their families" (Berlinghoff & McLaughlin, 2022, p. 12). In addition, *High-Leverage Practices in Special Education* emphasizes two specific practices regarding the collaborative role special educators have with professionals, including related service staff and paraeducators (McLeskey et al., 2017).

Paraeducator Competencies to Guide Training

Focusing on the instructional support role of paraeducators, the CEC established paraeducator competencies defining the essential knowledge and skills for special education paraeducators. CEC encourages agencies to ensure that all special education paraeducators possess, at a minimum, the knowledge and skills defined in these competencies through ongoing, effective, and pre-service and in-service training experiences targeted to their needs and provided by professional educators (CEC, 2015). In 2022, a revised set of core competencies, *Core Competencies for Special Education Paraeducators* (CEC, 2022a; Appendix D) were approved. These core competencies address the content of professional learning opportunities for paraeducators and provide clarity on the federal mandate "appropriately trained" (IDEIA, 2004). These paraeducator competencies can be used to guide professional learning opportunities, support the design of quality professional learning opportunities for pre-service and in-service training, offer a means to document quality training of paraeducators, and as an assessment of individual competency. Another specialty set serving these purposes is the *Specialty Set for Special Education Paraeducator Intervener for Individuals with Deafblindness* that defines specific knowledge and skills for special education paraeducators serving students with deafblindness (CEC, 2022b).

In their instructional support role in today's schools, paraeducators need training focused on instructional strategies and behavior management as they provide one-on-one and small group academic instruction (Chopra et al., 2018), facilitate social interactions, and assist with the implementation of individual behavior plans (Fisher & Pleasants, 2012). With innovations in education and the inclusion of students with diverse needs, training related to assistive technology, such as augmentative and alternative communication systems, is also necessary (Douglas et al., 2013). Early paraeducator training was primarily provided by teachers through on-the-job training opportunities, and this remains still today the most common form of training for paraeducators. On-the-job training supports paraeducators as they implement evidence-based strategies and requires teachers who observe, evaluate, and provide performance feedback on the paraeducator competencies. When given adequate training, paraeducators have been shown to successfully implement instructional strategies (Walker et al., 2020). Given the federal mandates for paraeducator utilization and training and professional guidelines, schools have an obligation to ensure paraeducators are appropriately trained for each of the various aspects of their job (e.g., instruction, behavioral support, daily living skills, communication).

Chapter Highlights

This text was designed and written so that the reader has the option to read it linearly from start to finish or to select specific chapters that are most relevant to the reader's needs. In order to assist in chapter selection, a brief overview of each chapter is provided.

- *Chapter 1—Roles and Responsibilities of Team Members in Relation to Paraeducators* describes the primary roles and responsibilities of paraeducators in various settings. In relation to paraeducators, the importance of defining individual roles of special education teachers, general education teachers, and administrators within special education and inclusive settings are explained. A focus on how to create a plan for establishing roles and/or responsibilities for paraeducators and the classroom environment to effectively utilize paraeducator supports is reviewed.

- *Chapter 2—Establishing Effective Communication and Collaboration With Paraeducators* provides methods of communication (e.g., emails, written notes) and suggestions for addressing planning times. The problem-solving and conflict management processes and how to provide effective feedback to support the work of paraeducators are described.
- *Chapter 3—Introduction to Paraeducator Supervision* describes the laws and guidelines relevant to paraeducator supervision and details that are included or missing. The rationale for special educators to hold the knowledge and skills to supervise paraeducators and importance of paraeducator supervision are explained. Tools to define the components of paraeducator supervision and practical strategies for effective supervision are provided.
- *Chapter 4—Supervision Responsibilities of Team Members* shares an in-depth discussion of the roles and team responsibilities of special education teachers, general education teachers, administrators, and related service personnel for the supervision of paraeducators. A formal paraeducator evaluation process is detailed with personnel involved, frequency of performance review, and the process to use. The importance of delegating tasks to paraeducators and the benefits of delegation are defined. The chapter justifies the importance of job descriptions, including pertinent items and a sample job description.
- *Chapter 5—Paraeducator Training* explains legal requirements and the key characteristics for high-quality practices useful in preparing paraeducators for their roles and responsibilities. A discussion of how teachers determine paraeducator training needs through observations, discussions, and employment practices are discussed. An example plan for paraeducator training is shared.
- *Chapter 6—Common Challenges and Areas for Growth* addresses the many issues that teachers, team members, and administrators experience within the interactions with paraeducators in their schools. Specifically, this chapter discusses paraeducator–family relationships, confidentiality, role clarification, overreliance of paraeducators, placement of students, hovering, person-first language, fading supports, collaboration, communication protocols, training, respect for paraeducators, and much more. These challenges are introduced and explained, and recommendations for addressing these challenges are mentioned briefly. Implications for practice and areas for continued growth are also shared.

Summary

Nearly half a million paraeducators are utilized to support students with disabilities in various educational settings today. It is important to be aware of the history of paraeducators, as well as the past and current legislation, standards, and competencies pertaining to paraeducators. The chapters in this text will provide insight on the roles and responsibilities of teachers and paraeducators, collaboration and communication of teacher–paraeducator teams, supervision of paraeducators, training for paraeducators, and challenges facing the field today. This text will help guide both special and general education teachers, school leaders, and professional development providers in their work to best support and manage with paraeducators.

References

Berlinghoff, D., & McLaughlin, V. L. (Eds.). (2022). *Practice-based standards for the preparation of special educators*. Council for Exceptional Children.

Biggs, E. E., Gilson, C. B., & Carter, E. W. (2019). "Developing that balance": Preparing and supporting special education teachers to work with paraprofessionals. *Teacher Education and Special Education*, 42(2), 117-131. https://doi.org/10.1177/0888406418765611

Chopra, R., Carroll, D., & Manjack, S. K. (2018). Paraeducator issues and strategies for supporting students with disabilities in arts education. In J. B. Crockett & S. M. Malley (Eds.), *Handbook of arts education and special education* (pp. 105-128). Routledge.

Council for Exceptional Children. (2015). *What every special educator must know: Professional ethics and standards* (7th ed.). Council for Exceptional Children.

Council for Exceptional Children. (2022a). *Core competencies for special education paraeducators*. https://exceptionalchildren.org/paraeducators/core-competencies-special-education-paraeducators

Council for Exceptional Children. (2022b). *Initial specialty set: Deafblind intervener*. https://tedcec.org/sites/default/files/2022-3/Deafblind%20Intervener%20SS%202022.pdf

Douglas, S. N., Chapin, S. E., & Nolan, J. F. (2016). Special education teachers' experiences supporting and supervising paraeducators: Implications for special and general education settings. *Teacher Education and Special Education, 39*(1), 60-74. https://doi.org/10.1177/0888406415616443

Douglas, S. N., McNaughton, D., & Light, J. (2013). Online training for paraeducators to support the communication of young children. *Journal of Early Intervention, 35*(1), 223-242. https://doi.org/10.1177/1053815114526782

Dukes, C., Darling, S. M., & Doan, K. (2014). Selection pressures on special education teacher preparation issues: Issues shaping our future. *Teacher Education and Special Education, 37*(1), 9-20. https://doi.org/10.1177/0888406413513273

Fisher, M., & Pleasants, S. L. (2012). Roles, responsibilities, and concerns of paraeducators: Findings from a statewide survey. *Remedial and Special Education, 33*(5), 287-297. https://doi.org/10.1177/0741932510397762

Individuals with Disabilities Education Improvement Act of 2004, 20 U.S.C. § 1400.

McLeskey, J., Barringer, M.-D., Billingsley, B., Brownell, M., Jackson, D., Kennedy, M., Lewis, T., Maheady, L., Rodriquez, J., Scheeler, M. C., Winn, J., & Ziegler, D. (2017). *High-leverage practices in special education*. Council for Exceptional Children & CEEDAR Center.

U.S. Department of Education. (2004). *Title I paraprofessionals: Non-regulatory guidance*. U.S. Department of Education. https://www2.ed.gov/admins/tchrqual/qual/paraprofessional.html

U.S. Department of Education, Office of Special Education and Rehabilitative Services, Office of Special Education Programs. (2021). *42nd Annual Report to Congress on the Implementation of the Individuals with Disabilities Education Act, 2020*, Washington, D.C. https://sites.ed.gov/idea/files/42nd-arc-for-idea.pdf

U.S. Department of Education, Office of Special Education and Rehabilitative Services, Office of Special Education Programs. (2022). *43rd Annual Report to Congress on the Implementation of the Individuals with Disabilities Education Act, 2021*, Washington, D.C. https://sites.ed.gov/idea/2021-individuals-with-disabilities-education-act-annual-report-to-congress/

Walker, V. L., Douglas, K. H., Douglas, S. N., & D'Agostino, S. R. (2020). Paraprofessional-implemented systematic instruction for students with disabilities: A systematic literature review. *Education and Training in Autism and Developmental Disabilities, 55*(3), 303-317.

Roles and Responsibilities of Team Members in Relation to Paraeducators

INTRODUCTION

Paraeducators play a variety of roles within the school. Chapter 1 explains why the roles held by paraeducators are crucial to student success and how to best support paraeducators with their numerous responsibilities. Specifically, this chapter identifies these primary roles, the roles of teachers and school administrators as they pertain to paraeducators, processes for conveying clear expectations, the importance of role clarification, and how to best utilize paraeducators across various settings.

CHAPTER OBJECTIVES

- Identify the primary roles and responsibilities of paraeducators across various school settings.
- Identify the roles of teachers and school administrators as they relate to paraeducators.
- Review a plan for establishing clear roles and responsibilities for paraeducators within the school and classroom setting.
- Discuss the structure of the classroom environment to utilize paraeducators effectively.
- Explain the importance of role clarification for paraeducators and key team members as it relates to paraeducators.

KEY TERMS

- **Behavioral Intervention Plan (BIP):** A written plan agreed upon by all team members based on student data and the outcome of the Functional Behavior Assessment (FBA). The FBA identifies the function of the behavior, and the BIP specifies the evidence-based steps and methods to modify or improve the behavior.
- **CEC Specialty Sets:** Knowledge and skills that are used by teacher education programs to develop curriculum and create assessments for their candidates to demonstrate mastery of standards.
- **Core Competencies for Special Education Paraeducators:** Refers to the required knowledge and skills all paraeducators must obtain to support students with disabilities safely and in kindergarten through 12 environments.
- **Council for Exceptional Children (CEC):** An international professional organization that strives to improve the experience of individuals with disabilities and/or gifts and talents through advocacy, professional development, resource sharing, and educational standards.
- **Council for the Accreditation of Educator Preparation:** An organization dedicated to evaluating preschool through 12th-grade educator preparation programs through an evidence-based accreditation process that includes continuous improvement, quality assurance, credibility, diversity and equity, innovation, and a strong foundation.
- **Highly Qualified Teacher:** This originated under NCLB (2001-2015). Teachers had to meet three additional qualifications beyond their state teaching certification to be employed by a school. Under the ESSA, any teacher who meets their state's certification qualifications is automatically deemed highly qualified.
- **Individualized Education Plan (IEP):** A formal and legal document that details an individualized school program developed to ensure that an eligible student with a disability who attends a kindergarten through 12th-grade school receives specialized instruction and related services.
- **Interstate New Teacher Assessment and Support Consortium:** An association made up of state education agencies, national educational organizations, and institutions of higher education, who strive to reform education, certify teachers, and provide continuous professional development for teachers.
- **Personal Care Support:** Hands-on services to assist an individual with daily activities that they cannot perform on their own.
- **Specialty Set of Knowledge and Skills for Interveners for Individuals with Deafblindness:** Specific competencies for candidates who will serve individuals with deafblindness.

CASE STUDY 1

Mrs. Lopez is a new paraeducator at Sunshine Elementary School who has been placed in a first-grade inclusive classroom. Although she will assist all students in the classroom, Mrs. Lopez is responsible for supporting four students with IEPs. She is 45 years old, holds an associate's degree in business, and has worked with students with disabilities during her time as a volunteer at her local Special Olympics. She has never worked in a school before, and this will be her first time providing specialized services to students with disabilities.

Mrs. Johnson is the first-grade teacher and is excited to have an extra set of hands in the classroom. She has organized a small desk and chair for Mrs. Lopez and is hopeful she will help manage some of the challenging behavior in the classroom. On Mrs. Lopez's first day, Mrs. Johnson shares a little bit about the class structure and shows Mrs. Lopez the four students with IEPs. She also tells her to let her know if she has any questions along the way.

Throughout the first week Mrs. Johnson notices that Mrs. Lopez sits near the students with IEPs and answers their questions, but does not intervene when the students become off their task. She also observes Mrs. Lopez's minimal involvement with the other students in the class, often only paying attention to the four specific students. By the end of Mrs. Lopez's first month, Mrs. Johnson continues to note that Mrs. Lopez does not take any initiative to use the sensory space in the classroom with the students, implement preventative strategies to manage challenging behavior, nor adapt materials for the students during instruction. Mrs. Johnson is frustrated and not sure why Mrs. Lopez is not being more hands-on and proactive in the classroom.

1. Why do you think Mrs. Lopez is not demonstrating the level of initiative that Mrs. Johnson is expecting?
2. How do you think Mrs. Lopez feels starting this new position? What do you think the teacher or school could do to help make her transition into this role smoother?
3. What could Mrs. Johnson do to help rectify her dissatisfaction?
4. What are some ways that Mrs. Johnson can prevent situations like this in the future?

CASE STUDY 2

Ms. Foster is the principal at Rockford Elementary School. She has recently learned that she will be getting a new third-grade student, Ian, who has an IEP that includes paraeducator services. Ms. Foster must decide which classroom to place Ian in so that he can get the services he needs. Currently, Ms. Foster has 10 paraeducators employed in her school, with three of them working in third-grade classrooms. Therefore, Ms. Foster must decide which of the three paraeducators will be best suited for Ian's needs.

1. What kind of information should Ms. Foster already know about her paraeducators' roles and responsibilities in order to best transition Ian into the school?
2. What type of student-specific information should Ms. Foster collect and review to aid in her decision making?
3. Considering her role in this process, as well as the teacher's and the paraeducator's roles, what steps should Ms. Foster implement in order to ensure a smooth transition for Ian?

Paraeducators have become an increasingly important part of the public education framework since No Child Left Behind (2001) was enacted. Across the United States, more than 458,000 paraeducators provide services to students with disabilities in public schools (U.S. Department of Education, 2018). Schools have looked to paraeducators to help meet the needs of students in overwhelmed inclusion classrooms (Sobeck & Robertson, 2019), resolve teacher shortages (Chopra et al., 2011), and provide specialized support in intensive special education settings (Biggs et al., 2018). Not only is the number of paraeducators employed nation-wide growing, but their role within these schools continues to be redefined. Paraeducators have become key team members in the provision of special education programs for students with disabilities throughout kindergarten through 12th-grade classrooms (Brock, 2021). When paraeducators were initially introduced into the school structure, their primary role was to offer support to the classroom teacher through completing clerical work tasks. Over time, their support role has changed significantly, with paraeducators implementing behavioral, functional, adaptive, social, and instructional support to students with disabilities. Responsibilities given to paraeducators include leading small group instruction, delivering one-on-one instruction, managing student behavior, executing BIPs, collecting student data, corresponding with parents, adapting academic materials, assisting students with daily living skills, and so much more. With such high levels of involvement, it is not uncommon for a paraeducator to be considered a student's primary service provider (Fisher & Pleasants, 2012). These responsibilities have been accompanied by much discussion in the literature about the appropriateness and impact of utilizing paraeducators in these ways (Giangreco, 2010), even more so due to paraeducators receiving limited training and preparation. Continued calls in the field have been made for examining not only how paraeducators are prepared and used but how their level of involvement impacts student outcomes as well.

Although paraeducators provide an array of services to students across school environments, researchers continue to reveal that paraeducators are often unsure of their exact role in each environment (Sobeck & Robertson, 2019). With this lack of understanding, paraeducators tend to find themselves unsure about their responsibilities and how to involve themselves in the classroom in the most efficient way (Majerus & Taylor, 2020). Further, classroom teachers who are often deemed the paraeducators' immediate supervisor are often ill-prepared to manage the paraeducators who work alongside them (Douglas et al., 2016), leaving these crucial roles and responsibilities within the classroom unclear to paraeducators. With an absence of clarity on the paraeducators' roles within the classroom, paraeducators end up being underutilized and at times can even have a negative impact on student success (Giangreco, 2010). For example, a paraeducator who is unsure of their role regarding the occurrence of challenging behavior may respond to a student's behavior disruption in a way that is not conducive to the student's plan. Or the paraeducator may not respond at all, waiting for the classroom teacher to respond. In another situation, a paraeducator who does not know their role during large group instruction may sit in the back of the classroom, appearing uninvolved. This may occur because they are not certain of their specific instructional responsibilities and do not want to be a distraction.

In order for paraeducators to be the support that they are intended to be, classroom teachers—both special and general educators—must develop a plan for communicating and articulating their expectations for the paraeducator in their classroom. Beyond the classroom, school- and district-level administrators must also be able to clearly share their expectations for each paraeducator.

ROLES AND RESPONSIBILITIES SPECIFIC TO KEY TEAM MEMBERS

Within the school setting, team members have differing perspectives of paraeducator roles and responsibilities. This is a natural occurrence due to the different roles team members hold. Each person within the school structure interacts with paraeducators in a different way. Therefore, not only is it important for all team members to understand their specific position in relation to the paraeducator, it is equally important that they be able to articulate their understanding and expectations. For example, the role of the paraeducator from the viewpoint of the building principal may be a little broader and more focused on procedures when compared to the role as perceived by the special education teacher, which tends to be more student-focused. It is imperative that all team members are aware of and comfortable with the responsibilities of paraeducators in relation to the specific position they hold. Further, they must have an active plan for conveying those responsibilities to paraeducators in a clear and professional manner.

Paraeducators

Approximately 458,676 full-time paraeducators are employed nationally to support students with disabilities ages 6 to 21 (U.S. Department of Education, 2020), often spending the majority of the school day supporting students in inclusive settings. With many schools turning to paraeducators to assist students with disabilities, the use of paraeducators has become a common practice within the field of education. Not only are paraeducators being used more, but their role has also evolved dramatically. In the past, paraeducators assumed primarily clerical roles for teachers (Chopra et al., 2011). They would complete tasks such as copy work, running errands within the building, assisting students with their classwork, and preparing lesson materials. Now, paraeducators are assuming some responsibilities that were traditionally carried out by a certified teacher. Paraeducators are providing one-on-one academic instruction, delivering large and small group instruction (Chopra et al., 2018), communicating with parents, and adapting student materials (Sobeck & Robertson, 2019). A large part of their role also focuses on providing both adaptive and behavior support services to students. Specifically, paraeducators now serve as primary behavior interventionists—facilitating peer interactions, collecting student behavior data, managing student behavior and BIPs, and providing personal care support (Fisher & Pleasants, 2012). Although many paraeducators' primary responsibility is to assist students with disabilities, their role in the classroom can extend to other students as well. They can provide support to students who are identified as being at-risk, as well as to students who do not have any specific area of identified need.

EXAMPLE OF PARAEDUCATOR ROLE IN AN INCLUSIVE SIXTH-GRADE CLASSROOM

Miss Melody is in her second year at Sunshine Middle School working as a paraeducator. This year one of her assignments is a sixth-grade social studies class in which she supports five students with IEPs for varying disabilities (e.g., autism, learning disability, ADHD). During this class session Miss Melody travels about the room during large group instruction answering students' questions and clarifying confusing information. During the second portion of the class period, Miss Melody works with seven students in a small group where she assists students in completing assigned work by the classroom teacher. While leading the small group, Miss Melody is responsible for guiding students through their work, answering questions, providing error correction, and extending student learning when appropriate. At the conclusion of each class session, Miss Melody checks in with each of the five students with IEPs to ensure they understand the homework or the current projects they are to be working on outside of class. Once a week, she also pulls students to a separate classroom to proctor the teacher's quizzes. Here, she ensures that test accommodations are provided as outlined in each student's IEP (e.g., extended time, questions read aloud, quiet environment).

When it comes to academic instruction, paraeducators are now being given responsibilities that were once carried out by certified teachers. It is important to understand that, although paraeducators can perform some instructional tasks, they *must* work under the direction of a highly qualified teacher, and therefore, any new material or content must be initially taught by the certified teacher (Every Student Succeeds Act, 2015). Then, once the material has been covered by the teacher, the paraeducator can provide additional practice of those skills and reteach as necessary. Therefore, paraeducators can teach a small group lesson, as long as the material is considered a review or a practice of skills. If a paraeducator is unsure of their role within the academic instructional process, they should ask their collaborating teachers for clarification.

In addition to supporting students academically, paraeducators spend a substantial portion of their workday managing student behavior (Walker et al., 2021), often serving as the primary behavior interventionist (Fisher & Pleasants, 2012) and collecting behavioral data (Mason et al., 2021). Paraeducators should be trained to implement BIPs, be proficient in specific data collection methods, and monitored to ensure strategies are implemented with fidelity. Further, it is important for the paraeducator to keep the cooperating teacher informed of any challenges so that the teacher can provide additional guidance to the paraeducator or so that changes can be made to their advancing roles. The Council for Exceptional Children (CEC) established the *Core Competencies for Special*

Education Paraeducators (see Appendix D; CEC, 2022). These seven competencies outline the specific knowledge and skills paraeducators should possess when supporting students with disabilities in the school setting. CEC also developed the *Specialty Set of Knowledge and Skills for Interveners for Individuals with Deafblindness* for those paraeducators working specifically with students who are deafblind. These competencies serve as a resource for various team members and are especially useful when considering targeted training for paraeducators. For paraeducators, these competencies provide a guide to the skills they need to learn or refine, while also providing guidance as to where they might need additional training.

Example of Paraeducator Role in an Alternative First-Grade Special Education Setting

Mr. Diaz has been working at The School of New Hope for 10 years. He currently works as a paraeducator in a first-grade classroom that contains eight students from local school districts with varying low incidence disabilities (e.g., autism, multiple disability, intellectual disability). There is one classroom teacher, and Mr. Diaz is one of the four paraeducators that provide support services to the students. During the morning session, Mr. Diaz assists two students as they participate in circle time. He uses picture cards to help the students understand the lesson, and he assists one student who is nonverbal as they respond with an alternative communication device. Halfway through the morning lesson, Mr. Diaz is responsible for taking three boys to the restroom, two of which require their diaper to be changed and one who is potty-training. During the latter portion of the morning, Mr. Diaz, along with a second paraeducator, monitors four students in the gross motor room. Here he helps students stretch and access the exercise balls, swings, and small trampoline. Mr. Diaz has consulted the physical therapist for each student, so he is aware of the various gross motor skills the students are working toward. In the afternoon, Mr. Diaz helps set up and assist students with a snack. He provides prompting and reinforcement procedures to help teach several of the students how to feed themselves. He also spoon-feeds one student who must consume puréed food. Mr. Diaz implements each student's BIP, with behaviors ranging from physical aggression or noncompliance, as directed by the classroom teacher and uses a visual schedule to help students who have a difficult time transitioning between tasks.

With so many roles held by paraeducators, it is important for paraeducators to advocate for themselves. Paraeducators should not be afraid to ask questions and seek clarification from their cooperating teachers on the specific responsibilities the teacher has for them. Very few teachers receive pre-service preparation and training on supervising paraeducators (Sobeck et al., 2020), therefore, paraeducators may need to seek clarification as they execute their responsibilities. It is completely appropriate for paraeducators to seek out performance feedback along the way and to reach out to their collaborating teacher when confusion arises (Dennis et al., 2021). Gerlach (2015) offers a variety of checklists for paraeducators to use to help ensure they are prepared for their roles and responsibilities in various classrooms. Within these checklists paraeducators are given topic areas to learn about, as well as specific questions to ask to help them become familiar with their duties. For example, paraeducators are given questions to ask regarding their primary responsibilities, school procedures, and getting started within a classroom. Guidance is also given for interacting with teachers and supervisors, responding to student behaviors, as well as executing their assigned tasks. Throughout each checklist paraeducators are provided with an opportunity for self-reflection, as well as a starting point for advocating for themselves.

Work style inventories, checklists, and other feedback tools can be used throughout the school year to discuss the classroom dynamic and expectations. Allocating time for routine meetings is a great way to ensure everyone starts out on the same page, stays consistent, has time to ask questions, and engages in performance feedback. If a teacher is not provided with time in their schedule to allow for a meeting, they should speak with a building administrator to advocate for this time within their schedule. Similarly, if a teacher does not initiate a regular meeting schedule, paraeducators are encouraged to inquire about setting time aside to meet.

Example of Paraeducator Role in a Public School Third- and Fourth-Grade Special Education Classroom

Mrs. Opal is a paraeducator at Rockville Elementary School. She is in her 15th year at the school and has been assigned to work in a third and a fourth-grade special education classroom this year. In this classroom, 21 students with varying disabilities are serviced. Most students have mild to moderate disabilities, while three students are classified as having a severe and profound disability. Throughout the day, Mrs. Opal travels to and from different classes taking students to and from the special education classroom, related service sessions (e.g., speech and language, occupational therapy, vision support), and helping students get situated in the cafeteria for lunch. In the classroom, Mrs. Opal works with several students in a one-on-one style where she teaches functional academics, and other students in a small group where she provides back-up support for the reading skills they are learning in their general education classroom. She also leads several social skills activities that help teach students how to interact with their peers. In the afternoon, Mrs. Opal attends special classes with students who need support while participating in music and art class. She also spends time in the special education classroom helping students complete targeted activities per their IEP goals. On a daily basis she assists those students who need help in the restroom, manages students' visual schedules, completes several parent communication logs, and implements BIPs per each student's needs. Each week, she assists the special education teacher in collecting progress monitoring data where she helps assess every student on each one of their IEP goals. She also helps the teacher maintain student records by helping graph student progress.

Special Education Teachers

Because the primary role of paraeducators is often to support students with IEPs, the paraeducator's immediate supervisor is often the special education teacher (Biggs et al., 2018). Moreover, the Individuals with Disabilities Education Improvement Act (IDEIA, 2004) mandates that paraeducators who support students with disabilities be adequately supervised by a special education teacher. As a result of this mandate, paraeducators are typically assigned to a special education teacher at the start of each school year. It then becomes the special education teacher's role to create the paraeducator's daily schedule, acclimate them to the specific roles they will hold, and review student information for students they will be supporting. It is important that the special education teacher ensures that the paraeducator is aware of the specific goals, accommodations, and behavior plans outlined in each student's plan. If the paraeducator spends some of their day in the special education classroom, the special education teacher must also review the classroom structure and procedures of the special education classroom. In addition to completing these introductory tasks with the paraeducator, the special education teacher is also responsible for assisting the paraeducator throughout the school year by providing on-the-job training, supervision, and answering questions regarding student progress. Specifically, the special education teacher should guide the paraeducator as they learn to support student academic, behavioral, and adaptive needs. They should also provide on-the-job training of evidence-based practices and strategies, clarify expectations around communicating with parents, problem-solve logistical challenges as they arise, implement instructional strategies, and much more. The special education teacher assumes these responsibilities for all paraeducators on their caseload, including those who work in their classroom and those who support students in inclusive settings. For the paraeducators who spend a portion of their day in the special education

5.0 Paraeducators	
Special education professionals:	
5.1	Ensure that special education paraeducators have appropriate training for the tasks they are assigned.
5.2	Assign only tasks for which paraeducators have been appropriately prepared.
5.3	Provide ongoing information to paraeducators regarding their performance of assigned tasks.
5.4	Provide timely, supportive, and collegial communications to paraeducators regarding tasks and expectations.
5.5	Intervene professionally when a paraeducator's behavior is illegal, unethical, or detrimental to individuals with exceptionalities.

Figure 1-1. *Standards for Professional Practice,* Standard 5. (Data source: Council for Exceptional Children. [2015]. *What every special educator must know: Professional ethics and standards* [7th ed.]. Council for Exceptional Children.)

classroom, the special education teacher should explicitly plan for how the paraeducator will be used. When lesson planning, for example, the special education teacher should state the role and expectations for the paraeducator throughout the lesson.

Within the *Initial Practice-Based Professional Preparation Standards for Special Educators* (*K-12*; Berlinghoff & McLaughlin, 2022) that accredited universities follow (Figure 1-1), several key areas are addressed that special education teachers should demonstrate proficiency in when managing paraeducators. Standard 7, *Collaborating with Team Members,* contains two subcomponents (i.e., 7.2 and 7.4) in which special education teachers are given specific competencies and skills as they pertain to their interactions with paraeducators. Standard 7.2 requires that special education teachers "... collaborate, communicate, and coordinate with... other professionals... to assess, plan, and implement effective programs and services that promote progress toward measurable outcomes for individuals with and without exceptionalities and their families." Standard 7.4 further directs special education teachers to "...work with and mentor paraprofessionals in the paraprofessionals' role of supporting the education of individuals with exceptionalities and their families." Collectively, these standards offer special education teachers a basic understanding of some of the responsibilities they hold when managing paraeducators.

There are several things a special education teacher can do at the beginning, throughout, and at the end of the school year to carry out their paraeducator-specific roles and responsibilities. Although this list is not exhaustive, Figure 1-2 outlines a few recommendations. Throughout this list, recurring themes arise. First, one of the most important roles a special education teacher has in relation to the paraeducators they manage is *clarification.* Special education teachers should clarify everything: introducing the paraeducator to the classroom procedures and teaching philosophies, policies, behavior management systems, process for disagreements, data collection, roles and responsibilities within different elements of the classroom, student-specific information, and their role within each lesson plan. It is important to remember that paraeducators work with numerous teachers, and every teacher executes a personalized classroom dynamic. It is unrealistic to assume that each paraeducator can simply infer what is expected of them. It is also helpful to consider that many paraeducators do not have a formal education or specific training in special education and, therefore, may not have a strong understanding of some of the practices and strategies being implemented.

Special education teachers should also attempt to build a positive working *rapport* with the paraeducators in their classrooms. With paraeducators being one of the least trained individuals in the school structure and working with the most challenging students (Giangreco et al., 2010) and with paraeducators often feeling overlooked as educational team members (Sobeck et al., 2019), special education teachers can help ease this dynamic by establishing a positive and personalized rapport with each paraeducator. This can be done by allocating time to check in with each paraeducator to hear how they are doing, offering on-the-job training with feedback for specific strategies, and

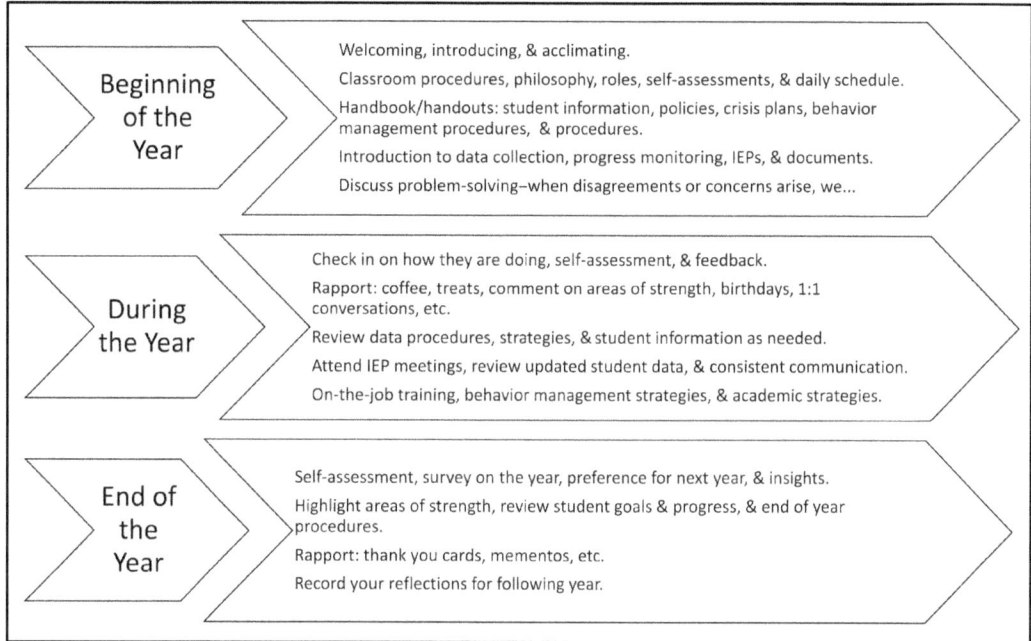

Figure 1-2. Recommendations for special education teachers to consider when managing paraeducators.

showing appreciation through thoughtful mementos. Establishing a mutual sense of respect and approaching decision making in a collaborative manner are crucial to ensuring a healthy working relationship. For example, research consistently reveals that paraeducators desire to be treated more professionally by having time to discuss their experiences, ask questions, and give input (Sobeck et al., 2019).

Obtaining *feedback* from paraeducators is also crucial. There are several ways special education teachers can seek feedback from paraeducators. Horner and colleagues (2003) suggest team members complete a self-assessment process where paraeducators engage in a Likert rating scale survey to determine if they have the skillset and an adequate level of comfort implementing strategies they are being directed to carry out. The Likert rating scale questions can be broken down through various subcategories, such as administrative support, resources, skills needed, values consistent with the plan, etc. For example, for paraeducator feedback on implementing BIPs, Horner and colleagues recommend questions such as, "I have the skills needed to implement this behavior support plan," "I have received the training that I need to be able to implement the Behavior Intervention Plan," and "My school provides the materials needed to implement this behavior support plan." Similarly, the PAR²A Center within the University of Colorado Denver (https://paracenter.org) offers a paraeducator work styles inventory that special education teachers can use to determine how to best utilize their paraeducators based on their personality, strengths, and work style. Within the inventory, paraeducators complete a Likert-style self-assessment with statements such as, "I like having a written schedule," "I speak slowly and softly," and "I like to get frequent feedback on my performance." Paraeducators also respond to a variety of responsibilities relative to their past experiences and their level of comfort. Statements such as, "Facilitate social interactions among students," "Carry out adapted instruction according to the adaptation list provided or specific directions," and "Observe and record student data" are included for paraeducators to reflect upon. Special education teachers can use tools like these to obtain insight about the paraeducator at the beginning and end of the school year. They should also seek intermittent feedback throughout the school year to identify any specific areas in which they require additional training or support.

General Education Teachers

With the increase in inclusive practices, paraeducators often work under the direction of general education teachers in addition to their assignment to the special education teacher. At times a paraeducator may support students in several general education classrooms, requiring the paraeducator to learn classroom dynamics for multiple settings. Initially, it is the general education teacher's responsibility to acclimate the paraeducator to the classroom, review the classroom structure and flow, and ensure that the paraeducator understands their active role within the classroom (Ashbaker & Morgan, 2012). Specific protocols and processes should be reviewed with the paraeducator and they should be given time to ask questions. Preparing an introductory handout for the paraeducator can help facilitate this information and guide the conversation. The general education teacher should make an effort to ensure that the paraeducator feels welcomed and part of the classroom. Similar to the special education teacher, it is equally important for the general education teacher to also clarify everything, build a positive working relationship with the paraeducator, and seek the paraeducator's feedback when possible. The general education teacher should also explicitly incorporate the paraeducator within their lesson plan. This plan can be shared with the paraeducator at the start of each class session, ensuring that the responsibilities and expectations of the paraeducator for each part of the lesson are clearly conveyed (Yates et al., 2020). General education teachers can use paraeducators in a variety of ways within the flow of the lesson. Paraeducators can work one-on-one with a student, lead a small group of students in an academic review exercise, help with lessons at centers, float around the classroom offering support to various students, and much more. It is important to note that although paraeducators are often placed in general education classrooms to provide services to students with IEPs, they are also able to support students without IEPs as well (O'Keeffe et al., 2013).

When a general education teacher is given a student with paraeducator support outlined in their IEP, not only should the general education teacher attend the IEP meeting but a brief meeting among the general education teacher, special education teacher, and paraeducator should be scheduled. During this meeting, the logistics of the paraeducator's schedule and schedule of students should be reviewed. A plan for responding to behavioral challenges, if any, should be discussed and time should be allocated for the paraeducator to ask any follow-up questions. This brief meeting will help the team make the student's experience in the inclusive classroom more successful.

The general education teacher should proactively establish a process for effective communication and working through disagreements with the paraeducator in their classroom. However, it is important for the general education teacher to keep the special education teacher informed of any challenges or decisions related to the paraeducator's performance, as these changes may impact the students being supported. The general and special education teachers must work together to use the paraeducator in the most effective way possible, ultimately providing the best service to the students being supported.

Although the CEC does not have a specific set of standards dedicated to general education teachers in regard to their work with paraeducators, the CEC standards discussed for special education teachers are applicable for general education teachers as well. Further, The Council for the Accreditation of Educator Preparation (CAEP) has provided guidance through their initial preparation standards, specifically within Standard 5 that states general education teachers are to "work collaboratively with colleagues, mentors, and other school personnel toward common goals that directly influence every learner's development and growth" (CAEP, 2018). Interstate New Teacher Assessment and Support Consortium (InTASC) also highlights the important role of the general education teacher in relation to paraeducators within their preparation standards. Standard 10 directs general education teachers to "...collaborate with... colleagues, and other school professionals... to ensure learner growth, and to advance the profession" (Council of Chief State School Officers, 2013). These standards should be used to provide insight into the knowledge and skills general education teachers should possess, learn, or continue to refine.

School Administrators

It is essential that school administrators (e.g., superintendents, principals) understand the role that paraeducators hold within the classroom, as their duties are crucial to school functioning. Although the administrator may be removed from interaction with the paraeducator in the classroom setting, they are often responsible for hiring paraeducators (Douglas et al., 2022). In order to hire the best candidate, the administrator must know the types of questions to ask and how to evaluate the candidate's responses. Further, with research continuing to reveal that paraeducators often feel overlooked by building- and district-level administrators (Fisher & Pleasants, 2012; Sobeck & Robertson, 2019), school administrators are encouraged to learn as much as they can about paraeducators through continuing education, discussions with teachers and paraeducators, observing in the classroom, and professional development opportunities. This not only helps administrators hire high-quality paraeducators but it can serve to establish strong working relationships among administrators and paraeducators. Currently, school administrators do not have a set of standards dedicated to supervising paraeducators specifically; however, the *Professional Standards for Educational Leaders* does include several standards that reference administrator competencies in relation to staff and team members. School administrators can look to Standards 6, 7, and 9 for guidance on their role in relation to the paraeducators employed in their schools (National Policy Board for Educational Administration, 2015). In addition to being aware of the responsibilities of paraeducators, it is essential for school administrators to know the particular laws pertaining to hiring and sustaining paraeducators. Section 1111 (g) (2) (J) of the Every Student Succeeds Act (ESSA) of 2015, requires that all paraeducators working in a state-funded school meet state certification. Further, Section 1111 (g) (2) (M) requires schools to have professional standards in place for paraeducators. Schools can use the *Initial K-12 Practice-Based Standards* (Berlinghoff & McLaughlin, 2022) and the *Core Competencies for Special Education Paraeducators* (CEC, 2022) as well. Examining both ESSA (2015) and state legislation can better inform school administrators as they hire and manage paraeducators.

Once administrators have established a strong understanding of who paraeducators are, the specific roles they hold in the classroom, and the legal mandates specific to paraeducators, administrators should begin to take several action steps to effectively support their paraeducators. First, school administrators should develop a plan for assessing the needs of their paraeducators on a routine or ongoing basis. Similar to teachers, paraeducators have certain aspects of their job that require consistent training and professional development. School administrators should develop a plan so they stay well-informed of the needs of their paraeducators (e.g., semester or yearly surveys, annual focus groups). Second, administrators should determine how to best use paraeducators within their school(s). In addition to input from teachers and paraeducators, examining student data to determine the most efficient way to use each paraeducator, based on identified needs, can be beneficial. Building-level administrators can also assess fit through a contextual fit survey to help guide their decision making on how to best place and use each paraeducator. As described earlier in the chapter, Horner and colleagues (2003) offer an example of a contextual fit survey for paraeducators implementing BIPs. A tool like this can be easily adapted to help administrators determine each paraeducator's areas of strength, as well as areas in which they need additional support. Third, it is important for administrators to convey their vision and expectations for how paraeducators are to be used and how the district will help them develop professionally. Detailing their vision not only gives paraeducators a sense of priority and establishes a line of communication, but it also helps to clearly articulate the paraeducator's roles and responsibilities from a school or district level. Lastly, establishing a way to convey specific expectations to the paraeducators is essential. These expectations should be made clear to not only the paraeducator but to the classroom teacher as well. Informing both paraeducators and teachers of these expectations allows for a collective understanding of the roles and responsibilities of each team member. This is especially important with the push for inclusion across schools today.

Related Service Providers

Related service providers have a unique relationship with paraeducators because paraeducators are often responsible for carrying out tasks outlined within the IEP by related service providers, in various school environments (Cole-Lade & Bailey, 2020). Therefore, paraeducators can find themselves responsible for implementing interventions related to fine motor skills, gross motor skills, speech and language, orientation and mobility, and many others. They may be responsible for taking the student to therapy, staying with the student during therapy if needed, implementing interventions, providing feedback to teachers, collecting student data, and updating the related service provider on student progress. Related service providers are responsible to implement direct services to students during therapy sessions. They are also often responsible for providing indirect services (i.e., consultation and training) to those who interact with the student frequently (e.g., paraeducators, teachers, school personnel) so the interventions can be carried out in the natural environment consistently (Cole-Lade & Bailey, 2020). Although related service providers and paraeducators interact frequently, a specific time for collaboration among the related service providers and paraeducators is needed. Allocating more time for discussion, setting aside time for the intervention skills to be modeled, providing on-the-job training, and allowing time for feedback are among the ways to incorporate effective collaboration. It is also important to include the paraeducator in conversations among the related service provider and the special education teacher, as the paraeducator tends to have the most interaction with the student throughout the school day. It is interesting to note that related service providers and paraeducators experience similar challenges within their disciplines. Both have faced a shortage of providers in their specialty area, inadequate training for the populations they serve, and high rates of attrition.

INCLUSIVE AND SPECIAL EDUCATION SETTINGS

Although paraeducators hold many roles and responsibilities across school environments, the specific instructional, behavioral, functional, adaptive, medical, and social supports that are required to students with disabilities often vary based on student needs or classroom settings. Their duties can look similar across settings, such as providing small group or one-on-one instructional support, implementing individualized BIPs, re-teaching social skills, reinforcing therapeutic skills such as the correct positioning of pencil grips, and following school and classroom rules. Across inclusive and special education settings, paraeducators might also monitor lunchroom, hallway, and playground activities; transition students between activities and settings; and provide medical assistance such as suctioning a tracheotomy tube. Due to the differing structure of each environment and the individual needs of students, a paraeducator may carry out distinct duties as noted in Table 1-1. Please note that schools can often have different expectations based on student and programmatic needs. Table 1-1 gives a general overview of possible paraeducator responsibilities; however, these responsibilities may vary from school to school and position to position.

In special education settings, paraeducators work side by side with the special education teacher. Therefore, paraeducators can ask questions in vivo and receive guidance from the special education teacher immediately. Often specific behavioral and academic interventions are implemented that require a thorough understanding of the strategies and protocols. Paraeducators in special education settings also tend to support students who require more support with adaptive skills. Paraeducators may find themselves supporting students with toileting, feeding, fine and gross motor skills, among many other self-help needs. In this environment paraeducators work with students in smaller ratios (e.g., 1:1 to 1:3) due to the students' more intense needs. At times a paraeducator may support a student using a one-on-one approach; however, this level of support has been criticized in the field due to the negative impact it can have on students, and many in the field are beginning to shift away from this approach (Giangreco, 2010). Students who receive paraeducator services through a one-on-one

TABLE 1-1. PARAEDUCATOR RESPONSIBILITIES ACROSS ENVIRONMENTS

TYPE OF CLASSROOM	SPECIFIC RESPONSIBILITIES
Inclusive Classroom	• Adapt curriculum materials as directed by teacher such as the use of note-taking strategies, reducing the number of math problems to solve, highlighting specific content in social studies • Assist with assessments, such as reading tests and record responses to test questions, collect work samples • Facilitate social interactions with peers and teachers using words, augmentative-alternative communication systems, gestures to greet, request assistance, or converse with classmates and teacher • Implement BIPs, such as reinforcing students for keeping hands to self, reminding students to acquire teacher signatures for individual BIPs • Implement planned instruction, such as small group instruction or one-on-one tutoring on grade-level subjects
Special Education Classroom	• Provide instructional support by pre-teaching lessons such as vocabulary in curriculum content areas, re-teaching concepts, and re-teaching academic math, reading, and writing skills • Supervise learning centers and independent work activities • Assist with assessment data such as frequency checks, reading fluency checks, curriculum-based assessments, and creating graphs of student data • Adaptive and life skills support such as assisting with classroom routines and following a pictorial schedule • Clerical work such as scoring student work, checking homework and communication folders, organizing and preparing classroom materials and activities • Offer behavioral support for following interventions outlined in BIPs and crisis intervention plans
Life Skills Classroom	• Re-teach adaptive and life skills support, such as self-care, use of communication strategies • Review social skills instruction, such as understanding social cues, obeying rules • Re-teach functional academic skills, such as counting money and making change, meal planning and preparation, creating shopping lists • Review community living skills such as doing laundry, shopping, public transportation, accessing community services • Offer behavioral support for following interventions outlined in BIPs and crisis intervention plans for more moderate and intense behaviors • Encourage self-determination skills such as problem solving, choice making, initiating and planning activities • Reinforce leisure skills such as playing simple games, taking responsibilities for personal activities • Assist with assessment data such as alternative assessment samples • Supervising employment activities such as cooperating with coworkers, being reliable and punctual, and following work standards (e.g., dress codes, absences)

style long-term can develop unnecessary dependence on the paraeducator, feel stigmatized with always having an adult with them, lose their sense of personal control, and display an increased rate of problem behavior.

In an inclusive classroom, paraeducators tend to support students in small groups (e.g., 1:2 to 1:6) and move throughout the classroom, aiding any student who needs help. The primary role of the paraeducator is to support students who have an identified disability and who have an IEP that includes paraeducator support services. However, they also support students who are considered at-risk and those who need additional help. Paraeducators in the inclusive setting implement both individual and class-wide behavior management plans, but these plans tend to be less intense. Although paraeducators spend a significant portion of their workday managing behavior (Walker et al., 2021), in an inclusive classroom paraeducators are continuing to become an integral part of the instructional process (Giangreco et al., 2010). In addition to providing small group instruction, paraeducators also adapt instructional materials, implement targeted reading interventions, and make pedagogical decisions (e.g., error correction procedures, style or presentation of material). In comparison to a special education setting, paraeducators who work in inclusive settings tend to engage in more academic instruction, support a larger number of students, and implement behavior management strategies under the direction of a general education teacher. Table 1-1 details the different types of content that paraeducators may be responsible to focus on per various settings.

Summary

Paraeducators have many roles and responsibilities within the school structure. It is important for all team members to understand the dynamics of paraeducator-specific duties and reflect on their own role as it pertains to paraeducators. Paraeducators are a fundamental piece of the service delivery for students with disabilities, as well as for those who are considered at-risk. To best support paraeducators in the field, teachers and administrators alike need to make thoughtful pedagogical decisions on how to best utilize the paraeducators working in their schools and classrooms. Using resources such as the CEC standards, paraeducator competencies, and referring to the current research base on paraeducators can help stakeholders understand their individual responsibilities—ultimately ensuring paraeducator support is implemented with the students' best interest in the forefront.

Chapter Review

1. What are the specific roles paraeducators hold? How are these roles different in special education and inclusive settings?
2. List three specific roles the special education teacher, general education teacher, and school administrator have as they pertain to paraeducators.
3. Why is it important for teachers and administrators to understand their responsibilities relative to paraeducators and clearly articulate their expectations to paraeducators?
4. How can special education teachers and general education teachers establish and maintain clear roles and responsibilities with the paraeducators who work in their classrooms?
5. Describe two ways a special education teacher and two ways a general education teacher can utilize a paraeducator during instruction in their classroom.
6. How can the *Core Competencies for Special Education Paraeducators* help paraeducators, teachers, and administrators?

Resources

- Ashbaker, B. Y., & Morgan, J. (2013). *Paraprofessionals in the classroom: A survival guide* (2nd ed.). Pearson.
- Connecticut State Department of Education. (2012). *Guidelines for training and support of paraprofessionals: Working with students birth to 21.* https://portal.ct.gov/-/media/SDE/Paraeducator/guidelines_paraprofessionals.pdf
- Council for Exceptional Children. (2023). https://exceptionalchildren.org/
- Gerlach, K. (2015). *Let's team up! A checklist for teachers, paraeducators, and principals.* National Professional Resources/Dude Publishing.
- Giangreco, M. F., Cloninger, C. J., & Iverson, V. S. (2011). *COACH 3: Choosing outcomes and accommodations for children: A guide to educational planning for students with disabilities.* (3rd ed.). Paul H Brookes Publishing.
- Hammeken, P. A. (2009). *The paraprofessional's essential guide to inclusive education* (3rd ed.). Corwin Press.
- Iowa Department of Education. (2013). *Appropriate paraeducator services matrix.* https://educateiowa.gov/sites/default/files/documents/Appropriate%20Paraeducator%20Duties.pdf
- Kansas State Department of Education. (2018). *Considerations for the effective use of paraprofessionals in schools.* Paraprofessional (ksde.org)
- Paraprofessional Resource and Research Center (PAR²A Center). (2023). *K-12 paraprofessional supervision.* Teachers - PAR²A Center (paracenter.org)
- State Education Resource Center. (2007). *Assessment checklist for paraprofessionals: Preschool-grade 12.* https://portal.ct.gov/SDE/Paraeducator/Paraeducator-Information-and-Resources/Documents

References

Ashbaker, B. Y., & Morgan, J. (2012). Team players and team managers: Special educators working with paraeducators to support inclusive classrooms. *Creative Education, 3*(3), 322-327. http://dx.doi.org/10.4236/ce.2012.33051

Berlinghoff, D., & McLaughlin, V. L. (Eds.). (2022). *Practice-based standards for the preparation of special educators.* Council for Exceptional Children.

Biggs, E. E., Carter, E. W., Bumble, J. L., Barnes, K., & Mazur, E. L. (2018). Enhancing peer network interventions for students with complex communication needs. *Exceptional Children, 85,* 66-85.

Brock, M.E. (2021). A tiered approach for training paraeducators to use evidence-based practices for students with significant disabilities. *TEACHING Exceptional Children, 54*(3), 224-233.

Chopra, R., Carroll, D., & Manjack, S. K. (2018). Paraeducator issues and strategies for supporting students with disabilities in arts education. In J. B. Crockett & S. M. Malley (Eds.), *Handbook of arts education and special education* (pp. 105-128). Routledge.

Chopra, R. V., Sandoval-Lucero, E., & French, N. K. (2011). Effective supervision of paraeducators: Multiple benefits and outcomes. *National Teacher Education Journal, 4*(2), 15-26.

Cole-Lade, G. M., & Bailey, L. E. (2020). Examining the role of paraeducators when supporting children with complex communication needs: A multiple case study. *Teacher Education and Special Education, 43*(2), 144-161. https://doi.org/10.1177/15407969211055127

Council for Exceptional Children. (2015). *What every special educator must know: Professional ethics and standards* (7th ed.). Council for Exceptional Children.

Council for Exceptional Children. (2022). *Core competencies for special education paraeducators.* https://exceptionalchildren.org/paraeducators/core-competencies-special-education-paraeducators

Council of Chief State School Officers. (2013, April). *Interstate teacher assessment and support consortium InTASC.* Model Core teaching standards and learning progressions for teachers 1.0: A resource for ongoing teacher development.

Council of Chief State School Officers, Council for the Accreditation of Educator Preparation. (2018). *CAEP 2018 K-6 elementary teacher preparation standards: Initial licensure program.* https://caepnet.org/~/media/Files/caep/program-review/2018-caep-k-6-elementary-teacher-prepara.pdf?la=en

Dennis, L.R., Weatherly, J., Robbins, A., & Wade, T. (2021). Practice-based coaching to support paraeducator implementation of shared book-reading strategies in preschool. *TEACHING Exceptional Children, 53*(6), 433-440.

Douglas, S. N., Bowles, R., & Kammes, R. (2022). Elementary principals' views on the policies and practices of paraeducators in special education. *Journal of the American Academy of Special Education Professionals,* Winter, 107-126.

Douglas, S. N., Chapin, S. E., & Nolan, J. F. (2016). Special education teachers' experiences supporting and supervising paraeducators: Implications for special and general education settings. *Teacher Education and Special Education, 39*(1), 60-74. https://doi.org/10.1177/0888406415616443

Every Student Succeeds Act of 2015, Pub L. No. 114-95 § 114 Stat. 1177 (215-2016).

Fisher, M., & Pleasants, S. L. (2012). Roles, responsibilities, and concerns of paraeducators: Findings from a statewide survey. *Remedial and Special Education, 33*(5), 287-297. https://doi.org/10.1177/0741932510397762

Gerlach, K. (2015). *Let's team up! A checklist for teachers, paraeducators, and principals.* Dude Publishing.

Giangreco, M. F. (2010). One-to-one paraprofessionals for students with disabilities in inclusive classrooms: Is conventional wisdom wrong? *Intellectual and Developmental Disabilities, 48*(1), 1-13. https://doi.org/10.1352/1934-9556-48.1.1

Giangreco, M. F., Suter, J. C., & Doyle, M. B. (2010). Paraprofessionals in inclusive schools: A review of recent research. *Journal of Educational and Psychological Consultation, 20*(1), 41-57. https://doi.org/10.1080/10474410903535356

Horner, R., Salentine, S., & Albin, R. (2003). *Self-assessment of contextual fit in schools.* University of Oregon.

Individuals with Disabilities Education Improvement Act of 2004, 20 U.S.C. § 1400 et seq. (2004) (reauthorization of the Individuals with Disabilities Education Act of 1990).

Majerus, C., & Taylor, D. M. (2020). Elementary music teachers' experience training and collaborating with paraprofessionals. *Applications of Research in Music Education, 39*(1), 27-37.

Mason, R. A., Gunersel, A. B., Irvin, D. W., Wills, H. P., Gregori, E., An, Z. G., & Ingram, P. B. (2021). From the frontlines: Perceptions of paraprofessionals' roles and responsibilities. *Teacher Education and Special Education, 44*(2), 97-116. https://doi.org/10.1177/0888406419896627

O'Keeffe, B. V., Slocum, T. A., & Magnusson, R. (2013). The effects of a fluency training package on paraprofessionals' presentation of a reading intervention. *Journal of Special Education, 47*(1), 14-27.

National Policy Board for Educational Administration. (2015). *Professional Standards for Educational Leaders 2015.* National Policy Board for Educational Administration.

Sobeck, E. E., & Robertson, R. (2019). Perspectives on current practices and barriers to training for paraeducators of students with autism in inclusive settings. *Journal of the American Academy of Special Education Professionals,* 131-159.

Sobeck, E. E., Robertson, R., & Smith, J. (2020). The effects of didactic instruction and performance feedback on paraeducator implementation of behavior support strategies in inclusive settings. *Journal of Special Education, 53*(4), 245-255. https://doi.org/10.1177/0022466919858989

U.S. Department of Education. (2018). *EDFacts submission system: FS112—Special education paraprofessionals file specifications.* https://www2.ed.gov/about/inits/ed/edfacts/sy-18-19-nonxml.html

U.S. Department of Education, Office of Special Education and Rehabilitative Services, Office of Special Education Programs. (2020). *41st annual report to Congress on the implementation of the Individuals with Disabilities Education Act, 2019.*

Walker, V. L., Kurth, J., Carpenter, M. E., Tapp, M. C., Clausen, A., & Lockman Turner, E. (2021). Paraeducator-delivered interventions for students with extensive support needs in inclusive school settings: A systematic review. *Research and practice for persons with severe disabilities, 46*(4), 278-295.

Yates, P. A., Chopra, R. V., Sobeck, E. E., Douglas, S. N., Morano, S., Walker, V. L., & Schulze, R. (2020). Working with paraeducators: Tools and strategies for instructional planning, performance feedback, and evaluation. *Intervention in School and Clinic, 56*(1), 1-8. https://doi.org/10.1177/1053451220910740

Establishing Effective Communication and Collaboration With Paraeducators

INTRODUCTION

It is essential for teachers and paraeducators to communicate efficiently. For this to occur, the teacher must establish protocols for problem solving, communicating, and managing conflict. Chapter 2 discusses the importance of communication and offers action steps that teachers, administrators, and paraeducators can take to ensure all team members have a way to discuss important information and concerns. Specific strategies are shared, *High-Leverage Practices* (HLPs) are described, and several resources are included. Chapter 2 also brings to light some important aspects of communication that school personnel should be made aware of and consider. Finally, conflict resolution is addressed as an important component of good communication.

CHAPTER OBJECTIVES

- Discuss the importance of establishing a positive and inclusive classroom culture for paraeducators.
- Explain the importance of conflict resolution and how to plan for and respond to conflict within a teacher–paraeducator relationship.
- Discuss the impact communication has on classroom culture.
- Review several prominent challenges that teachers and paraeducators experience with communication.

KEY TERMS

- **Conflict Resolution:** A formal or informal process in which two or more individuals work to find a solution to a disagreement in a respectful manner that satisfies everyone involved.
- **Contextual Fit Inventory:** An inventory tool that examines the extent to which the procedures of the student plan are consistent with the knowledge, beliefs, skills, resources, and supports of the school personnel who are expected to implement the plan.
- **High-Leverage Practices (HLPs):** Recommended practices supported by research that all teachers should implement in their classrooms classified under two aspects of practice, including collaboration, assessment, social/emotional/behavioral, and instruction.
- **LAFF Method:** An active listening strategy that emphasizes four main steps, including listening and demonstrating respect, asking questions, focusing on the main issue, and deciding on the first action step to resolve the situation.
- **Problem-Solving Approach:** Techniques and processes that individuals use to better understand a problem and to develop a solution.

CASE STUDY 1

Miss Lewis is a paraeducator in Ms. Markle's second-grade class where she is responsible for assisting several students who have an IEP, as well as several students who are considered at-risk. Currently, Miss Lewis does not attend IEP, behavior, or student data meetings; instead she is updated briefly by Ms. Markle after these meetings. One of the students Miss Lewis supports, Parker, has autism and engages in some challenging behavior throughout the day. During one instance of challenging behavior when Parker hit his hands on his desk when presented with math seatwork, Miss Lewis intervened by telling Parker to stop, threatening a time-out, and physically redirecting his hands back to his work. Ms. Markle immediately stepped in and told Miss Lewis that they are putting Parker's behavior of hitting on extinction and that she should continue to just redirect him back to work. She went on to stress the importance of being consistent with her response to Parker's hitting in order to improve Parker's behavior. She said this was outlined in Parker's BIP. Miss Lewis immediately felt embarrassed because she did not know she was supposed to be implementing the extinction strategy, nor did she exactly know what extinction was and how to employ it. With class needing to continue, Miss Lewis did not ask Ms. Markle to teach her about extinction; instead Miss Lewis apologizes and decides to learn about the strategy on her own. The next time Parker engages in hitting, Miss Lewis reacts according to what she learned on her own, and Ms. Markle again steps in and corrects Miss Lewis. Miss Lewis again feels embarrassed and begins to feel a sense of incompetence when it comes to supporting Parker. She is starting to think that Ms. Markle does not like her serving as a paraeducator in her classroom. Ms. Markle develops a sense of frustration because Parker's behavior is not improving, and from her perspective Miss Lewis is not doing what is outlined in Parker's BIP.

1. What is happening in this scenario between Miss Lewis and Ms. Markle? Why do you think it is occurring?
2. How could Ms. Markle improve the way she handles Miss Lewis's interactions with the students in the classroom? What preventative steps could Ms. Markle implement?
3. What could Miss Lewis do differently in this situation?
4. How could Ms. Markle's and Miss Lewis's working relationship be improved?

CASE STUDY 2

Mr. Rodriguez would like to try a new behavior management strategy with one of his fourth-grade students, Vashaun. He has already discussed the strategy with Vashaun's parents, as well as with the building principal. He wants to put the plan into place on Monday, but he is not sure when he is going to have time to review the plan with his classroom paraeducator, Mr. Thomas. Mr. Thomas lives far from the school, so he usually gets to school just a few minutes before his report time, which does not leave much time to meet. During the day, Mr. Thomas is given a 30-minute lunch break and one 15-minute break. He currently does not have a planning period or a designated time in which he can meet with Mr. Rodriguez to discuss the new plan. This is not the first time that Mr. Rodriguez has needed time to discuss information related to his students with Mr. Thomas. Mr. Rodriguez is unsure of how to keep Mr. Thomas informed of changes related to Vashaun and the other students.

1. Whose responsibility is it to ensure teachers and paraeducators have time to meet regularly?
2. Who should Mr. Rodriguez reach out to in order to help him?
3. What are some considerations Mr. Rodriguez needs to think through in order to make time to meet with Mr. Thomas?
4. Name three ways Mr. Rodriquez can design the meeting time to be most efficient.

CASE STUDY 3

Miss Ballard is a sixth-grade language special education teacher and has been assigned four paraeducators to help her teach and support a caseload of 25 students with IEPs for the upcoming school year. When organizing her daily schedule, as well as each of the four paraeducators' schedules, Miss Ballard became concerned with the lack of time available for her to meet with her paraeducators. She knows that she will need time to review student lessons, respond to questions regarding student behavior, and give the paraeducators some feedback on a variety of strategies and scenarios. Miss Ballard feels as though maintaining consistent and professional communication throughout the school year is critical when managing four paraeducators. She believes the more connected she is with her paraeducators, the more they can all work together to support the students as one unit. She has experienced a disconnect with a paraeducator in the past and observed the impact it has on the classroom culture as a whole, as well as on individual student performance. Miss Ballard wants to put some things in place in order to ensure she has time to talk and share information with her paraeducators on a regular basis.

1. What are some supports Miss Ballard can put into place to ensure her paraeducators can communicate with her on a consistent schedule?
2. How can Miss Ballard structure her communication and interactions to make sure the time spent with her paraeducators is effective and productive?
3. How can Miss Ballard's school leaders support her as she strives to incorporate effective communication into her class structure?

Paraeducators have been working in classrooms for decades, but their roles and responsibilities have dramatically changed in recent years (Mason et al., 2021). With this evolution, paraeducators have become active members of educational teams, specifically those including students with disabilities. Although paraeducators have assumed a more involved role in the classroom, they are often not included in the planning process or progress meetings. At times, paraeducators are not informed of changes or updates made to a student's educational program. This dearth of communication can be a disservice to everyone involved, especially with the impact on student learning. When a strong working relationship between adults in the classroom does not exist, a healthy environment in which students can play, learn, and develop is not fostered (Jones et al., 2012).

The teacher and paraeducator team must be comfortable with the one teach/one assist framework. Within this framework, the teacher and paraeducator work collaboratively; however, it is understood that the teacher takes the lead on instruction, educational decisions, and parent communication, and the paraeducator is available to contribute ideas and assist in various ways. In addition to embracing this structure of collaboration, it is also imperative that effective and open communication be established between teachers and paraeducators, as well as a positive and respectful classroom culture. In order for strong working relationships to develop and for healthy classroom culture to be established, Ashbaker and Morgan (2012) suggest that schools value and recognize paraeducator contributions, include paraeducators in the planning and review process to the greatest extent possible, designate time for teachers and paraeducators to meet regularly, and provide professional development where teachers and paraeducators can learn effective practices alongside one another.

COMMUNICATION AND HIGH-LEVERAGE PRACTICES

In 2016, the Collaboration for Effective Education Development, Accountability, and Reform (CEEDAR) and the Council for Exceptional Children created and published a set of 22 specific practices that in-service and pre-service special and general education teachers should strive to implement in their classrooms, known as the HLPs (McLeskey et al., 2017). HLPs are organized into four domains, including assessment, collaboration, instructional, and social/emotional/behavioral. With so much research emphasizing the need for, and impact of, effective communication, 3 of the 22 HLPs are dedicated to informing the ways in which collaboration efforts are executed within the school structure. Specifically, HLP 1 and HLP 2 target the interactions between teachers and paraeducators, while HLP 3 focuses on collaboration with parents. HLP 1 guides teachers to collaborate with professionals to increase student success. Within this HLP, it is recommended that teachers use effective collaboration behaviors, such as active listening, questioning, and problem solving, when interacting with paraeducators and other support staff. HLP 2 encourages teachers to organize and facilitate effective meetings with professionals and families. Teachers need to ensure that paraeducators participate in meetings that impact their specific roles and responsibilities, such as IEP and BIP meetings. Teachers should arrange these meetings, develop the agenda, and encourage participation from all members using effective collaboration behaviors (McLeskey et al., 2017). It is essential for teachers and paraeducators to know these HLPs and actively work toward establishing and maintaining effective communication.

COMMUNICATION

Communication is an essential part of most professional jobs. However, if a position is undervalued or if there is a lack of training, communication can suffer. This has been noted frequently within the literature related to paraeducators. Paraeducators report feeling as though they are not part of the educational team and that those around them do not value the work they do (Sobeck & Robertson, 2019). Research also reveals that most classroom teachers are ill-prepared to foster positive professional relationships with the paraeducators in their classrooms (Douglas et al., 2016; Jones et al., 2012).

TABLE 2-1. TEACHER–PARAEDUCATOR MEETING AGENDA	
Date:	Time:
Participants:	
Topic(s):	
Notes:	
Decision(s):	
Action Step(s):	
Items for Next Meeting:	Signature/Initials:

Due to these challenges, teachers must take active steps to ensure they establish a professional means for communication, as well as ways to convey their appreciation for the paraeducators who work in their classroom. Communication is most effective when it operates under a plan. With the overwhelmed schedules of teachers and paraeducators, it is essential to set routine time aside for communication to occur. An agreed-upon time must be built into the daily, weekly, or monthly schedule. The parameters of communication should also be set. At the beginning of the school year, the teacher and paraeducator should discuss the types of information that need to be discussed during the scheduled meetings so that each person can be prepared (Table 2-1). The length of the meeting should also be agreed upon and adhered to each time so it does not conflict with the other responsibilities of team members.

In addition to formal times for discussion, the teacher and paraeducator should also establish guidelines for "on-the-fly" communication, as some communication inevitably happens spontaneously as needs arise. Having a plan for when and where quick communication should happen is important. The teacher should inform the paraeducator of the best time of day or location to have quick conversations. For example, the teacher may want to let the paraeducator know that quick conversations are best before and after the lunch period, during the planning period, and during the afternoon math block where students tend to work a lot at learning stations. Or, if the teacher tends to arrive at school early each day, that time may also be offered to the paraeducator as time to briefly meet. Alternatively, the teacher can also let the paraeducator know the times of the day when interruptions for professional discussion should be limited. For example, a teacher may want to share with the paraeducator that quick check-ins or on-the-fly meetings would not be best before or during the morning reading intervention block due to the number of students they are working with, paired with a shorter class period. Or the teacher may share that this type of communication is not best at the very end of the day as they have to leave the school promptly to pick their child up from school. Teachers may also want to establish the best methods for communication such as text messages, a shared message board in the classroom, email, or verbally (Douglas et al., 2016). Setting parameters for formal and informal communication gives both the teacher and the paraeducator a clear time and path for effectively communicating.

In order to make communication as productive as possible, teachers and paraeducators should be familiar with the characteristics that make communication successful. Pickett and colleagues (2007) suggest that team members develop effective listening skills, as well as the ability to confirm and clarify information. Both the paraeducator and teacher need to demonstrate an interest in the message being delivered and a desire to understand the situation through active listening. Active listening involves confirming what was heard or clarifying information through summarizing (i.e., restating important facts), paraphrasing (i.e., stating the important facts in their own words), perception checking (i.e., combining a statement and a question), or asking questions (i.e., presenting a question when something is unclear). It can also be helpful for the teacher or paraeducator to take notes during or after the communication occurs in order to keep record of specific decisions and outcomes.

One specific strategy that has been found to be effective in promoting active listening among educator partnerships is the LAFF method (McNaughton et al., 2008). LAFF is a mnemonic term in which each letter represents a step or action to take while engaging in active listening. There are four steps within the strategy: (a) Listen, empathize, and convey respect; (b) Ask questions and take notes if permissible; (c) Focus on the main topic; and (d) Find a first step (Vostal et al., 2015). Within the first step, *listen,* teachers are encouraged to make an initial statement of empathy and understanding, demonstrate a neutral interest in the topic (Turnbull et al., 2010), maintain appropriate body language and expressions (Bodie et al., 2012), and offer an appreciative sentiment by thanking their colleague for meeting. Second, the teacher should *ask* permission to take notes and to ask a range of questions. Taking notes supports future reflection and communicates that what is being shared is important. Third, within the *focus* portion of the strategy, the teacher should summarize the problem or concern that was discussed, confirm their understanding of the issue, and ask for clarification as needed. Within this step, both teacher and paraeducator should demonstrate a shared understanding of the concern before moving on. The last step of the LAFF process is to *find a first step.* Teachers should identify a follow-up activity based on the conversation. First-step activities may include collecting more data, involving an additional person, putting a solution in place to try, or having follow-up conversations with other staff members. The steps within the LAFF process are evidenced-based ways to engage in active listening effectively. Each LAFF strategy component has also been deemed a valued communication skill by special educators (Turnbull et al., 2010) and professionals in general (Bodie et al., 2012; Figure 2-1).

In addition to intentional and active communication, teachers and paraeducators should be aware that, at times, some communication can be unintentional. Often, our most impactful form of communication is conveyed in nonverbal ways. For example, a teacher or paraeducator can unknowingly convey a communicative message to others by their body posture, gestures, facial expressions, and body language. Both teachers and paraeducators should ensure that their nonverbal communication aligns with the tone they want to portray. Effective communication along with these subtle forms of communication collectively help to create a positive classroom culture, an essential attribute of a successful classroom.

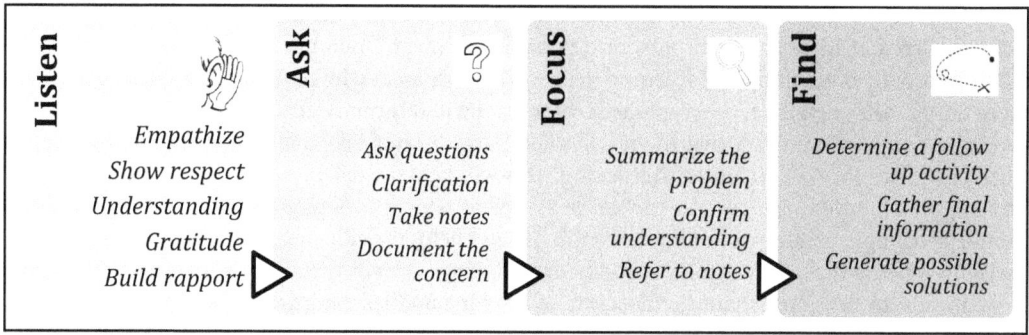

Figure 2-1. Flowchart depicting how to implement the LAFF active listening strategy.

EXAMPLE OF HOW NONVERBAL COMMUNICATION CAN IMPACT THE TEACHER–PARAEDUCATOR WORKING RELATIONSHIP

Mrs. Hernandez is a paraeducator in Mr. Joyce's eighth-grade classroom. She is new to the school this year as she transferred up from the elementary school. Mr. Joyce has repeatedly told Mrs. Hernandez that he is available to answer any of her questions and he does not mind explaining or demonstrating any strategies for questions she finds confusing. On several occasions Mrs. Hernandez has asked Mr. Joyce for some clarification on a few topics, and although he does respond to her, he is often looking at his computer or engaging in another task while talking to her. On another occasion Mrs. Hernandez needed to explain a behavioral situation she experienced with a student in order to get guidance from Mr. Joyce, and during her explanation she noticed Mr. Joyce constantly looking behind her and avoiding eye contact. Although Mr. Joyce had told her he did not mind providing guidance and support, Mrs. Hernandez is beginning to feel as though she is bothering Mr. Joyce. Over time she stopped asking for assistance and tried to handle the events of the day without clarification or guidance from Mr. Joyce. One day when Mrs. Hernandez did not follow a classroom routine correctly with a student, the student began to engage in anxiety-related behaviors of pacing, rocking, and self-talking. Mr. Joyce asked Mrs. Hernandez why she did not have the student following the routine as needed, and she shared that she was not sure about that specific routine. Again, Mr. Joyce reiterated that he is always available for questions. Mrs. Hernandez then shared that she had grown uncomfortable asking for assistance due his nonverbal gestures and that she did not want to bother him. Mr. Joyce apologized for any unintended messages his body language had sent, thanked Mrs. Hernandez for her honesty, and shared that he will try to be more cognizant of his nonverbal body language.

IMPORTANT TOPICS OF COMMUNICATION

Although there are numerous topics that can be discussed throughout the school year, there are several that are crucial to support a healthy working relationship between the teacher and paraeducator. Some topics need to only be covered once (e.g., informal paraeducator preference survey), while other topics are revisited often throughout the year (e.g., student performance). In the following section we discuss several topics that are important points of discussion for the teacher and paraeducator.

Everyone functions and navigates situations under different sets of principles, and often these principles are not identical from person to person. Each team member should take time to share their philosophy of teaching and learning to provide transparency in how they approach their classroom duties. Although the teacher–paraeducator team will rely on the teacher's professional training and expertise, it is important that the teacher and paraeducator take a few moments to discuss the what, how, and whys of teaching and learning. This will help the teacher know when more explanation might be needed with certain strategies, as well as which strategies the paraeducator may feel comfortable implementing or not implementing. It also helps provide meaning and reasoning for the decisions made at the student and classroom level. Having such conversations allows the teacher and paraeducator to develop a shared philosophy of teaching and learning where both perspectives are heard and represented (Table 2-2).

In addition to discussing the paraeducator's philosophy of teaching and learning, it is equally important to learn about their perspective of behavior management. A substantial portion of a paraeducator's workday is dedicated to managing student behavior (Brock & Carter, 2013; Douglas et al., 2022; Sobeck et al., 2020). Therefore, it is necessary for the teacher–paraeducator team to understand each other's views and approaches to behavior management. Having an upfront conversation and understanding relative to behavioral approaches can be extremely beneficial when it comes to responding to student behavior, implementing strategies with fidelity, and ensuring follow-through. Because the paraeducator provides support to the student's educational team, the paraeducator must understand the strategies outlined in a student's BIP, 504 Plan, or IEP. In addition to discussing behavioral approaches with the paraeducator and providing training to understand these strategies, the teacher can ask the paraeducator to complete a contextual fit inventory. This inventory (Table 2-3) is designed to evaluate the paraeducator's level of confidence and comfort with specific behavior management strategies they are required to implement. This quick and easy tool, adapted from Horner and colleagues (2003), can be used prior to a paraeducator implementing a new behavior management strategy.

Another topic that should be discussed is each person's approach to work. Discussing aspects of work ethic, collaboration, and what the teacher and paraeducator feel is most important to a strong working relationship can bring clarity and understanding to the classroom dynamic. For example, the teacher might rate punctuality as a very important component of a solid work ethic, while the paraeducator might place more emphasis on task completion. Communicating about various aspects of work gives the teacher and paraeducator an opportunity to share their opinions and helps maintain a reciprocal level of respect. It also allows each person to demonstrate consideration for the aspects of work ethic and collaboration that their colleague values. For example, if the paraeducator knows the teacher places high value on punctuality, then they can be more aware and intentional with their timing. Alternatively, the teacher may decide to give the paraeducator a sufficient amount of time to complete certain tasks because they know the paraeducator finds task completion important.

The PAR^{2}A Center at the University of Colorado Denver has a teacher–paraeducator work styles inventory that can be used to help the teacher and paraeducator evaluate the conditions in which they work best. When using this resource, both the classroom teacher and paraeducator complete a self-assessment survey specific to the ways in which they work best in the classroom (PAR^{2}A Center, 2021). Having this information about both team members can help with collaboration, roles and responsibilities, and expectations.

TABLE 2-2. PHILOSOPHY OF TEACHING AND LEARNING INVENTORY

Respond to the statements below using numbers 1 through 5. The numbers represent the following indicators:

1—Strongly Disagree, 2—Disagree, 3—Neutral, 4—Agree, 5—Strongly Agree

1.	Students should be given external reinforcement to help them behave appropriately in class.	☐1 ☐2 ☐3 ☐4 ☐5
2.	Students with disabilities should be given individual learning opportunities outside of the general education classroom.	☐1 ☐2 ☐3 ☐4 ☐5
3.	All students learn differently, so content should be presented in different ways.	☐1 ☐2 ☐3 ☐4 ☐5
4.	The curriculum should focus on essential knowledge, not the students' personal interests, likes, and dislikes.	☐1 ☐2 ☐3 ☐4 ☐5
5.	If a student is not learning a skill, content, or behavior, the teaching staff is responsible, not the student.	☐1 ☐2 ☐3 ☐4 ☐5
6.	Students should progress through skills at their own individualized pace and only complete tasks they want to, when they are ready.	☐1 ☐2 ☐3 ☐4 ☐5
7.	Instruction should be presented in an inquiry-based manner, allowing the student to construct their own understanding.	☐1 ☐2 ☐3 ☐4 ☐5
8.	Students should be taught to mastery before moving on to the next skill or content level.	☐1 ☐2 ☐3 ☐4 ☐5
9.	The classroom should be structured with routines and processes in place so students know the expectations.	☐1 ☐2 ☐3 ☐4 ☐5
10.	Instruction should be presented in a direct way where the student is explicitly taught the essential skills or content specific to the learning target.	☐1 ☐2 ☐3 ☐4 ☐5
11.	Students with disabilities should be included with their peers for all classes of the day.	☐1 ☐2 ☐3 ☐4 ☐5
12.	The curriculum and content presented in class should be the same for every student.	☐1 ☐2 ☐3 ☐4 ☐5
13.	Actively ignoring a behavior can be an effective method for behavior modification.	☐1 ☐2 ☐3 ☐4 ☐5
14.	Students with disabilities should be provided extra support from a teacher or paraeducator only as needed.	☐1 ☐2 ☐3 ☐4 ☐5

Table 2-3. Contextual Fit of Behavior Management Strategies Inventory

Name:

Strategy:

Respond to the statements below using numbers 1 through 5. The numbers represent the following indicators:

1—Strongly Disagree, 2—Disagree, 3—Neutral, 4—Agree, 5—Strongly Agree

1. I understand my role in implementing this strategy.	☐1 ☐2 ☐3 ☐4 ☐5
2. I have the skills needed to implement this strategy.	☐1 ☐2 ☐3 ☐4 ☐5
3. I do not require any additional training in order to implement this strategy with fidelity.	☐1 ☐2 ☐3 ☐4 ☐5
4. I am comfortable with the elements of this strategy.	☐1 ☐2 ☐3 ☐4 ☐5
5. This strategy aligns with my personal opinion on how students should be supported.	☐1 ☐2 ☐3 ☐4 ☐5
6. I have all of the materials and space needed to effectively implement this strategy.	☐1 ☐2 ☐3 ☐4 ☐5
7. There are components of this strategy I find difficult and/or may require some clarification.	☐1 ☐2 ☐3 ☐4 ☐5
8. I have an adequate amount of support needed to implement the strategy accurately.	☐1 ☐2 ☐3 ☐4 ☐5
9. I believe that the strategy is an effective strategy that may help improve the student's behavior.	☐1 ☐2 ☐3 ☐4 ☐5
10. I believe it is in the best interest of the student to try this behavior management strategy.	☐1 ☐2 ☐3 ☐4 ☐5
11. The amount of time and effort needed in order to implement this strategy effectively and with fidelity is reasonable.	☐1 ☐2 ☐3 ☐4 ☐5
12. I am able to collect data accurately on the student's performance and the effectiveness of this strategy.	☐1 ☐2 ☐3 ☐4 ☐5

Adapted from Horner, R. H., Salentine, S., & Albin, R. W. (2003). *Self-assessment of contextual fit in schools*. University of Oregon.

As mentioned in Chapter 1, the roles and responsibilities of the paraeducator also need to be conveyed. In addition to making the paraeducator aware of their role within the classroom, they also need to learn about the policies, routines, and protocols. Sometimes these aspects of classroom functioning can be learned by spending time in the classroom, but reviewing common practices can help the paraeducator have a clear understanding of classroom functioning from the start. With guidance from the teacher, paraeducators can develop a sense of independence working with students, reduce potential conflicts in teacher–paraeducator relationships, and support productive work—which ultimately prompts a level of respect by students. When the paraeducator has a greater level of independence and authority within the classroom, students tend to assume a higher level of respect for the paraeducator. Additionally, paraeducators may have a stronger sense of pride and accomplishment in their work when they are given some independence.

Classroom Culture

Beebe and colleagues (2014) suggest that when two individuals have a professional working relationship, a common culture must be established. Each person brings their own personal culture to the classroom. However, in order to cultivate a collaborative classroom dynamic, teacher–paraeducator teams need to create a new, third culture that represents each person's perspectives. Often the quality of services provided to students can depend on the positive dynamic established between the teacher and paraeducator (Biggs et al., 2018). Both individuals need to feel comfortable to discuss, debate, and exchange ideas professionally. Once this common culture is negotiated and expectations are agreed upon, effective communication can thrive.

To negotiate a positive classroom culture, teachers and paraeducators should consider one another's cultural and ethnic background, as well as the life experiences they bring to the classroom. Consideration should also be given to how each individual works best, their understanding of behavior management and academic learning, as well as past experiences with conflict resolution. One way to organize and obtain this type of information is to create a questionnaire for both the teacher and the paraeducator to complete. This questionnaire can then serve as a starting point for a conversation. See Tables 2-1, 2-2, and 2-3, as well as the PAR^{2}A Center survey referenced earlier for examples of inventories to use. Gerlach (2015) and Morgan and Ashbaker (2001) also offer questionnaires and checklists within their texts that can guide this type of conversation. By addressing these areas, generating an agreed-upon plan for communication, and clarifying expectations, the teacher–paraeducator team can set the stage for a supportive classroom culture to emerge.

Teachers can also take steps to establish a positive classroom culture. Knowing that paraeducators often feel undervalued and of low priority within the school, teachers can take small steps to make the paraeducator feel valued (Douglas et al., 2016). Things like buying coffee for their paraeducator, writing a personalized card sharing their gratitude for how the paraeducator handled a specific situation, engaging in brief check-ins with the paraeducator to see how they are doing and if additional support can be given, or even bringing in small treats to share can all have a big impact. Having the paraeducator complete a preference survey at the start of the school year can give the teacher ideas to carry out these demonstrations of appreciation. The survey could include questions like:

- What do you like to do in your spare time?
- What is your favorite type of coffee?
- What is your favorite type of candy?
- How do you unwind after a long day?
- What is your go-to place to get a good meal?

Getting to know the classroom paraeducator through an informal survey gives the teacher a resource throughout the year to show the paraeducator how much they are valued. Table 2-4 shows an example of an inventory that can be used to learn about a paraeducator's preferences.

TABLE 2-4. PREFERENCE SURVEY TO ASSESS A PARAEDUCATOR'S LIKES AND DISLIKES TO ASSIST THE TEACHER IN ESTABLISHING STRONG RAPPORT

Respond to the following questions by writing in your answer on the line provided.

1. In my spare time, I enjoy ...	
2. My favorite foods are ...	
3. My favorite types of candy are ...	
4. If I had a day off of work I would ...	
5. My closest family members are ...	
6. I do/do not have pets. They are ...	
7. In order to relax or calm myself down I tend to ...	
8. I am most encouraged by ...	
9. My least favorite part about work is ...	
10. The holiday I enjoy the most is ...	
11. My favorite coffee/drink is ...	
12. I prefer to come in early to work or stay late because ...	
13. I feel appreciated by others when ...	
14. My favorite outdoor activity is ...	
15. Something unique about me is ...	

Example of How a Teacher Can Do Extra Things to Make the Paraeducators Feel Appreciated

Mrs. Wilson is a third- and fourth-grade special education teacher who works half of her day in inclusive classrooms and the other half in the special education classroom delivering small group instruction. She manages five paraeducators who help support her caseload of 22 students. Prior to becoming a certified teacher, Mrs. Wilson spent 6 years as a middle school paraeducator supporting students with disabilities. Now in her third year of being a classroom teacher, Mrs. Wilson has seen, second hand, the impact that paraeducators have on the students and the classroom as a whole. At the start of the school year she had each paraeducator complete a preference survey so that she would be aware of her paraeducators' likes and dislikes and be able to show her appreciation periodically and have some ideas on how to uplift her paraeducators on more challenging days. During an in-service day early in the school year, Mrs. Wilson brought in a coffee for each paraeducator and wrote an uplifting message on each cup. Then, a month later, one of the paraeducators had a particularly challenging day due to some intense behavior demonstrated by one of their students. The following day Mrs. Wilson carved out an additional 20-minute break for the paraeducator to take a walk outside around the school, as they had indicated on their preference survey that walking is a stress reliever. Around winter recess, Mrs. Wilson wrote each paraeducator a message of appreciation in a holiday card and attached their favorite type of candy. Mrs. Wilson found these instances of showing appreciation to their paraeducators to be encouraging and plans to continue to incorporate small acts of kindness as the school year continues.

The climate of the classroom can be impacted by the interactions between the teacher and paraeducator. Both individuals need to demonstrate trust, kindness, and respect. It is important for students to see that the paraeducator has authority and should be given respect, just like the classroom teacher. If a conflict arises, it should be handled privately following conflict resolution procedures rather than be addressed in the presence of students.

Conflict Resolution

Although practices can be implemented to create a positive classroom culture, the teacher and paraeducator should be prepared to address conflict when it arises. Conflict can occur between the paraeducator and a student, the paraeducator and a parent, the paraeducator and another team member, or between the paraeducator and the teacher. Handling conflicts appropriately helps to maintain a positive classroom culture and a strong working relationship between the teacher and paraeducator. Navigating conflict should follow a protocol similar to establishing an effective plan for communication. The teacher and paraeducator can come up with their own plan when responding to conflict; however, many researchers have noted effective steps that can be taken. Pickett and colleagues (2007) identified the following nine-step process to support conflict resolution:

1. Identify and define the problem
2. Determine the cause of the problem
3. Identify the needs and desired results
4. Brainstorm possible solutions
5. Select the solution that will address the identified needs
6. Create a plan of action
7. Implement the plan
8. Evaluate the solution
9. Respond to conflict

Alternatively, paraeducator and teacher teams can approach conflict using a problem-solving approach. Within this approach each person is encouraged to maintain an objective perspective and systematically create a solution. It involves reflecting on the situation, deciding what could be done to improve the situation, and determining who will complete specific tasks to help bring the solution to fruition. Morgan and Ashbaker (2001) suggest writing down each person's reflections and the agreed-upon plan.

Example of How a Teacher and Paraeducator Can Use a Conflict Resolution Protocol When a Conflict Arises

Mrs. Yang is a kindergarten special education teacher with a caseload of 12 students. She manages three paraeducators who support her students. One of her paraeducators works with a student who requires the use of a daily picture schedule. In order to accommodate this student's need, the paraeducator, Miss Zuhm, carries and implements a traveling schedule as she is always with the student. When an outside agency support personnel visited the school to give feedback to Mrs. Yang on her program, she recommended that Miss Zuhm use a visual schedule with her student. Mrs. Yang was surprised as Miss Zuhm should have been using one all along. Mrs. Yang knew she needed to address this with Miss Zuhm so she followed the conflict resolution protocol.

The following day Mrs. Yang met with Miss Zuhm during the half hour before school started. This was a time they had agreed upon at the start of the year as a good time for meeting. Mrs. Yang **identified the problem**—*not implementing the picture schedule as outlined in the student's IEP. She went on to* **determine the cause of the problem** *by asking Miss Zuhm why the picture schedule was discontinued. Miss Zuhm explained that she thought the student might not need the picture schedule anymore and figured she would try to fade the support. Mrs. Yang then* **identified the desired results**—*re-implementing the picture schedule and explained why this was important for this specific student. She also encouraged Miss Zuhm to talk to her first before fading an intervention, as the student's team was responsible for a decision such as this. She then asked Miss Zuhm for some* **possible solutions** *for how to help her remember to use the schedule moving forward. They agreed that taking the time to discuss the rationale for the schedule was an adequate solution and was all that was needed. As a* **plan of action** *moving forward, Mrs. Yang said she will check in with Miss Zuhm every 2 weeks to see how the schedule is going and to discuss possible options for eventually fading the schedule. Mrs. Yang and Miss Zuhm* **implemented the plan,** *and Mrs. Yang checked in every 2 weeks. After 2 months they* **evaluated the solution,** *and both agreed the* **conflict had been resolved** *and therefore bi-weekly check-ins were no longer needed.*

Whether following the identified nine-step process, using the problem-solving approach, or developing a personalized protocol, it is important for both the teacher and paraeducator to be comfortable with the plan. Having prepared protocol easily accessible and using an agreed-upon process will allow the teacher and paraeducator to navigate and resolve conflicts more efficiently. The protocol should also identify what should be done when a solution cannot be identified by the teacher–paraeducator team. In these cases it may be necessary to involve an administrator, such as a building principal. The conflict resolution plan can be included in the topics teachers review with their paraeducator at the start of the academic year. This way, the plan is developed, reviewed, and agreed upon when no conflict is present.

Common Areas of Conflict

Although disagreements can develop regarding any number of topics or situations, there are common challenges that teachers often experience when managing one or more paraeducators. The following conflicts are common; however, each teacher–paraeducator team is unique and therefore may experience all, some, or none of these conflicts.

Paraeducator's Age and Experience

In some situations, a more novice teacher may accept a position in which the classroom paraeducator is older or has more experience in the classroom setting than the teacher. This can present a challenge for the teacher as the lines of the one-lead, one-assist model may blur. The more experienced paraeducator may be inclined to give the teacher directions or tell them how to teach or handle certain situations. Ultimately, the classroom teacher is responsible for the learning and behavior management of the students, however, seeking information or guidance from the paraeducator can serve to establish a healthy working relationship. Asking the paraeducator for insights on specific aspects of the school, students, or classroom can give the paraeducator a chance to be heard and can also provide some helpful knowledge to the newer teacher. Writing down a list of the specific elements of the school or classroom that the teacher feels would be helpful to discuss with the paraeducator is a great way to ensure time is set aside for the paraeducator to share their experiences and knowledge.

Lack of Follow-Through

At various points throughout the school year a paraeducator may demonstrate a lack of follow-through with a task or a written plan. This might include not fully implementing strategies as directed, not following protocols for specific situations, or not completing given tasks. It is important for the teacher to address such instances with the paraeducator; however, the teacher should also remember the specific roles and responsibilities, training, and preparation provided to the paraeducator. In many instances, paraeducators have minimal to no formal training on behavior management, teaching, or implementing interventions (Sobeck et al., 2020). Therefore, when addressing a concern with the paraeducator, it is important to use language that is easy to understand, explain the reasoning for the task or strategy, and provide an overview of the steps or components. Leaving time for the paraeducator to ask questions or seek clarification on the task is also helpful. Taking the time to explain the principles of the strategy or the "why" behind it, instead of just telling them to do a specific task, can support paraeducator follow-through. Research has also consistently revealed that follow-up instruction with coaching can help alleviate issues with paraeducator follow-through. See Chapter 5 for additional guidance on coaching.

Parent Communication

With paraeducators often working so closely with individual students, it is common for the paraeducator to develop a relationship with the student's parents or guardians. Paraeducators are often left with a responsibility to write a note to the parents in a daily communication log or checklist, and they may also engage in brief verbal exchanges when the parent drops off or picks up their child each day. Paraeducators often live in the community in which they work (Dai et al., 2007) and therefore may experience interactions with their students' parents outside of school. Additionally, paraeducators who support students with extensive support needs may also be approached to provide respite care for the child outside of school hours.

These interactions may result in a shift in the relationship between the paraeducator and parent that can pose challenges for the teacher. This might include the paraeducator becoming the primary contact with parents for gaining information about the child's school day, communicating directly with the parent via phone and text, making the parent feel uneasy about a potential new paraeducator assignment in the following school year, or discussing information about other students or class happenings that violates confidentiality. At times a parent or guardian may even talk to a paraeducator about a situation at school and brainstorm ideas to help the situation without keeping the teacher in the loop. The teacher can set boundaries for the communication practices at the start of the school that are specific to their classroom and students to prevent these challenges from occurring. The school or district may also have guidelines for paraeducators involving parent interactions that the teacher can refer to as well. Reviewing parent communication protocols before problems arise will let the paraeducator know the expectations for interacting with parents. It is also good to review these guidelines throughout the year; this can be incorporated into a review of other classroom processes.

EXAMPLE OF HOW A PARAEDUCATOR AND PARENT/GUARDIAN RELATIONSHIP CAN GO BEYOND THE BOUNDARIES SET FORTH BY THE CLASSROOM TEACHER

Mr. Vitullo is a fifth-grade special education teacher and has a caseload of 12 students. He manages two paraeducators who support his students. For the last 2 years, one of his paraeducators, Miss Robinson, has supported one of her students with Down syndrome, Jacob. During this time Miss Robinson has assisted Jacob not only with daily classroom and social routines but also for special events at the school. She completes a checklist at the end of each school day that informs Jacob's parents about how his day went at school. The checklist not only keeps his parents in the loop but also serves as a discussion starter for Jacob and his parents. Miss Robinson also sees Jacob's mother during pickup at the end of the school day, and they speak briefly. Over the past 2 years, Miss Robinson has established a friendly relationship with Jacob's mom. She has even assisted Jacob's mother with taking Jacob to a few family outings and events outside of school as an extra set of hands to help. Recently, Jacob's mother and Miss Robinson saw one another at a local coffee shop. While they were waiting for their drinks, Jacob's mom asked Miss Robinson about one of Jacob's behaviors at school. The two ended up having a 30-minute conversation about the behavior and brainstormed some ideas to try to help Jacob diminish the unwanted behavior. At school the next day, Miss Robinson shared with Mr. Vitullo the strategies and techniques that Miss Robinson and Jacob's mother would like to try. Mr. Vitullo did not know how to respond as Miss Robinson not only discussed confidential information about a student outside of school but also agreed on strategies to try with the parents without his approval. Mr. Vitullo reminded Miss Robinson that although he appreciates her eagerness to help the student, all communication with the parent regarding behavior, academics, and plans need to be made through him. He also made a phone call home to Jacob's parents to discuss the situation and explain where they will go from here.

If a problem arises and the teacher feels as though the paraeducator is sharing too much information or communicating with the parents outside the parameters of the working relationship, the teacher can have a conversation with the paraeducator in which the teacher shares their concerns. If needed, the teacher can also utilize the problem-solving approach or the steps of conflict resolution to help resolve the concern. If after engaging in conflict resolution strategies the paraeducator continues to communicate with the parents outside the identified parameters of the working relationship, or if the communication interferes with the student's education or creates challenges for the teacher, then the teacher should consult the building-level administrator for guidance and support.

Lack of Involvement in the Classroom

Walk into various classrooms and you observe paraeducators engaging in the class at varying levels. Some paraeducators take an active role supporting students and assisting in instruction, while other paraeducators are more passive, supporting students only as needed. As mentioned earlier, it is important for classroom expectations to be clearly outlined with the paraeducator so they know how much involvement the teacher expects. It can also be helpful to assign specific tasks for the paraeducator to complete at certain times throughout the day. By giving specific tasks based on student and classroom needs, the paraeducator is aware of what needs to be done. When given explicit directions on tasks to complete, paraeducators also tend to feel more comfortable because they know these duties fall within their responsibilities. The teacher can use the information collected from the paraeducator surveys to identify areas of strength. Knowing the paraeducator's strengths can help the teacher assign appropriate tasks and can help teachers focus on the positive attributes of the paraeducator.

There will be times in which the paraeducator must participate in class activities or tasks that may not be favorable. When it comes to these responsibilities, the teacher will need to provide scaffolding and support to teach the paraeducator the steps or skills needed to successfully complete the task. If a paraeducator seems to continue to lack in their level of involvement, even after they are provided with instruction and support for specific responsibilities, the teacher can have several responses. One option is the teacher can talk with the paraeducator and discuss any concerns. Alternatively, the teacher could offer additional guidance and support. The teacher could also revisit the paraeducator's areas of strengths and areas for improvement and switch around paraeducator duties accordingly. Each person brings various abilities and strengths to the classroom, and it is important to consider these when organizing student supports, classroom duties, and responsibilities within the classroom. It is also important to note that teachers must be willing to join in on supporting students in nonpreferred tasks and activities of daily living skills, such as toileting and feeding. By sharing the responsibility of these self-help skills, a sense of mutual respect can be fostered between the teacher and the paraeducator (Douglas et al., 2016).

ADMINISTRATOR'S ROLE WITHIN COMMUNICATION

Although effective communication is primarily carried out between the teacher and paraeducator, the building administrator must acknowledge the importance of this communication. Teachers have packed schedules; therefore, it is essential that school administrators build in time for teachers and paraeducators to communicate. This can occur daily, weekly, or bi-weekly, and should be incorporated into each teacher's schedule. Administrators are encouraged to think creatively on times and ways (e.g., before or after school, during planning times, arranging substitutes, participating in video chatting, alternating schedules) to ensure teachers and paraeducators have protected meeting time. This might require coverage within the classroom by other school personnel. If a school currently does not have dedicated time for the teacher and paraeducator to engage in training, data sharing, and performance feedback, the teacher should talk with the building principal to identify the steps that need to be taken to include this time into their schedule. Alternatively, the teacher and paraeducator can examine their specific schedules to identify adjustments that can be made to free up time for communication. The building administrator should also be willing to step in and support the teacher–paraeducator team when they are unable to resolve a conflict on their own.

Summary

It is important to establish effective communication practices and conflict resolution protocols early in the school year. Having these processes in place will help to maintain a balanced and efficient classroom. Paraeducators can bring a wealth of experience, talent, support, and assistance to the classroom. It is crucial that educators not only acknowledge this, but take steps to actively support the paraeducators they work with and convey their value to the team. When the paraeducator and the teacher keep an open line of communication and have established steps in place for when conflict arises, students experience a much more balanced and healthy learning environment. We want to strive for this type of an environment so that the students not only see an excellent model for communication and teamwork but so that the classroom culture remains steady and positive.

Chapter Review

1. What are some factors that contribute to creating a welcoming and supportive classroom culture?
2. Why should teacher and paraeducator dyads strive to create a balanced and positive classroom culture?
3. What are some strategies and tools that a teacher can use in order to understand and utilize their classroom paraeducator to the fullest?
4. Name and describe two ways to address conflict when it arises between a paraeducator and a teacher.
5. Identify two common areas of conflict and how it can be resolved or addressed.

Resources

- Council for Exceptional Children. (2023). *High-leverage practices for students with disabilities.* https://highleveragepractices.org/
- Council for Exceptional Children. (2023). https://exceptionalchildren.org/
- Doyle, M. B. (2008). *The paraprofessional's guide to the inclusive classroom: Working as a team* (3rd ed.). Brookes Publishing.
- Fitzell, S. G. (2010). *Paraprofessionals and teachers working together: Highly effective strategies for inclusive classrooms* (2nd ed.). Cogent Catalyst Publications.
- French, N. K. (2003). *Managing paraeducators in your school: How to hire, train, and supervise non-certified staff.* Corwin Press.
- Gerlach, K. (2015). *Let's team up! A checklist for teachers, paraeducators, and principals.* National Professional Resources/Dude Publishing.
- Montana Office of Public Instruction. (2017). *Paraprofessionals in Montana: A resource guide for administrators, educators, and paraprofessionals.* https://opi.mt.gov/Portals/182/Page%20Files/Special%20Education/Guides/2017%20Revised%20PARA%20Resource%20Guide%20FINAL%206-6-17A.pdf?ver=2017-08-31-125132-977
- Pickett, A. L., & Gerlach, K. (2003). *Supervising paraeducators in educational settings: A team approach* (2nd ed.). Pro Ed.
- Pickett, A. L., Gerlach, K., Morgan, R., Likins, M., & Wallace, T. (2007). *Paraeducators in schools: Strengthening the educational team.* Pro Ed.
- State Education Resource Center. (2007). *Assessment checklist for paraprofessionals: Preschool-grade 12.* https://portal.ct.gov/SDE/Paraeducator/Paraeducator-Information-and-Resources/Documents

- The University of Kansas. (2023). *Collaboration: Working effectively with paraeducators.* https://specialconnections.ku.edu/collaboration/working_effectively_with_paraeducators/teacher_tools
- Virginia Department of Education. (2005). *The Virginia paraprofessional guide to supervision and collaboration with paraprofessionals: A partnership.* https://vcuautismcenter.org/resources/paraprofessionals.cfm

REFERENCES

Ashbaker, B. Y., & Morgan, J. (2012). Team players and team managers: Special educators working with paraeducators to support inclusive classrooms. *Creative Education, 3*(3), 322-327. http://dx.doi.org/10.4236/ce.2012.33051

Beebe, S. A., Beebe, S. J., & Redmond, M. V. (2014). *Interpersonal communication relating to others* (7th ed.). Pearson.

Biggs, E. E., Gilson, C. B., & Carter, E. W. (2018). "Developing that balance": Preparing and supporting special education teachers to work with paraprofessionals. *Teacher Education and Special Education, 42*(2), 1-15. https://doi.org/10.1177/0888406418765611

Bodie, G. D., St. Cyr, K., Pence, M., Rold, M., & Honeycutt, J. (2012). Listening competence in initial interactions I: Distinguishing between what listening is and what listeners do. *International Journal of Listening, 26*, 1–28.

Brock, M., & Carter, E. W. (2013). Systematic review of paraprofessional-delivered educational practices to improve outcomes for students with intellectual and developmental disabilities. *Research & Practice for Persons with Severe Disabilities, 38*(4), 211-221.

Dai, C., Sindelar, P. T., Denslow, D., Dewey, J., & Rosenberg, M. S. (2007). Economic analysis and the design of alternative-route teacher education programs. *Journal of Teacher Education, 58*(5), 422-439. https://doi.org/10.1177/0022487107306395

Douglas, S. N., Bowles, R., & Kammes, R. (2022). Paraeducators: An important member of the educational team for students with disabilities. *Journal of the American Academy of Special Education Professionals,* Spring/Summer, 134-150.

Douglas, S. N., Chapin, S. E., & Nolan, J. F. (2016). Special education teachers' experiences supporting and supervising paraeducators: Implications for special and general education settings. *Teacher Education and Special Education, 39*(1), 60-74. https://doi.org/10.1177/0888406415616443

Gerlach, K. (2015). *Let's team up! A checklist for teachers, paraeducators and principals.* Dude Publishing.

Horner, R. H., Salentine, S., & Albin, R. W. (2003). *Self-assessment of contextual fit in schools.* University of Oregon.

Jones, C. R., Ratcliff, N. J., Sheehan, H., & Hunt, G. H. (2012). An analysis of teachers' and paraeducators' roles and responsibilities with implications for professional development. *Early Childhood Education Journal, 40,* 19-24. https://doi.org/10.1007/0643-011-0487-4

Mason, R. A., Gunersel, A. B., Irvin, D. W., Wills, H. P., Gregori, E., An, Z. G., & Ingram, P. B. (2021). From the frontlines: Perceptions of paraprofessionals' roles and responsibilities. *Teacher Education and Special Education, 44*(2), 97-116. https://doi.org/10.1177/0888406419896627

McLeskey, J., Barringer, M.-D., Billingsley, B., Brownell, M., Jackson, D., Kennedy, M., Lewis, T., Maheady, L., Rodriguez, J., Scheeler, M. C., Winn, J., & Ziegler, D. (2017). *High-leverage practices in special education.* Council for Exceptional Children & CEEDAR Center.

McNaughton, D., Hamlin, D., McCarthy, J., Head-Reeves, D., & Schreiner, M. (2008). Learning to listen: Teaching an active listening strategy to preservice education professionals. *Topics in Early Childhood Special Education, 27*(4), 223-231.

Morgan, J., & Ashbaker, B.Y. (2001). *A teacher's guide to working with paraeducators and other classroom aides.* Association for Supervision and Curriculum Development.

Pickett, A. L., Gerlach, K., Morgan, R., Likins, M., & Wallace, T. (2007). *Paraeducators in schools: Strengthening the educational team.* Pro Ed.

Sobeck, E. E., & Robertson, R. (2019). Perspectives on current practices and barriers to training for paraeducators of students with autism in inclusive settings. *Journal of the American Academy of Special Education Professionals,* 131-159.

Sobeck, E. E., Robertson, R., & Smith, J. (2020). The effects of didactic instruction and performance feedback on paraeducator implementation of behavior support strategies in inclusive settings. *Journal of Special Education, 53*(4), 245-255. https://doi.org/10.1177/0022466919858989

Turnbull, A., Turnbull, H. R., Erwin, E. J., Soodak, L. C., & Shogren, K. A. (2010). *Families, professionals, and exceptionality: Positive outcomes through partnerships and trust* (6th ed.). Pearson.

Vostal, B. R., McNaughton, D., Benedek-Wood, E., & Hoffman, K. (2015). Preparing teachers for collaborative communication: Evaluation of instruction in an active listening strategy. *National Teacher Education Journal, 8*(2), 5-14.

Introduction to Paraeducator Supervision

INTRODUCTION

Supervision is an essential aspect of ensuring paraeducators have the knowledge and skills to successfully support students with disabilities. Chapter 3 provides an overview of laws and guidelines related to paraeducator supervision. Key components of supervision are outlined including creating a supportive work environment, directing the work of paraeducators, training paraeducators, and observing and providing feedback to paraeducators.

CHAPTER OBJECTIVES

→ Describe the laws and guidelines related to paraeducator supervision and the details that are included or missing.

→ Explain the importance of paraeducator supervision and provide a rationale for pre-service and in-service teacher knowledge and skills related to paraeducator supervision.

→ Describe the components of paraeducator supervision and practical strategies for implementing effective supervision with paraeducators.

KEY TERMS

- **CEC Specialty Sets:** Knowledge and skills that are used by teacher education programs to develop curriculum and create assessments for their candidates to demonstrate mastery of standards.
- **Council for Exceptional Children (CEC):** An international professional organization that strives to improve the experience of individuals with disabilities and/or gifts and talents through advocacy, professional development, resource sharing, and educational standards.
- **Every Student Succeeds Act (ESSA):** One of the main education laws for public schools in the United States that holds schools accountable for student performance. This law ensures equal opportunities for students from disadvantaged backgrounds and students who qualify for special education services.
- **Individuals with Disabilities Education Act (IDEA):** Established in 1990 and reauthorized in 2004, this federal law details special education and related service programming for students with disabilities.
- **Individuals with Disabilities Education Improvement Act (IDEIA):** A law that was established in 2004 as the reauthorization of IDEA (1990), in which several amendments were added that further detailed special education and related service programming for students with disabilities.
- **Initial Practice-Based Professional Preparation Standards for Special Educators (K-12):** Standards that define what a pre-service teaching candidate must know and be able to demonstrate prior to becoming a teacher.
- **No Child Left Behind Act (NCLB):** One of the leading laws for kindergarten through 12th-grade general education in the United States from 2002 to 2015 that sought to hold schools accountable for both student and overall school performance.

CASE STUDY 1

Mr. Garcia is a recent college graduate with a major in special education. He is in the first few months of his first year as a special education teacher at Saguaro Middle School. Mr. Garcia is working in a resource classroom and oversees one paraeducator in his classroom and three other paraeducators supporting students in inclusive classroom settings. Mr. Garcia had very little pre-service training and has had no in-service training since starting his current position to know how to best supervise paraeducators. Although no major issues have arisen yet, Mr. Garcia feels he needs additional support to learn how to best supervise the paraeducators who work with his students and reaches out to his building administrator, special education district administrator, and mentor teacher for support.

1. What does Mr. Garcia need to know about the supervision of paraeducators?
2. What are the different components of supervision that Mr. Garcia is likely to carry out with his paraeducators?
3. What kind of information should the building administrator, district administrator, and mentor teacher provide to Mr. Garcia to support him in his paraeducator supervision responsibilities?

CASE STUDY 2

Several years ago special education directors across the region, including Mrs. Main, the special education director from the Middleway School District, came together to discuss the necessity for paraeducator supervision and training. This is a relevant issue due to changes in federal law and new state legislation on supervision and training to ensure paraeducators have skills to support students with disabilities. After the regional meeting, Mrs. Main met with the superintendent and school board and, with their permission, developed and facilitated teacher in-service on the importance of paraeducator supervision and specific responsibilities of teachers in relation to paraeducators including ongoing training and coaching. Mrs. Main also worked with district and building personnel to clarify the roles and responsibilities of administrators, teachers, and paraeducators. She found that the paraeducators held many different responsibilities, depending on the building and program they served. At the end of each school year, Mrs. Main asked teachers for input on the specific knowledge and skills needed by paraeducators. She used this information to inform policy, procedures, and training opportunities in the Middleway School District. Teacher input consistently noted benefits from the in-service training related to paraeducator supervision and the transparency in role clarification of paraeducators and their supporting administrators and teachers. Teachers also indicated that training and role clarification helped them better understand supervision responsibilities and address problems with school administrators. However, teachers identified several key areas of focus for future paraeducator training to support current skill gaps. Mrs. Main provides a report to the school board that includes a recap of the paraeducator training topics and activities during the school year, along with plans for the following year based on teacher feedback.

1. *Who else should Mrs. Main solicit feedback from in her district to understand current paraeducators needs and inform adjustments to paraeducator related policies, procedures, and training opportunities? Provide a rationale for the individuals you identified and discuss the ways in which feedback might be obtained.*
2. *Mrs. Main attends another regional meeting with special education directors from surrounding school districts. Two special education directors approach her with concerns about the high paraeducator turnover they are experiencing in their districts. They know Mrs. Main has not had this issue in her district and asked her for advice on how they might reduce paraeducator turnover. What suggestions should Mrs. Main provide to these special education directors?*
3. *After a couple of years of funding to support in-service training for teacher supervision of paraeducators, the superintendent and school district are facing budget cuts. Mrs. Main has an upcoming meeting with the superintendent and school board and must provide a compelling case to justify why these funds are needed. Draft a rationale Mrs. Main can use to justify continued funding for teacher in-service related to paraeducator supervision.*

One of the important aspects of ensuring effective paraeducator support for students with disabilities is high-quality supervision of paraeducators. Supervision entails several components and responsibilities are shared between administrators, special education and general education teachers, and at times related service providers. While supervision components are detailed in this chapter, the specific supervision responsibilities of team members are detailed in Chapter 4.

Federal laws clearly outline the importance of paraeducator supervision. IDEA of 1997 was the first to indicate the use of paraeducators in "the provision of special education and related services ... to children with disabilities" and the need for paraeducators "who are appropriately trained and supervised" (20 U.S.C. 1412[a][14]). This language was maintained in the reauthorization of the act in 2004—renamed the IDEIA. Similarly the NCLB of 2001 acknowledged the use of paraeducators to provide services to students with and without disabilities. NCLB also indicated that paraeducators "may not provide any instructional service to a student unless the [paraeducator] is working under

Table 3-1. State-Adopted Paraeducator Certification Requirements

STATE	WEBSITE LINK
Delaware	https://www.doe.k12.de.us/Page/3501
Georgia	https://www.gapsc.com/Certification/LicensesPermits/paraprofessional.aspx
Illinois	https://www.isbe.net/licensure-requirements
New York	http://www.highered.nysed.gov/tcert/certificate/ta.html
Ohio	http://education.ohio.gov/Topics/Teaching/Licensure/Apply-for-Certificate-License/Educational-Aides-and-Monitors
Oklahoma	https://sde.ok.gov/faqs/oklahoma-title-i-paraprofessional-teaching-credential-teaching-assistant
Washington	https://www.pesb.wa.gov/paraeducator-certificate-program/minimum-employment-requirements

the direct supervision of a teacher" (2002). In 2015, the ESSA replaced NCLB and included further articulation of the role of paraeducators in educational settings and provided clarity regarding proficiency and training requirements for paraeducators. However, each of these laws are vague in their reference to supervision of paraeducators and lack specificity about how to best carry out paraeducator supervision.

Several legal decisions have provided some clarity around paraeducator supervision and have emphasized the need for paraeducators to be appropriately supervised. In two separate cases—Hingham Public Schools (2000) and Sioux City Community School District (2003)—rulings sided with parents who brought forth cases addressing concerns about paraeducator supervision practices in schools. The rulings emphasized the need for paraeducator supervision by a professional with expertise in the interventions and services being utilized and clarified that the paraeducator cannot serve as a substitute for intervention and services with certified professionals. In other words, paraeducators should not carry out primary instruction but can provide follow-up instruction or practice skills previously taught to students by a certified professional. Two other cases emphasized the need for supervision that includes appropriate training to paraeducators to carry out their duties. The Board of Education of the City of New York (1998) and Silsbee Independent School District (1997) cases both clarified the need for teachers, paraeducators, and related professionals to be adequately trained to address the specific needs of students with disabilities including their individual behavior and medical needs.

Guidelines Related to Paraeducator Supervision

Given the lack of specificity in federal law, rulings within case law, and research indicating poor supervision practices of paraeducators, several states (Table 3-1) have adopted specific certification requirements for paraeducators to ensure minimum proficiency upon hire and reduce the supervisory burden on teachers and administrators. Proficiency requirements often include documentation of completed education requirements (e.g., associate's degree, college coursework, specific workshops), passing scores on educational assessments (e.g., ParaPro, Workkeys, state-developed paraeducator exam), and/or professional learning plans to address deficits in performance identified in the annual evaluation. Other states follow federal guidelines but do not have specific certification requirements. Additionally, few states provide policies or procedures to guide paraeducator supervision, which places the burden on local educational agencies to develop and implement these policies.

For example, Douglas and colleagues (2022a) discovered the lack of state-level policies in Michigan related to paraeducator evaluation meant that many administrators did not have evaluation procedures, materials, or policies specific to paraeducators. As a result they often used teacher evaluation materials, which are inappropriate to the roles of paraeducators. In some cases, administrators admitted that they did not carry out paraeducator evaluation despite a recognition of its importance because it was not mandated like teacher evaluations.

Professional organizations have also developed guidelines to support paraeducator supervision. The CEC provides initial preparation standards for special education teachers including acknowledgment of skills and knowledge to supervise paraeducators (Berlinghoff & McLaughlin, 2022). In the *Initial Practice-Based Professional Preparation Standards for Special Educators* (*K-12*; see Appendix A), a section is dedicated to work with team members. This section includes the teacher's role collaborating, communicating, and coordinating paraeducators (Component 7.2), as well as working with and mentoring paraeducators (Component 7.4). Furthermore, the *Deafblindness Standards* (Standards DB.1.K5, DB.1.S2, DB.1.S4, DB.7.K1, DB.7.S9), *Advanced Specialty Set for Inclusion Specialists* (Standard SEIS.7.S6), and *Developmental Disabilities and Autism Spectrum Disorder Specialists* (Standard SEDAS.5.S3) all include references to special education teachers' roles supervising paraeducators (CEC, 2022a). The CEC standards also include *Core Competencies for Special Education Paraeducators* (see Appendix D), which can guide teachers in their supervisory roles with paraeducators (CEC, 2022b). See Table 3-2 for a list of the CEC standards related to paraeducator supervision.

IMPORTANCE OF PARAEDUCATOR SUPERVISION

Consistent with the current hiring practices in most states and federal requirements, the majority of paraeducators enter positions without formal training, especially in the area of special education. This lack of preparation often results in paraeducators questioning their competence, and when coupled with insufficient supervision, these feelings are exacerbated (Capizzi & Da Fonte, 2012). Furthermore, the limited training of paraeducators before hiring makes the need for high-quality supervision and training opportunities for paraeducators of top importance. Although special education teachers regularly supervise paraeducators, there is a clear need for additional training for teachers related to their supervisory roles with paraeducators (Sobeck, Douglas et al., 2020). Specifically, teachers have indicated a lack of pre-service preparation and in-service training, which results in teachers who are reluctant to supervise paraeducators and feel unprepared to carry out supervisory roles (Douglas et al., 2016; Giangreco et al., 2010). Research has also indicated that there is a need for in-service training to support teachers in their supervisory roles with paraeducators (Douglas et al., 2022a; Mason et al., 2021). In a study by Sobeck, Douglas, and colleagues (2020), teacher education faculty were surveyed to understand the pre-service preparation practices of teachers in relation to paraeducators. Findings indicated that although faculty noted the importance of paraeducator supervisory skills, insufficient coursework and instructional activities were provided in pre-service programs to prepare teachers for paraeducator supervision responsibilities. This trend is concerning since we know that the lack of preparation results in teachers who engage in ineffective supervision practices (Giangreco et al., 2010).

The reality is that teachers need skills to effectively instruct students *and* work with paraeducators (Biggs et al., 2019). The existing challenges in paraeducator supervision result in paraeducators and teachers learning on the job together (Capizzi & Da Fonte, 2012). Additionally, with the increasing use of paraeducators in inclusive settings but limited meeting time to support shared planning and on-the-job training (Douglas et al., 2016; Giangreco et al., 2011), the field consistently notes poor supervision practices and increased paraeducator turnover (Fisher & Pleasants, 2012; Giangreco et al., 2010).

TABLE 3-2. COUNCIL FOR EXCEPTIONAL CHILDREN STANDARDS RELATED TO SUPERVISION

STANDARD SET	STANDARD
Initial Practice-Based Professional Preparation Standards for Special Educators (K-12)	7.2 Candidates collaborate, communicate, and coordinate with families, paraprofessionals, and other professionals within the educational setting to assess, plan, and implement effective programs and services that promote progress toward measurable outcomes for individuals with and without exceptionalities and their families. 7.4 Candidates work with and mentor paraprofessionals in the paraprofessional's role of supporting the education of individuals with exceptionalities and their families.
Initial Specialty Set: Deafblindness	DB.1.K5 Specialized roles of educators of learners who are deafblind, including teacher of deafblind, in their various capacities (e.g., itinerant teacher, classroom teacher, and consultant) and as supervisors of interveners and other support staff. DB.1.S2 Support, train, communicate and, when appropriate, supervise interveners and other direct support staff. DB.1.S4 Determine, recommend, and support appropriate services and providers, including, when appropriate, the services of an intervener, based on evaluation. DB.7.K1 Role of the intervener to ensure optimal access to age and developmentally appropriate communicative interactions that establish shared meanings. DB.7.S9 Provide leadership to the team in defining the roles of interveners, interpreters, and other specialized assistants across multiple environments according to the needs of the learner.
Advanced Specialty Set: Inclusion Specialist	SEIS.7.S6 Ensure effective roles, responsibilities, and professional learning for paraeducators.
Advanced Specialty Set: Special Education Developmental Disabilities and Autism Spectrum Disorder Specialist	SEDAS.5.S3 Provide structure, ongoing training, and support to families, professionals, and paraprofessionals.
Core Competencies for Special Education Paraeducators	See Appendix D.

Finding quality individuals to serve in paraeducator positions begins with the hiring process and continues through actions that demonstrate appreciation for their contributions. Paraeducators who are valued as members of the educational team, orientated to their position, entrusted with instructional responsibilities, and receive ongoing support through supervision are more likely to stay in their positions (Ghere & York-Barr, 2007). Conversely, paraeducators who receive low wages and limited benefits, lack clarity in their roles, have little input into decisions for students they support, and experience stressful working conditions—such as conflicts within teams—are more likely to leave their positions (Ghere & York-Barr, 2007). Paraeducator turnover comes with substantial financial

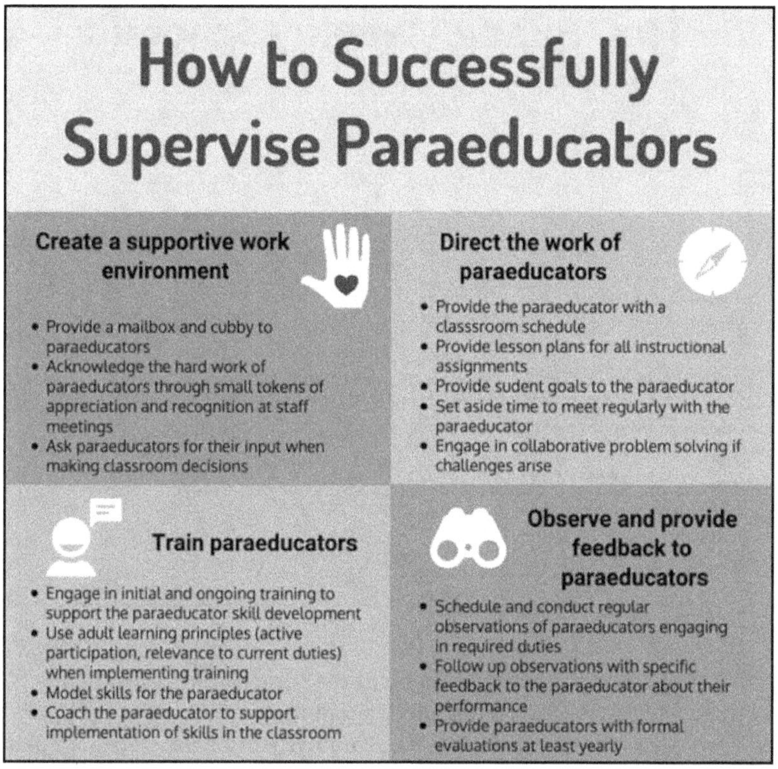

Figure 3-1. Tips for successful supervision of paraeducators.

How to Successfully Supervise Paraeducators

Create a supportive work environment
- Provide a mailbox and cubby to paraeducators
- Acknowledge the hard work of paraeducators through small tokens of appreciation and recognition at staff meetings
- Ask paraeducators for their input when making classroom decisions

Direct the work of paraeducators
- Provide the paraeducator with a classroom schedule
- Provide lesson plans for all instructional assignments
- Provide student goals to the paraeducator
- Set aside time to meet regularly with the paraeducator
- Engage in collaborative problem solving if challenges arise

Train paraeducators
- Engage in initial and ongoing training to support the paraeducator skill development
- Use adult learning principles (active participation, relevance to current duties) when implementing training
- Model skills for the paraeducator
- Coach the paraeducator to support implementation of skills in the classroom

Observe and provide feedback to paraeducators
- Schedule and conduct regular observations of paraeducators engaging in required duties
- Follow up observations with specific feedback to the paraeducator about their performance
- Provide paraeducators with formal evaluations at least yearly

and educational costs due to time required by administrators and teachers to recruit, screen, and interview applicants (Douglas et al., 2022a; Ghere & York-Barr, 2007). When paraeducators leave a position, their responsibilities need to be covered by substitutes or other paraeducators and often involves reassignment of responsibilities to ensure the safety and appropriate education of students. Additionally, new paraeducators require substantial training and must meet frequently with teachers to establish new supervisory relationships.

SUPERVISION DEFINED

There are numerous components that are encompassed into paraeducator supervision—each essential to ensure a good working relationship with paraeducators and appropriate supports for students with disabilities. The components of paraeducator supervision include: (a) creating a supportive work environment, (b) directing the work of paraeducators, (c) training paraeducators, and (d) observing and providing feedback to paraeducators (Figure 3-1).

Creating a Supportive Work Environment

It is important for the supervisor to set the right tone for the work environment. The supervisor should establish and maintain a positive work setting that ensures all team members feel included, respected, valued, and acknowledged (Biggs et al., 2016; Douglas & Uitto, 2021). Administrators at the school and district level might contribute to a supportive work environment by knowing each paraeducator by name, providing training and orientation to the school when a paraeducator is hired, and ensuring adequate compensation (Douglas et al., 2022a; 2022b). Teachers can contribute to a supportive work environment by seeking input from paraeducators when making decisions in the classroom, showing appreciation, and sharing equally in nonpreferred tasks (Bagawan et al., 2022; Biggs et al., 2016; Douglas et al., 2016). A supportive work environment also includes clear,

Figure 3-2. Sample classroom schedule for paraeducators.

	MON	TUE	WED	THU	FRI
8:30 am	Bus Duty				
9:00am	Circle Time Braxton (K)	Math Group Grades 1-2 (Novak)	Circle Time Braxton (K)	Math Group Grades 1-2 (Novak)	Circle Time Braxton (K)
9:30am	Inclusion Reading Xander, Sam, Mimi (Grade 1)		Reading/Writing Group Grade 3 (Novak)		Inclusion Reading Xander, Sam, Mimi (Grade 1)
10:00am		PE - Braxton (K)		Art - Braxton (K)	
10:30am					
11:00am	Reading Group Grade 2 (Novak)	Math Group Grade 3 (Novak)	PT - Emma (2)	Math Group Grade 3 (Novak)	Reading Group Grade 2 (Novak)
11:30am	Lunch Support - Maisy, Albert, Roberto				
12:00pm	Recess Duty				
12:30pm	Lunch Break				
1:00pm	Inclusion Math Deon, Riley, Ben (K)	Free Play Support Braxton, Deon, Ben (K)	Life Skills Group (Novak)	Free Play Support Braxton, Deon, Ben (K)	Inclusion Math Deon, Riley, Ben (K)
1:30pm					
2:00pm	Reading/Writing Group Grade 3 (Novak)	Library - Yakov (3)	Social Skills Group with Peer Models (Novak)	OT/Art - Yakov (3)	Reading/Writing Group Grade 3 (Novak)
2:30pm		Music - Mandy (1)		PE/PT - Mandy (1)	
3:00pm	Bus Duty				
3:30pm	End of Day Meeting with Mrs. Novak				

Mrs. Huang - Weekly Schedule
K-3 Inclusion/Learning Support

active, and frequent communication between the supervisor and the paraeducator. (See Chapter 2 for additional ideas on ensuring good team relationships and communication.) Creating a supportive work environment will help educational teams develop a shared vision for the classroom and will ensure paraeducators feel encouraged, which will increase motivation and reduce paraeducator burnout and turnover (Bagawan et al., 2022; Biggs et al., 2016; Douglas et al., 2016).

Directing the Work of Paraeducators

The supervisor also directs the day-to-day work of the paraeducator (Douglas et al., 2016). This involves setting clear expectations for the paraeducator by assigning specific tasks, providing schedules, and providing lesson plans for paraeducators to use with students (Capizzi & Da Fonte, 2012; Yates et al., 2020). Schedules for paraeducators should be developed by the classroom teacher or collaboratively between the special education and general education teacher for students in inclusive placements. The schedule should include each location and activity during the day and the students whom the paraeducator will support (Stewart, 2019; Figure 3-2). Sometimes things may come up in the schedule that are not planned, so teachers should be ready to troubleshoot and adjust the schedule as needed—always be prepared with a back-up plan!

It is also vital to provide lesson plans to the paraeducator. Lesson plans should be developed by the classroom teacher responsible for the instruction. As with schedules, lesson plans may be created collaboratively with input from the special education and general education teachers in instances where the student is in an inclusive placement. Lesson plans should list the supervising teacher; the setting; student goals that are being addressed; specific accommodations, modifications, and behavior supports that might be needed for the student; materials that are needed; the lesson content and sequence; and assessment information when applicable. Figure 3-3 gives a sample lesson plan in an inclusive fourth-grade classroom with roles for the special education teacher, general education teacher, and paraeducator.

The day-to-day management of paraeducators requires numerous qualities from the supervisor. Supervisors should have good interpersonal skills (Ashbaker & Morgan, 2012) and be confident in their ability to manage other adults in the classroom (Biggs et al., 2016). Supervisors must also be prepared, organized, and willing to delegate tasks to paraeducators (Biggs et al., 2016). Good supervisors are also willing to address challenges and engage in collaborative problem solving when issues arise (Biggs et al., 2016; Douglas et al., 2016). For example, if a paraeducator comes to the

PRE-PLANNING	
Task: Place value lesson *Grade Level:* Fourth CCSS 4.NBT.A.3 *Lesson Objective:* I can use place value to round numbers	*Rationale/Purpose of the Lesson:* Students will use place value understanding to round whole numbers to the nearest tenths place *Short-Term Goal:* Students will identify place value and rounding to the nearest tenths (IEP Goal: Mary/Tim) *Long-Term Goal:* The students will apply skills to estimation in dollars, cents, and budgeting

Other Skills Addressed
Social/Emotional: Taking turns (review fair game play)   *Transition:* Rounding dollars and cents

STUDENT NEEDS AND STRENGTHS	ACCOMMODATIONS/MODIFICATIONS/ BEHAVIOR SUPPORTS
Mary: Second-grade math level, works well in pairs	*Mary:* Behavior goal—keep hands to herself
Tim: First-grade math level, works hard	*Tim:* Read test aloud/modified test

GENERAL ANTICIPATED NEEDS	
Common Academic Errors: Confusion of tens with the tenths place	*Behavioral Challenges:* Plan for Jane's tardiness and disruption upon entry to class

THREE-PERSON INSTRUCTIONAL TEAM ROLES (ITALIC=SUPPORT ROLE)

Sequence	General Ed Teacher	Special Ed Teacher	Paraeducator
Introduce Topic (full class)	*Support content being introduced, monitor Jane's entry into class, and record behavior data*	Introduce topic, lead discussion on place value/round numbers, money	*Walk through rows, redirect student attention, add details to discussion*
Main Lesson (full class)	Discuss vocabulary, provide problem examples, dry erase boards for student responses	*Support content being taught, help students with incorrect answers*	*Help students with incorrect answers, collect behavior data for Mary*
Next (full class)	Describe Station 1 activities	Describe Station 2 activities	Describe Station 3 activities
Next (stations)	Station 1: Large-screen activity to review, after 10 minutes rotate to Station 2, use timer	Station 2: Small group review of place value, after 10 minutes rotate to Station 3	Station 3: Comparing numbers, after 10 minutes rotate to Station 1
Next (transition to full class)	Return students to large group on cue, begin cue with countdown	Return students to large group on cue	Return students to large group on cue
Next (full class)	Review key concepts, detail how skills can be applied to money	*Support content being taught*	*Watch Mary for disruptive behavior, monitor student behavior in classroom*
Formative Assessment (groups as assigned)	Hand out tests, collect papers, grade all student work	Have modified test ready for Mary and Tim, monitor completion	Read test to Tim

Formative Assessment: Mary and Tim, 70%; three out of four times is considered passing

Supervisor: General and special education teachers

Figure 3-3. Sample lesson plan for inclusive fourth-grade classroom. (Adapted from Yates, P. A., Chopra, R. V., Sobeck, E. E., Douglas, S. N., Morano, S., Walker, V. L., & Schulze, R. [2020]. Working with paraeducators: Tools and strategies for instructional planning, performance feedback, and evaluation. *Intervention in School and Clinic, 56*[1], 1-8. https://doi.org/10.1177/1053451220910740)

teacher supervisor with a complaint about another team member, the teacher supervisor should work with the paraeducator and team member to find a solution. Many challenges that arise among educational teams who utilize paraeducators can be avoided by clearly defining roles and engaging in frequent communication. All members of the team should know their role and the role of others on the team. Times should be set aside where paraeducators and teachers can meet regularly to discuss schedules, provide training, discuss student instruction, address questions, and resolve any conflicts (Bagawan et al., 2022; Douglas et al., 2016). These meetings do not have to be long and can often be accomplished in as little as 15 minutes a day. What is important is that a routine is established so the teacher and paraeducator know when they will touch base. Administrative support is important to ensure a meeting time, as it may place additional demands on other school scheduling and budgets (Biggs et al., 2016; Douglas et al., 2016). Furthermore, regular meeting times between teachers and paraeducators can help supervising teachers identify and advocate for any ongoing professional development needs (Douglas et al., 2016).

Training Paraeducators

Supervision also includes providing paraeducator training. Paraeducators require both formal and informal training (Douglas & Uitto, 2021). While formal training is usually provided through the local educational agency, informal on-the-job training is often provided by the supervising teacher and, as stated previously, requires protected meeting time for the teacher to conduct training (Solis et al., 2012). Paraeducator training should include orientation to the work setting, outline the paraeducator's professional duties and responsibilities, and include the administration of professional development based on paraeducator roles/responsibilities and needs (Table 3-3). The *Core Competencies for Special Education Paraeducators* (CEC, 2022b; see Appendix D) should be used as a guide for paraeducator supervisors. The resource provides a clear outline of the knowledge and skills needed by paraeducators. The supervisor can also conduct a needs assessment with paraeducators to identify specific professional development needs, set priorities, and create a training plan (Capizzi & Da Fonte, 2012; Douglas et al., 2016). The PARAprofessional resource and research center provides several resources to help identify professional development needs (http://paracenter.org).

Professional development for paraeducators should take into consideration the unique learning needs of adults. Adult learners benefit from active participation in professional development programs—professional development that is relevant and application to current roles and responsibilities, instructor guidance, and performance assessment to measure knowledge and skills (Dunst et al., 2010). Research indicates that beyond including the principles of adult learning, paraeducator training should also include: (a) content aligned with federal/state laws and professional standards, (b) modeling by the supervising teacher, and (c) feedback/coaching to ensure the implementation of trained skills (Brock & Carter, 2015; Douglas et al., 2016; Mason et al., 2021). Chapter 5 provides additional details on implementing paraeducator training.

Observing and Providing Feedback to Paraeducators

Coaching and feedback are essential to ensure paraeducators effectively implement trained skills. Research indicates that didactic training alone is often insufficient to ensure proper implementation by paraeducators (Mason et al., 2021; Sobeck, Robertson et al., 2020; Walker et al., 2020). Therefore, coaching and feedback become an important component to paraeducator supervision. When providing feedback, Gerlach (2015) suggests that supervisors discuss evaluation criteria with the paraeducator, and then schedule and conduct regular observations. Each observation is then followed by structured feedback that is constructive. This process should occur regularly for optimum outcomes. Resources have been developed to illustrate training cycles that can be used with paraeducators (Douglas & Uitto, 2021; Yates et al., 2020; Figures 3-4 and 3-5). Similarly, resources exist to support administrators and teacher supervisors in selecting and evaluating training materials and programs (Douglas et al., 2019; Figure 3-6).

TABLE 3-3. PARAEDUCATOR TRAINING CATEGORIES

CATEGORY	DETAILS
Orientation	- Identification of the supervising teacher - Introduction to administrator(s) and other key school personnel - Introduction to school setting, with focus on places where the paraeducator will primarily work and need to access - Expectations for professionalism (arrival/departure times, appropriate dress, policies for reporting absences, confidentiality, person-first language) - Emergency procedures for fire, inclement weather, etc. - Contacts for communication (email/phone numbers for team members) - Other relevant school policies and procedures - Schedule
Professional Duties/Responsibilities	- Job description for paraeducator/teacher/relevant team members - Classroom responsibilities, with indication of which responsibilities are paraeducators, teachers, or shared - Documentation of when training or discussion occurred for each paraeducator responsibility
Professional Development	- Reference *CEC Specialty Set for Paraeducators in Special Education Standards* - Conduct needs assessment with paraeducator - Set priorities and create a plan for professional development - Document professional development - Provide follow-up coaching

Adapted from Capizzi, A. M., & Da Fonte, M. A. (2012). Supporting paraeducators through a collaborative classroom support plan. *Focus on Exceptional Children, 44*(6), 1-16.

As part of the feedback process, it is important for paraeducators to be provided with formal evaluations. Formal evaluations ensure that expectations are clear and paraeducators understand how they are performing. Evaluation processes should be transparent to administrators, paraeducators, and teachers (Douglas et al., 2022b). Paraeducators should be told who will evaluate their performance, how often performance will be evaluated, and how evaluation results will be shared (Douglas et al., 2022a; Stewart, 2019). Although administrators hold primary responsibility for formal evaluations, teachers should provide feedback for the evaluation and be involved in the evaluation process (Douglas et al., 2016, 2022a, 2022b). Annual evaluations are recommended, but benefits have also been noted from mid-year evaluations (Douglas et al., 2022a). The State Education Resource Center in Connecticut provides some valuable resources that can aid districts in developing paraeducator evaluations that are aligned to job descriptions and paraeducator responsibilities (see https://portal.ct.gov/SDE/Paraeducator/Paraeducator-Information-and-Resources).

48 Chapter 3

Instruction	Modeling	Rehearsal	Feedback
• Provide a rationale for the strategy being used. • Describe the skill with explicit and clear details. • Provide written steps of the strategy using the fidelity checklist.	• Demonstrate the correct use of the strategy following the steps in the fidelity checklist. • Modeling can be *live* by a person or *symbolic* through video. • Teacher draws attention to the important components of the strategy. • Scaffold in varying scenarios to model. • Repeat the model several times.	• Provide an opportunity for the paraeducator to practice the skill with the teacher. • Rehearse the skill in the natural environment when possible. • Rehearse the strategy until the paraeducator demonstrates it correctly per an established critera. • Remodel if needed.	• Provide reinforcement for correct implementation of the strategy and corrective feedback for errors. • Feedback provided during rehearsal and ongoing thereafter with routine fidelity checklists. • Always comment on at least one area of strength. • Offer feedback as immediately as possible. • Maintain a positive or neutral tone and focus on one corrective area at a time.
Example • Prior to the start of the lesson provide the paraeducator with instruction on how to use picture cues. • Give a rationale for picture cues, explicitly discuss the steps using the fidelity checklist as a guide, and provide a tangible copy of fidelity checklist for the paraeducator.	*Example* • Model using the visual following the fidelity checklist steps. • Demonstrate several scenarios of using the visuals and how to respond according to student behavior.	*Example* • The paraeducator practices using the visual cue with the teacher, then with a student. • The paraeducator implements the visual cues over 5 consecutive times with 90% accuracy.	*Example* • Upon rehearsing using the visual cue with the teacher, the teacher comments on how well the paraeducator modeled the strategy. • The teacher encourages the paraeducator to incorporate additional wait time when using the visual. • Immediately after working with a student, the teacher reviews the fidelity checklist with the paraeducator.

Figure 3-4. Example of Behavior Skills Training to use when training paraeducators. (Reproduced with permission from Yates, P. A., Chopra, R. V., Sobeck, E. E., Douglas, S. N., Morano, S., Walker, V. L., & Schulze, R. [2020]. Working with paraeducators: Tools and strategies for instructional planning, performance feedback, and evaluation. *Intervention in School and Clinic, 56*[1], 1-8. https://doi.org/10.1177/1053451220910740)

Figure 3-5. Example of a general training cycle to use with paraeducators. (Reproduced with permission from Douglas, S. N., & Uitto, D. J. [2021]. A collaborative approach to paraeducator training. *Beyond Behavior, 30*[1], 4-13. https://doi.org/10.1177/1074295621997177)

PARAEDUCATOR TRAINING PLAN STEPS	
 Define Paraeducator Training Needs	• Define paraeducator roles/responsibilities • Define paraeducator knowledge/skills needed for responsibilities • Provide orientation to paraeducator • Conduct observation of paraeducator • Identify training needs through discussion
 Create Paraeducator Training Plan	• Set a goal for each training component • Identify time commitments • Identify personnel involved in training • Determine location of training • Determine materials needed for training

STEP 3
Provide Paraeducator Training
	• Conduct initial workshop
	• Conduct intervention-focused workshop
	• Provide coaching with performance feedback
	  ○ Model intervention
	  ○ Observe paraeducator/collect performance data
	  ○ Provide feedback to paraeducator

 Document Paraeducator Performance	• Maintain a log of training activities • Document evidence of paraeducator growth • Determine next training steps

Title:	Author:
Publisher:	Copyright Date:

Material Overview		What is the purpose defined in the training material?
Content		What is the content focus of the training (e.g., general overview, autism, instructional strategies)?
Time Commitment		How long does it take to complete the training?
Cost		How much does the training material cost?
Content Background		How was the training material developed? Is it research-based? Check all that apply: ☐ Field tested with paraprofessionals (tested and modified based on input) ☐ Author experience (statement indicating materials were created based on author experience) ☐ Data-based literature ☐ Non–data-based literature ☐ Survey of training needs (developed based on paraprofessional needs identified in survey)
ADULT LEARNING APPROACHES	*Presentation Format/ Instructional Approach*	How is the training material presented to the paraprofessional? Facilitated by professional to paraprofessionals—Check all that apply: ☐ Book study with guided discussions (designed for a team to read and discuss together) ☐ Lecture (presentation to a group of paraprofessionals may include manual, slide notes, or DVD) ☐ Opportunities for modeling, practice of skills, and feedback in simulated setting (active engagement) ☐ Opportunities for planned observation/feedback/coaching in actual classroom (outside of training) ☐ Suggestions for practice (materials include techniques for paraprofessionals to use with students) Self-directed learning materials for paraprofessionals (may lack collaborative discussion with a licensed professional, understate role of direct supervision, and/or overstate level of paraprofessional autonomy): ☐ Book (designed for independent reading similar format to educational textbooks)

	Performance Measure	Does the material support an ongoing learning and promote performance for the paraprofessional?
		☐ Does not provide a way to measure performance of skills by paraprofessional
		☐ Provides a system to measure performance of skills by paraprofessional such as:
		  ☐ Joint teacher/paraprofessional assessment ☐ Teacher assessment
		  ☐ Paraprofessional self-assessment ☐ Portfolio

Figure 3-6. Paraprofessional training material rubric. (Adapted from Douglas, S. N., Uitto, D. J., Reinfelds, C. L., & D'Agostino, S. [2019]. A systematic review of paraprofessional training materials. *Journal of Special Education, 52*[4], 195-207. https://doi.org/10.1177/0022466918771707) *(continued)*

Congruence of Materials with NCLB/ IDEA 2004	Does the training material establish the teacher as supervisor to the paraprofessional? ☐ Materials clearly establish the teacher as responsible for the primary education of students and supervision of paraprofessionals *(list specific statements found)*. ☐ Materials clearly establish the paraprofessionals as providing support under the direction of a licensed professional (teacher; *list specific statements found*). ☐ Materials encourage a collaborative approach for students that includes the established roles of teachers and paraprofessionals *(list specific statements found)*.
Training Resources	What materials are available for the facilitator and/or participant? Check all that apply: Facilitator manual including:　　　　☐ DVD with slide presentation ☐ Handouts　　　　　　　　　　　　☐ Quizzes with answer keys Participant book including:　　　　　☐ Reproducible forms/templates ☐ Workbook　　　　　　　　　　　　☐ Online modules

Scoring Rubric to rate the level of learning with the *Core Competencies for Special Education Paraeducators* (CEC, 2022b).

1	Training material does not include any content, mentions it with minimal development, or supports content only at the knowledge-recognition level for selected *Core Competencies for Special Education Paraeducators*
2	Training material requires content at the **knowledge recall** level using quizzes or informal assessments to be discussed with/by licensed professional
3	Training material requires content at a **comprehension level** assessed through assignments or projects to be reviewed with/by licensed professional (e.g., reaction paper, journal writing, create an example to share, case scenarios)
4	Training material requires content used for the **application of skills** or competencies in simulated setting with feedback by licensed professional (e.g., modeling activities, practicum exercises, role play, practice of a strategy)
5	Training material requires content be used for the application of **skills or competencies within natural environment** with feedback by a licensed professional

Note: Licensed professional may include a presenter, teacher, administrator, etc.

Based upon the scoring rubric (1 to 5 above), score linkage to the *Core Competencies for Special Education Paraeducators* (i.e., Standard 1—Professional learning and ethical practice, Standard 2—Learner development and individual learning differences, Standard 3—Special education services and supports in the learning environment, Standard 4—Assessment, Standard 5—Instructional supports and strategies, Standard 6—Social, emotional, and behavior supports, Standard 7—Collaboration with team members). The *Core Competencies for Special Education Paraeducators* (CEC, 2022b) are provided in Appendix D.

Standards Assessment (see rubric and standards)

Standard 1 _____　Standard 2 _____　Standard 3 _____　Standard 4 _____
Standard 5 _____　Standard 6 _____　Standard 7 _____

Figure 3-6 (continued). Paraprofessional training material rubric. (Adapted from Douglas, S. N., Uitto, D. J., Reinfelds, C. L., & D'Agostino, S. [2019]. A systematic review of paraprofessional training materials. *Journal of Special Education, 52*[4], 195-207. https://doi.org/10.1177/0022466918771707)

SUMMARY

Paraeducator supervision is essential to ensure high-quality paraeducator supports to students with disabilities. Federal and state laws have included supervision as an essential component of paraeducator supports, while case law findings and professional organizations provide additional clarification of the specific skills that are needed for teacher supervisors. Supervision is essential given the lack of training paraeducators have when they enter their position. It is important for teachers and supervisors to understand their supervisory responsibilities with paraeducators. This chapter outlined the key components of supervision. However, given the varied roles of administrators and teachers, Chapter 4 will focus on the specific supervisory roles and responsibilities of special education teachers, general education teachers, and administrators.

CHAPTER REVIEW

1. How is paraeducator supervision addressed in federal and state laws? What detail is provided and what detail is lacking?
2. Why is paraeducator supervision essential? Provide a rationale with five supporting reasons.
3. List and describe the components of paraeducator supervision.
4. Reflect on any jobs you have held in the past. Consider the reasons for wanting to stay and not wanting to remain in a particular job. State features of the jobs that motivated you to continue to work with rationale. State five specific things you plan to do to retain the paraeducators who support you in your role as teacher.

RESOURCES

General Supervision Resources

- Causton, J., & Tracy-Bronson, C. (2015). *The educator's handbook for inclusive school practices.* Brookes Publishing.
- Connecticut State Department of Education. (2012). *Guidelines for training and support of paraprofessionals: Working with students birth to 21.* https://portal.ct.gov/-/media/SDE/Paraeducator/guidelines_paraprofessionals.pdf
- Council for Exceptional Children. (2023). https://exceptionalchildren.org/
- French, N. K. (2003). *Managing paraeducators in your school: How to hire, train, and supervise non-certified staff.* Corwin Press.
- Gerlach, K. (2015). *Let's team up! A checklist for teachers, paraeducators, and principals.* National Professional Resources/Dude Publishing.
- Kansas State Department of Education. (2018). *Considerations for the effective use of paraprofessionals in schools.* Paraprofessional.
- Montana Office of Public Instruction. (2017). *Paraprofessionals in Montana: A resource guide for administrators, educators, and paraprofessionals.* https://opi.mt.gov/Portals/182/Page%20Files/Special%20Education/Guides/2017%20Revised%20PARA%20Resource%20Guide%20FINAL%206-6-17A.pdf?ver=2017-08-31-125132-977
- Morgan, J., & Ashbaker, B. Y. (2009). *Supporting and supervising your teaching assistant.* Continuum.

- Paraprofessional Resource and Research Center (PAR²A Center). (2023). *K-12 paraprofessional supervision.* Teachers - PAR²A Center (paracenter.org)
- Pickett, A. L., & Gerlach, K. (2003). *Supervising paraeducators in educational settings: A team approach* (2nd ed.). Pro Ed.
- Pickett, A. L., Gerlach, K., Morgan, R., Likins, M., & Wallace, T. (2007). *Paraeducators in schools: Strengthening the educational team.* Pro Ed.
- State Education Resource Center. (2007). *Teacher supervisory checklist: Preschool to grade 12.* https://portal.ct.gov/SDE/Paraeducator/Paraeducator-Information-and-Resources/Documents
- Virginia Department of Education. (2005). *The Virginia paraprofessional guide to supervision and collaboration with paraprofessionals: A partnership.* https://vcuautismcenter.org/resources/paraprofessionals.cfm
- William & Mary Training & Technical Assistance Center. (2015). *Paraeducators' tools for supporting the instructional process considerations packet.* https://education.wm.edu/centers/ttac/documents/packets/paraeducatortools.pdf

Professional Journals That Provide Research and Guidance on Paraeducator Supervision

- Council for Exceptional Children. (2023). *Exceptional children.* https://exceptionalchildren.org/improving-your-practice/publications
- Council for Exceptional Children. (2023). *TEACHING exceptional children.* https://exceptionalchildren.org/improving-your-practice/publications
- Division for Early Childhood of the Council for Exceptional Children. (2022). *Young exceptional children.* https://www.dec-sped.org/young-exceptional-children
- Council for Learning Disabilities. (2022). *Intervention in school and clinic.* https://council-for-learning-disabilities.org/intervention-in-school-and-clinic/
- Taylor & Francis Online. (2023). *Preventing school failure: Alternative education for children and youth.* https://www.tandfonline.com/toc/vpsf20/current
- TASH. (2023). *Inclusive practices.* https://tash.org/publications/inclusive-practices/
- Teacher Education Division of the Council for Exceptional Children. (2020). *Teacher education and special education.* Teacher Education and Special Education: SAGE Journals.

REFERENCES

Ashbaker, B. Y., & Morgan, J. (2012). Team players and team managers: Special educators working with paraeducators to support inclusive classrooms. *Creative Education, 3*(3), 322-327. https://doi.org/10.4236/ce.2012.33051

Bagawan, A., Douglas, S. N., & Gerde, H. (2022). *Components of effective supervision and training for paraeducators.* Intervention in School and Clinic. https://doi.org/10.1177/10534512221093778

Berlinghoff, D., & McLaughlin, V. L. (Eds.). (2022). *Practice-based standards for the preparation of special educators.* Council for Exceptional Children.

Biggs, E. E., Gilson, C. B., & Carter, E. W. (2016). Accomplishing more together: Influences to the quality of professional relationships between special educators and paraprofessionals. *Research and Practice for Persons With Severe Disabilities, 41*(4), 256-272. https://doi.org/10.1177/1540796916665604

Biggs, E. E., Gilson, C. B., & Carter, E. W. (2019). "Developing that balance": Preparing and supporting special education teachers to work with paraprofessionals. *Teacher Education and Special Education, 42*(2), 117-131. https://doi.org/10.1177/0888406418765611

Board of Education of the City of New York. 28 IDELR (SEA NY 1998).

Brock, M. E., & Carter, E. W. (2015). Effects of a professional development package to prepare special education paraprofessionals to implement evidence-based practice. *Journal of Special Education, 49,* 39-51. https://doi.org/10.1177/0022466913501882

Capizzi, A. M., & Da Fonte, M. A. (2012). Supporting paraeducators through a collaborative classroom support plan. *Focus on Exceptional Children, 44*(6), 1-16.

Council for Exceptional Children. (2022a). *Initial and advanced specialty sets.* https://exceptionalchildren.org/standards/specialty-sets-specific-practice-areas

Council for Exceptional Children. (2022b). *Core competencies for special education paraeducators.* https://exceptionalchildren.org/paraeducators/core-competencies-special-education-paraeducators

Douglas, S. N., Bowles, R., & Kammes, R. (2022a). Elementary principals' views on the policies and practices of paraeducators in special education. *Journal of the American Academy of Special Education Professionals,* Winter, 107-126.

Douglas, S. N., Bowles, R., & Kammes, R. (2022b). Paraeducators: An important member of the educational team for students with disabilities. *Journal of the American Academy of Special Education Professionals,* Spring/Summer, 134-150.

Douglas, S. N., Chapin, S. E., & Nolan, J. F. (2016). Special education teachers' experiences supporting and supervising paraeducators: Implications for special and general education settings. *Teacher Education and Special Education, 39*(1), 60-74. https://doi.org/10.1177/0888406415616443

Douglas, S. N., & Uitto, D. J. (2021). A collaborative approach to paraeducator training. *Beyond Behavior, 30*(1), 4-13. https://doi.org/10.1177/1074295621997177

Douglas, S. N., Uitto, D. J., Reinfelds, C. L., & D'Agostino, S. (2019). A systematic review of paraprofessional training materials. *Journal of Special Education, 52*(4), 195-207. https://doi.org/10.1177/0022466918771707

Dunst, C. J., Trivette, C. M., & Hamby, D. W. (2010). Meta-analysis of the effectiveness of four adult learning methods and strategies: Supplemental tables and references. *International Journal of Continuing Education and Lifelong Learning, 3,* 91-112.

Every Student Succeeds Act of 2015, 20 U.S.C. § 1177.

Fisher, M., & Pleasants, S. L. (2012). Roles, responsibilities, and concerns of paraeducators: Findings from a statewide survey. *Remedial and Special Education, 33*(5), 287-297. https://doi.org/10.1177/0741932510397762

French, N. (2003). *Managing paraeducators in your school: How to hire, train, and supervise non-certified staff.* Corwin Press.

Gerlach, K. (2015). *Let's team up! A checklist for teachers, paraeducators and principals.* Dude Publishing.

Ghere, G., & York-Barr, J. (2007). Paraprofessional turnover and retention in inclusive programs: Hidden costs and promising practices. *Remedial and Special Education, 28*(1), 21-32. https://doi.org/10.1177/07419325070280010301

Giangreco, M. F., Broer, S. M., & Suter, J. C. (2011). Guidelines for selecting alternatives to overreliance on paraprofessionals: Field-testing in inclusion-oriented schools. *Remedial and Special Education, 32*(1), 22-38. https://doi.org/10.1177/0741932509355951

Giangreco, M. F., Suter, J. C., & Doyle, M. B. (2010). Paraprofessionals in inclusive schools: A review of recent research. *Journal of Educational and Psychological Consultation, 20*(1), 41-57. https://doi.org/10.1080/10474410903535356

Hingham Public Schools, 33 IDELR 292 (SEA MA 2000).

Individuals with Disabilities Education Act of 1997, 20 U.S.C. § 1400.

Individuals with Disabilities Education Improvement Act of 2004, 20 U.S.C. § 1400.

Mason, R. A., Gunersel, A. B., Irvin, D. W., Wills, H. P., Gregori, E., An, Z. G., & Ingram, P. B. (2021). From the frontlines: Perceptions of paraprofessionals' roles and responsibilities. *Teacher Education and Special Education, 44*(2), 97-116. https://doi.org/10.1177/0888406419896627

Morgan, J., & Ashbaker, B. Y. (2009). *Supporting and supervising your teaching assistant.* Continuum International.

No Child Left Behind Act of 2002, P.L. 107-110, 20 U.S.C. § 6319.

Pickett, A. L., & Gerlach, K. (2003). *Supervising paraeducators in educational settings: A team approach* (2nd ed.). Pro Ed.

Pickett, A. L., Gerlach, K., Morgan, R., Likins, M., & Wallace, T. (2007). *Paraeducators in schools: Strengthening the educational team.* Pro Ed.

Silsbee Independent School District, 25 IDELR 1023 (SEA TX 1997).

Sioux City Community School District and Western Hills Area Education Agency (AEA 12), 104 LRP 10804 (SEA IA 2003).

Sobeck, E., Douglas, S. N., Chopra, R., & Morano, S. (2020). Paraeducator supervision in pre-service teacher preparation programs: Results of a national survey. *Psychology in the Schools, 58*(4), 669-685. https://doi.org/10.1002/pits.22383

Sobeck, E. E., Robertson, R., & Smith, J. (2020). The effects of didactic instruction and performance feedback on paraeducator implementation of behavior support strategies in inclusive settings. *Journal of Special Education, 53*(4), 245-255. https://doi.org/10.1177/0022466919858989

Solis, M., Vaughn, S., Swanson, E., & Mcculley, L. (2012). Collaborative models of instruction: The empirical foundations of inclusion and co-teaching. *Psychology in the Schools, 49,* 498-510. https://doi.org/10.1002/pits.21606

Stewart, E. M. (2019). Reducing ambiguity: Tools to define and communicate paraprofessional roles and responsibilities. *Intervention in School and Clinic, 55*(1), 52-57. https://doi.org/10.1177/1053451218782431

Walker, V. L., Douglas, K. H., Douglas, S. N., & D'Agostino, S. (2020). Paraprofessional-implemented systematic instruction for students with disabilities: A systematic literature review. *Education and Training in Autism and Developmental Disabilities, 55*(3), 303-317.

Yates, P. A., Chopra, R. V., Sobeck, E. E., Douglas, S. N., Morano, S., Walker, V. L., & Schulze, R. (2020). Working with paraeducators: Tools and strategies for instructional planning, performance feedback, and evaluation. *Intervention in School and Clinic, 56*(1), 1-8. https://doi.org/10.1177/1053451220910740

Supervision Responsibilities of Team Members

INTRODUCTION

The supervision of paraeducators requires the coordination of various educational team members. Chapter 4 provides details about the relevant supervisory roles for special education teachers, general education teachers, administrators, and related service providers. We outline how specific team members create supportive work environments for paraeducators, direct the work of paraeducators, train paraeducators, and observe and provide feedback to paraeducators. Topics include tasks such as hiring, orientation, delegation of tasks, creating plans, teaming, overseeing tasks, and evaluation.

CHAPTER OBJECTIVES

- → Describe the paraeducator supervision roles for various team members including special education teachers, general education teachers, administrators, and related service providers.
- → Detail the formal evaluation process for paraeducators, including who is involved, frequency, and the process to follow.
- → Explain the importance of delegating tasks to paraeducators and benefits noted in relation to delegation for teachers, paraeducators, and students.
- → Justify the importance of paraeducator job descriptions and list items that should be included in job descriptions.

KEY TERMS

- **Augmentative and Alternative Communication (AAC):** Describes multiple temporary or permanent ways to supplement or compensate for the impairment or disability patterns of individuals with a profound expressive communication disorder, such as impairments in speech/language production and/or comprehension.
- **English-Language Learner (ELL):** A diverse group of students, with varying language, academic, and social/emotional needs between the ages of 5 through 21 years enrolled in a kindergarten through 12th-grade school and whose native language is not English. These individuals can also be referred to as English learners (EL).
- **Occupational Therapist:** A hands-on therapist who treats and supports students with physical and/or cognitive disabilities who experience difficulty with fine motor skills (e.g., cutting, printing, grasping).
- **Physical Therapist:** A therapist who supports individuals in developing, maintaining, or rehabilitating gross mobility skills, such as ambulating and positioning.
- **Speech-Language Pathologist:** A therapist who supports individuals in developing communication skills including speech sounds, language, social communication, voice, fluency, and augmentative and alternative communication.

CASE STUDY 1

During their weekly planning session Ms. Glass, a special educator, and Mr. Kalani, the middle school science teacher, discussed the upcoming unit in science. As they shared content and discussed accommodations for individual students, they also wrote the responsibilities for the paraeducator, Mrs. Thomas. When writing next week's lesson plans, Ms. Glass states how much she appreciates the work of Mrs. Thomas and feels that she could not function in her special education classroom nor provide inclusive services without her.

"I give her the planned lessons we create and provide her with the accommodations or modifications for the students she supports in your classroom. She follows my lessons and returns from your class with details about how students respond to activities. Although our meeting time is brief, we talk about how the lesson went and how the accommodations worked and make plans for future lessons."

As the teachers finished their planning, Ms. Glass shared a recent interaction with the paraeducator.

"Yesterday I pulled Mrs. Thomas aside. I told her how much we both appreciate her work with students and the feedback she provides us for improvements. She smiled and thanked me for my comments. Just like us, she wants acknowledgment for her work and feedback to improve her practices."

Ms. Glass considers reaching out to the principal, who performs formal evaluations on all staff members, to provide an update about performance and share her appreciation of Mrs. Thomas.

1. Why is shared planning important for paraeducators working in inclusive settings?
2. How did collaborative discussions between Mr. Kalani and Ms. Glass support the supervision of Mrs. Thomas?
3. What type of feedback should Ms. Glass share with the school principal related to paraeducators she oversees in the school?

Case Study 2

Ms. Decker, principal at Windsong Elementary School, is planning for the upcoming school year and is conducting a needs assessment to identify the students who have individualized needs, current staff available to meet those needs, and hiring to address unmet needs. She has identified six students who have specific needs that are not met by existing staff and will require at least some support this coming year. After a thorough assessment of the student's needs, she determines that to support them properly she will need to hire four new paraeducators. She develops job descriptions and posts positions to start the hiring process. She also develops interview questions and invites the special education teacher to sit in on interviews. Overall, they interview six individuals and select the four best matched for the positions. As soon as hiring is complete, Ms. Decker works with the educational teams to plan orientation and training for each paraeducator.

1. Are there other school personnel Ms. Decker should consider next time she conducts a needs assessment, develops paraeducator job descriptions, or interviews paraeducator candidates?
2. Why is it important to have clear job descriptions before paraeducators are hired? In what ways are paraeducator job descriptions used?
3. Who should be involved in the orientation and training of new paraeducators? What should their involvement look like?
4. How can Ms. Decker support the supervision of new paraeducators as they start their positions?

Case Study 3

Mrs. Ramirez is a speech-language pathologist in a large urban middle school. She is one of three speech-language pathologists in the school and primarily supports students with developmental disabilities. In this role she conducts all augmentative and alternative communication (AAC) evaluations, programs AAC systems, and creates and carries out treatment plans for students who use AAC. Mrs. Ramirez wants to involve paraeducators who support students who use AAC, but she is not sure where to begin. She reaches out to the two special education teachers in the school—Mr. Riley and Miss Singh—who work closely with these students, to see how she can delegate tasks and help the paraeducators support the communication needs of students who use AAC.

1. What are some important things that Mrs. Ramirez, Mr. Riley, and Miss Singh should consider when determining which tasks to delegate?
2. What are some of the specific tasks that would be appropriate to delegate to paraeducators who support students who use AAC?
3. Are there any tasks that Mrs. Ramirez should not delegate to paraeducators in this instance?
4. What training and coaching considerations should be made when delegating tasks?
5. How can Mr. Riley and Miss Singh support the delegation of AAC-related tasks to paraeducators?

The supervision of paraeducators requires the coordination of various educational team members. There are relevant supervisory roles for special education teachers, general education teachers, administrators, and related service providers. Although some supervisory roles are clearly the responsibility of specific team members, others are shared or must be defined. This chapter will outline the specific and shared roles of the most common individuals who provide supervision to paraeducators. Keep in mind that supervision is defined broadly and as discussed in Chapter 3 includes: (a) creating a supportive work environment, (b) directing the work of paraeducators, (c) training paraeducators, and (d) observing and providing meaningful feedback to paraeducators. Let's look at the individual supervisory responsibilities of each team member in these areas, starting with the special education teacher.

SPECIAL EDUCATION TEACHERS

As pointed out in Chapter 3, special education teachers often hold the primary responsibility for directing, supporting, and monitoring the day-to-day tasks of paraeducators (Chopra et al., 2011; Douglas et al., 2016). As such, special education teachers engage in a number of supervision tasks related to creating a supportive work environment, directing the work of paraeducators, as well as training, observing, and providing feedback to paraeducators.

Creating a Supportive Work Environment

It is often up to the supervising special education teacher to create a supportive work environment for the paraeducator, but this requires a number of specific skills (Figure 4-1). These include clear communication, rapport, trust, and openness (Biggs et al., 2016; Douglas et al., 2016). Special education teachers also act as leaders, role models, mentors, and advocate for paraeducators (Biggs et al., 2016; Chopra et al., 2011; Gerlach, 2015). Supervising teachers must be problem solvers, organized, prepared, flexible, willing to delegate, collaborative, work well with the team, address conflicts, and treat paraeducators with respect—as an important member of the team (Biggs et al., 2016; Chopra et al., 2011; Gerlach, 2015). Teachers often need training, support, and mentorship from experienced teachers to develop these skills (Douglas et al., 2016), but once obtained these skills can help teachers more effectively carry out their supervision responsibilities with paraeducators.

One of the first ways the supervising special education teacher can establish a supportive work environment is by providing paraeducators with orientation when they are assigned to support new students with disabilities. Orientation includes helping them get comfortable with the classroom and school. The supervising special education teacher should provide paraeducators with a tour of the school—share where items are kept, introduce them to members of the team, establish a place where they can keep their belongings, and show them locations they will frequent (Gerlach, 2015). During orientation teachers should also clearly outline the policies and procedures that paraeducators must follow in the classroom and the school (Capizzi & Da Fonte, 2012). A school or paraeducator handbook can be especially helpful in providing these details in a systematic and consistent manner. During orientation it is also essential to set clear expectations (Biggs et al., 2016). Supervising teachers should locate the paraeducator's job description, if it exists, and verify that it identifies the roles and responsibilities the paraeducator will hold on the team. Teachers should be sure that any roles in lesson planning, delivery of instruction, management of student behavior, assessment, and clerical duties are included (Gerlach, 2015). Teachers should also clearly outline the roles and relationships paraeducators should have with students and parents including any boundaries they should respect (Chopra et al., 2011). A written copy of these roles and responsibilities should be provided to the paraeducator (Gerlach, 2015; Stewart, 2019). The roles and responsibilities of others on the team should also be shared (Gerlach, 2015) so the paraeducator knows where their role ends and other roles begin.

Figure 4-1. Skills needed by supervising teachers. (Artwork created by Claire Douglas.)

Directing the Work of Paraeducators

A primary task of supervising special education teachers is to direct the work of paraeducators. As discussed in Chapter 3, this involves working collaboratively with the paraeducator and other professionals, such as the general education teacher, special area teachers (e.g., art, music, physical education), and related service providers. Key to making this collaboration happen is advocating for meeting times with the paraeducator and other team members. Meeting times will allow you to provide schedules, share lesson plans, and discuss student progress. Meeting times can also provide time where you can delegate tasks to paraeducators, one of the most challenging aspects of supervising paraeducators.

Teachers by nature are very capable and independent workers—used to handling things on their own. However, when a paraeducator is part of the educational team, teachers must recognize that they are there to assist and support students, and as such the teacher must learn to delegate tasks to them. Figure 4-2 outlines some important reasons that teachers should delegate to paraeducators. Delegation benefits the teacher (e.g., saves time, shares workload), the paraeducator (e.g., empowers and challenges paraeducators), and the students (e.g., improves efficiency and effectiveness in the classroom). Despite its importance, delegation can be challenging for teachers to carry out. Figure 4-3 provides a six-step process to help teachers maximize the efficiency and effectiveness of teacher–paraeducator teams through delegation.

> - Delegation makes the most of your time.
> - Delegation supports teamwork.
> - Delegation empowers paraeducators.
> - Delegation means you don't have to do everything yourself.
> - Delegation maximizes your personal resources.
> - Delegation gives paraeducators direction.
> - Delegation challenges paraeducators.
> - Delegation helps the whole team gain skills and competence.
> - Delegation allows limited budgets to be used most efficiently and effectively.
> - Delegation allows us to work smarter—not harder.

Figure 4-2. Why should I delegate? (Adapted from French, N. [2003]. *Managing paraeducators in your school: How to hire, train, and supervise non-certified staff*. Corwin Press.)

Identify Tasks

First, teachers must identify the tasks that need to be completed in the classroom. This might include clerical duties, instructional preparation, assessment, data collection, behavior management, and more. As teachers identify tasks they should consider both student and program needs (Gerlach, 2015). During the process of identifying tasks, teachers should break down large tasks into their components. Teachers should also assess the urgency and importance of each task, which will help them later as they determine priorities. As they identify tasks, the teacher should note tasks that could be completed by a paraeducator.

Decide Tasks to Delegate

Next, the teacher must make decisions about which tasks are best to delegate to the paraeducator. Just because a task can be completed by a paraeducator does not mean that is the best option for their classroom or setting. Tasks that are most urgent and important, and within the paraeducator's existing roles and responsibilities, are best for delegation. For each task that is delegated, the teacher must identify what training is required. For some tasks informal or minimal training will be required (e.g., clerical duties), while others will require specific training and coaching (e.g., data collection, instructional support). The teacher should work with the educational team to determine who will provide training and coaching.

Develop a Plan

After individual tasks have been identified for delegation, the teacher must develop a plan to provide to the paraeducator for each task (Douglas et al., 2016; Gerlach, 2015; McGrath et al., 2010). This requires that the teacher have clear knowledge of roles and responsibilities of paraeducators related to instruction, intervention, and direct services (Berlinghoff & McLaughlin, 2022). Where possible, the teacher should involve the paraeducator in the development of the plan, which will reduce ambiguity, ensure appropriate detail, and reduce the likelihood that they assign inappropriate tasks (Gerlach, 2015). The plan should list the task, include a rationale for the task, clearly list the steps of the task, and note how they should be carried out (Ashbaker & Morgan, 2012). The teacher should also share any limits that might be relevant to the task—sharing where their role starts and ends—and indicate who will serve as the supervisor for the task. This will help clarify who the paraeducator should go to with questions. Figure 4-4 gives an example of a non-instructional paraeducator plan.

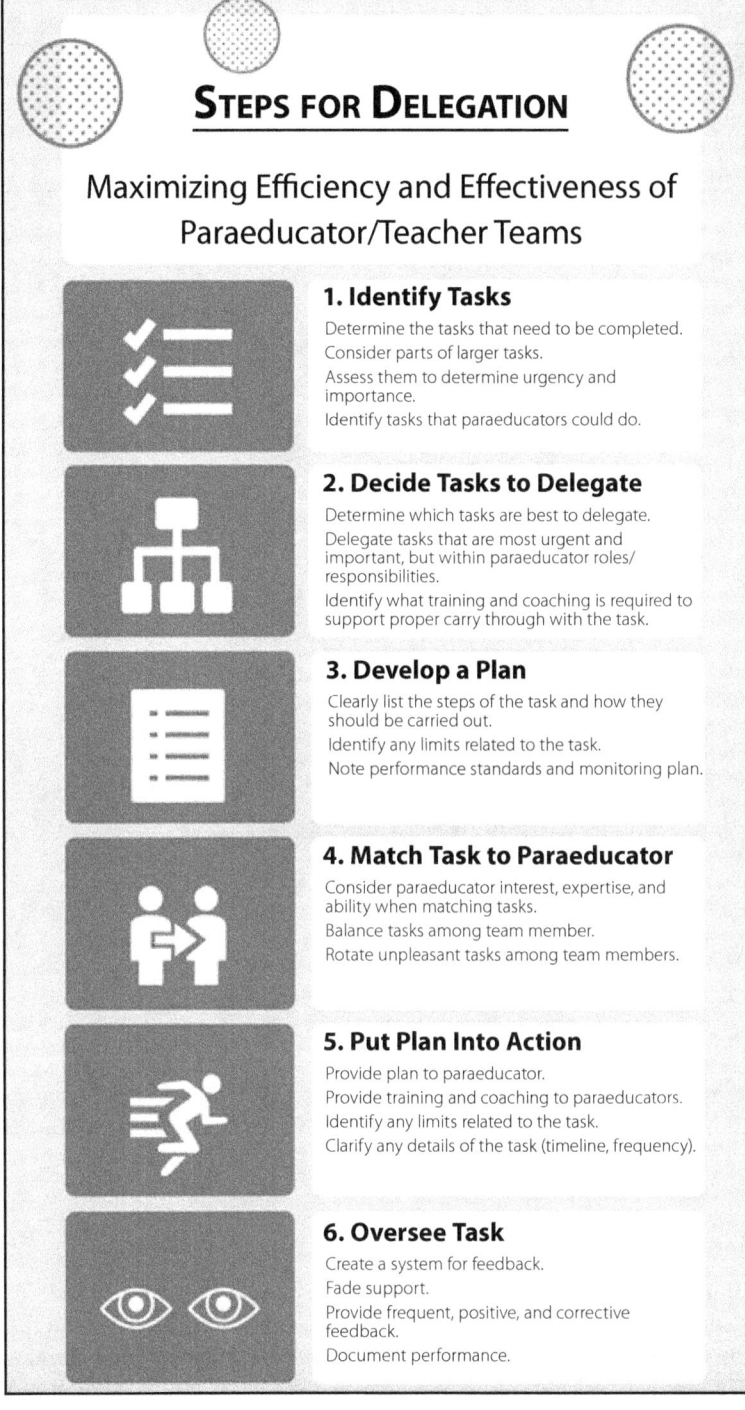

Figure 4-3. Steps for delegation. (Adapted from French, N. (2003). *Managing paraeducators in your school: How to hire, train, and supervise non-certified staff.* Corwin Press.)

Within the plan the teacher should note any performance standards that are expected and share the plan for monitoring the paraeducator. Tasks that are instructional in nature or involve students should include information about the setting; student goals that are being addressed; specific accommodations, modifications, and behavior supports that might be needed for the student; such as materials that are needed; the lesson content and sequence; and assessment information when applicable (see Figure 3-3 for an example).

PARAEDUCATOR PLAN
Task: Classroom attendance/lunch count
Rationale: Attendance must be provided to the office by 9:15 am each day to comply with record-keeping policies. Lunch count must be provided to the cafeteria by 9:15 am each morning to ensure the correct amount of food is ready for students at lunch.
Task Steps: 1. As students enter the classroom each morning, have each student make their lunch selection on the lunch choice board (Home, Lunch 1, Lunch 2).  2. Ensure all students present have made a lunch choice selection. 3. At 9:00 am record absent students on attendance sheet. 4. At 9:00 am record lunch choice selection counts on lunch count slip. 5. Provide lunch count slip to student assigned as the messenger for the week. Have them deliver to the office and cafeteria.
Supervisor: Classroom teacher

Figure 4-4. Paraeducator plan example—non-instructional task.

Match Task to Paraeducator

Before putting the plan into action, the teacher should do their best to match delegated tasks to the paraeducator's interests, expertise, and abilities (Biggs et al., 2016). Consulting directly with the paraeducator can be useful during this step (Biggs et al., 2016). Ensuring a match between tasks and the paraeducator can support a positive work atmosphere, reduce the need for extensive training and coaching, and help ensure that the paraeducator is provided with tasks that are meaningful and interesting to them—which will boost motivation. When matching tasks, the teacher should also be sure to balance tasks among team members, especially when they are responsible for supervising multiple paraeducators. Teachers should also be careful to not overdelegate, which can lead to paraeducators assuming too many instructional responsibilities and making curricular decisions (McGrath et al., 2010). Furthermore, teachers should be sure to rotate unpleasant tasks and, when appropriate, include themselves in the rotation. This will help paraeducators see the teacher as a team player, which will further support a positive work environment.

Training Paraeducators

Training paraeducators is another essential component of supervision often carried out by the special education teacher. Training is also essential to delegation and *putting the plan into action* (see Figure 4-3, Step 5) and supports the paraeducator in carrying out all tasks to which they are assigned. The paraeducator should be provided with the plan and given any training and coaching required to carry out the task within the plan (Brock & Carter, 2015; Chopra et al., 2011; Douglas et al., 2016). In instances where extensive training and coaching is needed, teachers may need to advocate to administrators on behalf of paraeducators to obtain the time and resources needed to support paraeducator training and coaching (Douglas et al., 2016). Chapter 5 provides more details about how to best carry out training and coaching with paraeducators. Although provided in the written plan, the teacher needs to be sure to clearly articulate any limits to the task so the paraeducator does not overstep boundaries. The teacher should also clarify details of the task, such as timeline and frequency. When putting the plan into action, it is important to provide a schedule for the paraeducator so they know when and where tasks should be carried out (Capizzi & Da Fonte, 2012; Douglas et al., 2016; Gerlach, 2015; Yates et al., 2020). Chapter 3 (specifically Figure 3-2) provides some information on the details that should be included in schedules.

Observing and Providing Feedback to Paraeducators

Supervision of paraeducators also requires that teachers *oversee tasks* that have been delegated (see Figure 4-3, Step 6). The teacher should create a system for providing feedback, which should be included within the paraeducator schedule or written plan. Additionally, the teacher should fade any support they originally provided to paraeducators. When providing feedback, teachers should ensure it is frequent, positive, and corrective (Brown et al., 2014; Douglas et al., 2016; Gerlach, 2015). This will increase paraeducator accuracy in tasks, motivation, and clarity in their assigned roles. Lastly, teachers should document paraeducator performance to ensure their growth does not go unrecognized (Capizzi & Da Fonte, 2012; Douglas & Uitto, 2021). If performance concerns arise that cannot be resolved, they should be discussed with administrators (Gerlach, 2015). Teachers should also be sure to share paraeducator successes with the administrator, as both concerns and successes can be used to inform formal evaluations.

GENERAL EDUCATION TEACHERS

Although special education teachers often hold primary supervisory roles with paraeducators, general education teachers serve as collaborative partners in the supervision of paraeducators when they support students with disabilities (Douglas et al., 2016). This collaborative relationship is especially relevant when students with disabilities are included in general education settings. Furthermore, general education teacher supervision responsibilities are more involved when paraeducators spend the majority of their time supporting students in the general education setting.

Creating a Supportive Work Environment

Just like special education teachers, general education teachers help create a supportive work environment for paraeducators. This responsibility is most obvious when children are supported by paraeducators in inclusive settings. First, general education teachers should ensure they treat paraeducators with respect and as part of the team (Biggs et al., 2016; Capizzi & Da Fonte, 2012; Douglas et al., 2016). This might include involving paraeducators in decision making and providing a space for them in the classroom. General education teachers should also communicate roles and responsibilities of the paraeducator to the educational team and paraeducator (Stewart, 2019). Without the appropriate communication from the general education teacher, there might be unintended gaps in job descriptions, training, and performance. General education teachers must also be willing to engage in shared decision making with the special education teacher and educational team (Capizzi & Da Fonte, 2012) to ensure a supportive work environment for paraeducators.

Directing the Work of Paraeducators

As part of their collaborative leadership, the general education teacher provides important insights and information about the general education curriculum, standards, and classroom structure—all which help direct the work of paraeducators. This requires regular meetings with the team to collaborate and delegate tasks to paraeducators. These discussions should include how paraeducator time will be divided when they provide support to multiple students, under the direction of more than one teacher, or in more than one setting (Gerlach, 2015). This division of responsibilities should be outlined within job descriptions, paraeducator schedules, and written plans (Douglas et al., 2016; Stewart, 2019).

Training Paraeducators

Once plans are outlined for paraeducators with the general education curriculum, standards, and classroom structure all in mind, the general education teacher then works with the team to determine what training is required (Douglas et al., 2016). The team should work together to outline a plan for training, determine the observation and feedback that will be required to ensure the paraeducator carries out plans as designed, and who will be responsible for training and observation of the paraeducator.

Observing and Providing Feedback to Paraeducators

Lastly, the general education teacher should provide input about paraeducator performance to the educational team. This might include formal observations and feedback directly to the paraeducators, or it might include sharing information about performance with the educational team. If the general education teacher has any concerns about paraeducator performance, this should be shared promptly with the educational team and administrators (Douglas et al., 2016; Stewart, 2019). Information about paraeducator performance can inform formal evaluations performed by administrators.

ADMINISTRATORS

Different administrators might be involved in the supervision of paraeducators. While district-level administrators (e.g., special education director, professional development coordinator) might support some supervision responsibilities, principals often assume the majority of administrator-related supervisory responsibilities with paraeducators. Knowing how to meet the supervision responsibilities of paraeducators requires a clear understanding of appropriate paraeducator roles, the needs of students, and supports that might be provided by paraeducators. Administrators can make informed decisions by conducting a needs assessment. The needs assessment can help them determine the needs of students, classrooms, and programs, and then select appropriate supports to meet these needs—including those that can be provided by paraeducators (Capizzi & Da Fonte, 2012; Douglas et al., 2016). Schools might find the resources from the PARAprofessional resource and research center helpful in conducting a needs assessment (http://paracenter.org). Administrators should also be careful to ensure that paraeducators are not misused or overused in the support of students with disabilities (Giangreco et al., 2010).

Position Title: Inclusion paraeducator

Position Setting: Middle school general education classrooms

Qualifications for the Position

- High school diploma, GED, or equivalent
- 18 years or older

Roles/Responsibilities

1. Carry out instructional activities as planned and directed by teachers.
2. Assist teachers in implementing classroom management procedures.
3. Collect data about student progress under the direction of teachers.
4. Provide updates to teachers about student performance.
5. Assist in preparing instructional materials.
6. Perform clerical duties assigned by teachers.
7. Follow district procedures to maintain student safety and promote learning as outlined during orientation.
8. Follow guidelines for professionalism (e.g., attendance, punctuality, interaction with family).
9. Maintain student confidentiality and follow ethical and legal guidelines as directed by administrators and teachers.
10. Communicate concerns about student behavior, development, or progress to appropriate team members.

Training Requirements

Attend 2-day orientation at the beginning of the school year and 10 hours of formal in-service training during the school year. On-the-job training will also occur during teacher work days.

Supervision Guidelines

The special education teacher will work in coordination with classroom teachers to supervise the daily work of the paraeducator, provide schedules and daily plans, and conduct regular meetings to discuss student progress. The paraeducator will report to teachers regarding instructional and student support.

Evaluation Guidelines

Paraeducators are responsible for performing assigned tasks and following instructions from supervising teachers and the principal. The principal will conduct annual evaluations (bi-annual for new paraeducators in their first year or those with identified performance issues) with input from the educational team, and the paraeducator will work with the principal to develop goals for improvement.

Figure 4-5. Sample paraeducator job description. (Adapted from Vasa, S., Steckelberg, A., & Pickett, A. L. [2003]. Paraeducators in educational settings: Administrative issues. In A. L. Pickett & K. Gerlach [Eds.], *Supervising paraeducators in educational settings: A team approach* [pp. 255-288]. Pro Ed.)

Creating a Supportive Work Environment

Just like general and special education teachers, administrators are critical to creating a supportive work environment for paraeducators. As a first step, administrators can use information from the needs assessment and supervising teachers to develop accurate job descriptions for paraeducators (Figure 4-5). Administrators can also set a positive tone during hiring. After hiring, they can continue to create a positive work environment by learning each paraeducator's name, including paraeducators in school meetings, and ensuring paraeducators are recognized for their hard work. Administrators also provide important support to teacher–paraeducator teams.

Hiring Paraeducators

Hiring paraeducators is a responsibility that is often held solely by administrators. Using the job description that was created as part of the needs assessment, the administrator works with school and/or district personnel to post paraeducator positions. When possible, these positions may be filled by existing paraeducators, but when new paraeducators are needed, positions are posted for outside candidates. Next, applications are reviewed and applicants are carefully selected for interviews. Ideally the principal includes key members of the educational team (e.g., special education teacher, general education teacher, and key related service providers) in the interview process (Douglas et al., 2016, 2022a). Involving educational team members in the interview process helps ensure a good fit between the paraeducator, students, and educational teams—which is critical to ensuring a positive work environment for the paraeducator after hiring. The interview process might include measures to ensure paraeducator proficiency, such as degree/credit requirements or a proficiency exam (Douglas et al., 2022a). These steps are often taken to meet federal "highly qualified" requirements for paraeducators (Every Student Succeeds Act of 2015; No Child Left Behind Act of 2002). The face-to-face interview can be the most informative part of the interview process. The hiring committee should develop an interview protocol that ensures that key roles and responsibilities of the position are discussed and questions are written to help determine fit with the applicant (Figure 4-6). Principals might find the interview instrument from Dillon and Ebmeier (2009) helpful in creating interview protocols specific to the needs of their school. Once a paraeducator is hired, administrators should clearly outline and communicate the paraeducator's roles both verbally and in writing (Stewart, 2019), as well as ensure that appropriate orientation occurs (Capizzi & Da Fonte, 2012; Douglas et al., 2016).

Supporting Teacher–Paraeducator Teams

Both teachers and paraeducators have expressed the importance of administrative support in ensuring positive work environments. Teachers indicate their need for administrator support in their supervisory roles with paraeducators, including support for conflict resolution—an area that is often uncomfortable for teachers to navigate alone (Douglas et al., 2016). Furthermore, administrators have a responsibility to advocate for better work conditions for paraeducators including improved pay, benefits, and involvement of paraeducators in team meetings (Douglas et al., 2022a).

Directing the Work of Paraeducators

The day-to-day work of paraeducators is usually directed by supervising teachers, but administrators often hold important supportive roles. First, administrators might work with teachers to establish paraeducator schedules. This is especially important when paraeducators hold numerous responsibilities around the school (e.g., cafeteria and playground supervision, behavior management tasks, small group instruction). The paraeducator job description, created by administrators, can also assist teachers in directing the work of paraeducators.

Training Paraeducators

Administrators are key to ensuring high-quality training for paraeducators. The job description can be used as a guide to determine what training the paraeducator requires. Administrators often facilitate formal training, such as workshops provided to paraeducators across the school or district on topics of relevance across positions (Douglas et al., 2016; Stewart, 2019). However, administrators also help ensure time and resources are available for teacher–paraeducator teams to meet and provide ongoing training and support (Capizzi & Da Fonte, 2012; Douglas et al., 2016).

> **Candidate:** _____
>
> **In Attendance:** Ms. Kilgo (principal), Mrs. Bennett (special education teacher), Mrs. Flores (general education teacher), Mr. Wang (ELL coordinator)
>
> **Introduction:** Thank you for your interest in a paraeducator position in our school. We are filling a couple of positions in the school to support students with disabilities. Mrs. Bennett is our special education teacher who oversees the support of these students. Paraeducators within these positions are expected to perform self-care activities with students, provide supplementary instruction, supervise peer interactions, and support the teacher in clerical duties. This often includes classroom management, lifting, toileting, and playground duty. Our school has a high number of students who are English-language learners, including those with disabilities, so I've invited Mr. Wang our ELL coordinator. We also include most of our students within general education classrooms, so Mrs. Flores is here to represent those settings.
>
> **Interview Questions**
>
> 1. What made you interested in this position?
> 2. Based on the roles and responsibilities we have outlined, are there any duties that you are unwilling or unable to perform? Please explain.
> 3. What training or experience have you had that is relevant to this position? What specific experience do you have supporting individuals with disabilities?
> 4. Name one strength you have that will help you in this position.
> 5. Name one weakness you have that will challenge you in this position and indicate how you will work to overcome that challenge.
> 6. Describe a time when you worked closely with another adult. What obstacles did you encounter and how did you work through them?
> 7. How would you handle a student who is displaying challenging behavior?
> 8. Many of our students are English-language learners. What kind of additional considerations would you make in your work with these students?
> 9. We value inclusion, so much of the support you will provide will be social support in the general education classroom. Please describe how you might support peer interactions.
> 10. Many of our students have medical and therapy needs. As a paraeducator, what steps will you take to ensure a student is supported in all aspects of their education and needs?

Figure 4-6. Sample interview protocol for paraeducator interviews.

Observing and Providing Feedback to Paraeducators

The most commonly noted supervisory responsibility of administrators in relation to paraeducators is the formal evaluation process. Although teachers serve in day-to-day supervision of paraeducators, building principals and other administrators often carry out the formal evaluation of the paraeducator (Douglas et al., 2022a). Formal evaluation of paraeducators ideally includes observation of paraeducators in the classroom, input from supervising teachers, and a written evaluation accompanied by a meeting (Biggs et al., 2016; Douglas et al., 2016). Evaluation should occur at least once per year, or bi-yearly for new paraeducators or those who are underperforming (Douglas et al., 2022b). The formal evaluation should mirror the job description provided to the paraeducator (Figure 4-7). Some districts opt for a more general evaluation with standardized forms for all paraeducators and only assess areas that are applicable to the paraeducator's assigned roles.

Paraeducator: _____	Paraeducator Assignment: _____
Evaluation Completed By: _____	Date: _____

Input Provided By: _____

Rate the paraeducator's performance below using the following scale:

O—Outstanding, consistently performs task at a high level/exceeded standard

S—Satisfactory, consistently performs task at an acceptable level/met standard

D—Developing, evidence of developing skills to an acceptable level/working toward standard

N—Needs improvement, requires improvement to perform at an acceptable level/performing below standard

U—Unsatisfactory, requires immediate improvement and remedial support to reach acceptable performance/did not meet standard

X—Not observed

N/A—Not applicable (provide justification)

Training Requirements

__ Attended orientation prior to the start of the position.
__ Completed 10 hours of in-service training.
__ Completed on-the-job training as outlined by supervising teachers and administrators.

Instructional/Student Supports

__ Carried out instructional activities as directed by supervising teacher(s).
__ Followed instructional plans provided by supervising teacher(s).
__ Carried out classroom management procedures as directed by supervising teacher(s).
__ Collected data about student progress by supervising teacher(s).
__ Provided teacher(s) with updates about student progress.
__ Prepared instructional materials for students as directed by teacher(s).
__ Followed district procedures to maintain student safety and promote learning as outlined during orientation.

Team Supports

__ Carried out clerical duties assigned by supervising teacher(s).
__ Attended regular planning/student progress meetings.
__ Communicated concerns about student behavior, development, or progress to appropriate team members.

Professionalism

__ Maintained professional behavior in interactions with families and school professionals.
__ Strictly maintained student confidentiality.
__ Followed ethical and legal guidelines as directed by the administrators and/or teachers.
__ Demonstrated appropriate attendance, punctuality, and open communication about illness or absences to supervising teacher(s).

Overall Rating (circle one)

Outstanding   Satisfactory   Developing   Needs Improvement   Unsatisfactory

Comments: _____
Areas for Improvement: _____
Paraeducator-Identified Goals to Address Areas for Improvement: _____

Evaluator's signature: _____ Date: _____
Paraeducator's signature: _____ Date: _____

Paraeducator signature acknowledges receipt of the evaluation, not necessarily agreement with the evaluation.

Figure 4-7. Sample formal paraeducator evaluation.

Either approach is appropriate, but it is important to be transparent throughout the process and provide supervising teachers and paraeducators with information about the evaluation process, including copies of the evaluation that will be used (Douglas et al., 2022b; Stewart, 2019).

RELATED SERVICE PROVIDERS

Beyond the three core supervisors of paraeducators (i.e., special education teachers, general education teachers, administrators), there are numerous related service providers that support students with disabilities and interface with paraeducators. As described in the Individuals with Disabilities Act (IDEA; 2004) this might include speech-language pathologists, occupational therapists, physical therapists, school nurses, rehabilitation counselors, and psychological services. Although not specifically outlined in IDEA, students with disabilities might also receive support from behavior specialists when challenging behaviors occur, and paraeducators will often hold important roles in implementing behavior supports with these students (Chopra et al., 2011; Douglas et al., 2022b). This might include coordination and training with behavior consultants to carry out behavior plans (Douglas & Uitto, 2021). Additionally, students who are English-language learners (ELL) or from different cultures might require support from ELL providers and home–school liaisons. In these instances, the paraeducator often serves in instructional roles and as a cultural broker (Chopra et al., 2011). Furthermore, students with visual impairments might be supported by vision specialists and orientation and mobility specialists, while students with hearing impairments might receive translator or hearing specialist support. In these instances, specialists will work closely with paraeducators to provide appropriate student support.

Related service providers often have a unique relationship with paraeducators because paraeducators are often responsible for carrying out tasks assigned by related service providers across various school environments (Chopra et al., 2011). Given this delegation, related service providers often hold important supervision responsibilities related to paraeducators. Related service providers can be involved in all aspects of supervision, but are generally involved to a lesser degree than special education teachers, general education teachers, and administrators. Additionally, supervision responsibilities will vary based on student needs. It is important that the educational team clearly defines the roles of related service providers to ensure they understand their supervisory and training roles with paraeducators. Educational teams should meet regularly to communicate these roles and discuss any training and supervision needs. Furthermore, related service providers should follow guidelines established by their associated professional organizations related to the supervision of paraeducators (see American Speech-Language-Hearing Association, 2022 for an example related to speech-language pathologists). Following are some examples of how related service providers might create supportive work environments for paraeducators, direct the work of paraeducators, train paraeducators, and observe and provide feedback to paraeducators.

Speech-Language Pathologist

The speech-language pathologist creates a positive work environment by working with the paraeducator to support students with communication challenges. For example, in the case of a student with complex communication needs, the speech-language pathologist communicates with the paraeducator regularly about the student's communication goals and adjustments that need to be made to support their communication. The speech-language pathologist also provides training to the teacher and paraeducator on the use of an AAC system used by the student. Then the speech-language pathologist creates an intervention plan for the student to support AAC use throughout the school day (Figure 4-8). The speech-language pathologist provides instruction to the student, with the paraeducator present, during speech-language sessions. The speech-language pathologist also provides the paraeducator with training to implement AAC with the student outside of therapy sessions. They provide ongoing oversight and input to support the student and educational team.

PARAEDUCATOR PLAN	
Task: Model AAC for Annabelle	**Setting:** All areas of the school

Rationale: Modeling AAC for Annabelle will help her learn how to use her AAC system.

IEP Goals Addressed: When given a choice or asked a question by others, Annabelle will respond by communicating using her AAC system 80% of the time. Annabelle will initiate communication with others (unprompted) at least three times per day.

Task Steps

- When you model AAC
    - Be face-to-face with Annabelle and make sure you have her attention.
    - Have the AAC system within reach of both of you.
    - Model AAC as you talk. Press symbols on the device within 2 seconds of your verbal messages. You do not need to press a symbol for every word you speak. Aim for two to three symbols per message.
    - Model AAC as you provide choices, ask questions, comment about what you/Annabelle are doing, and respond to Annabelle's communication.
    - Wait for 3 to 5 seconds after each AAC model to give Annabelle a chance to communicate.
- Model AAC throughout the day during a variety of tasks and in a variety of locations within the school. Right now aim for 50 instances of AAC models per day.

Things to Avoid

- Make sure you have Annabelle's attention when you model AAC.
- Do not use hand-over-hand to have Annabelle use her AAC.
- Do not require Annabelle to communicate each time you use AAC—remember you are teaching her how to use it, even if she does not try it right then she is still learning.
- Be sure you are waiting long enough after you model. This helps Annabelle know it is her turn to communicate.

Supervisor: Speech-language pathologist

Figure 4-8. Paraeducator plan example—related service provider.

Occupational Therapist

The occupational therapist creates a positive work environment by working with the paraeducator to support the fine motor skills of students. For example, the occupational therapist might design an intervention to support a student in developing self-feeding skills. After implementing and demonstrating the intervention during occupational therapist sessions, the occupational therapist provides training to the paraeducator, who carries out the intervention during mealtimes at school when the occupational therapist is not present. The paraeducator collects data after training from the occupational therapist to document student progress and shares student progress and challenges faced when implementing the intervention. The occupational therapist periodically observes the paraeducator, provides feedback, makes adjustments to the intervention, and evaluates student progress.

Physical Therapist

The physical therapist creates a positive work environment by working with the paraeducator to support the gross motor skills of students. For example, the physical therapist is helping one student learn to ambulate using a walker. They invite the paraeducator to join therapy sessions to learn how they provide this support and provide training to the paraeducator to carry out practice with the walker as the student travels around the school. The paraeducator is assigned to work with the student on walking 20 steps with the walker each day and collects data on the student's walking practice. During therapy sessions the physical therapist observes the paraeducator implementing the walking practice, provides feedback to the paraeducator, modifies the therapy as needed, models additional therapy supports for the student as they progress, and evaluates the student's progress.

Nurse

The school nurse creates a positive work environment by working with the paraeducator to support the medical needs of students. The school nurse provides training at the beginning of the school year to a paraeducator who will support a student who requires medication and feeding through a gastrointestinal tube. The nurse demonstrates the procedure to the paraeducator and observes the paraeducator when carrying out the procedure. The nurse creates a form to record all medication administration and feeding and instructs the paraeducator on recording medical procedures. The nurse monitors the procedure and record-keeping periodically to ensure the procedure is being carried out as planned.

Rehabilitation Counselor

The rehabilitation counselor works with the paraeducator to support students as they transition from high school to work settings. The rehabilitation counselor provides instruction and intervention support to paraeducators as they support students in gaining job skills. This includes the development of instructional plans for transition-related skills, formal and informal training to the paraeducator to carry out these plans, observation of and feedback to paraeducators with students in transition activities and settings, and monitoring student progress and adjusting plans to meet their changing needs.

Behavior Specialist

The behavior specialist works with the paraeducator to support students with behavioral needs. For example, the paraeducator may support a student who is engaging in self-injurious behavior. The behavior specialist is asked to help the team and conducts a Functional Behavior Assessment with input from the team. They determine that the behavior occurs when the student wants to escape a task. With input from the educational team, including the paraeducator, the behavior specialist develops a Behavior Intervention Plan and provides training to the whole team to carry out the plan. The paraeducator is most closely supporting the student, so the behavior specialist makes sure to observe the paraeducator when they carry out the plan. This includes teaching the paraeducator how to collect data about the student's behavior. As needed, the behavior specialist makes adjustments to the Behavior Intervention Plan after analyzing the data and discussion with the educational team, including the paraeducator.

English-Language Learner Teacher

The ELL teacher works with paraeducators who support ELL students. For example, the ELL teacher is working with an ELL student who also has a learning disability. They coordinate with the classroom teacher and classroom paraeducator to provide appropriate accommodations for the student's learning needs related to their English language acquisition level. This includes training, consultation, and observation of support. The ELL teacher joins the teacher–paraeducator team meeting once a month to discuss the student's needs and makes adjustments to their educational plan as needed.

Home–School Liaison

The home–school liaison supports the paraeducator by serving as a link to the home environment for students. The home–school liaison is providing support to a family who has a student with a disability and is experiencing an eviction. Beyond connecting the family with community resources to help them through this challenging time, the home–school liaison meets with the teacher and paraeducator to inform them of what is happening with the family and provides additional strategies they can carry out with the student in the classroom.

SUMMARY

Supervision is a shared responsibility among educational team members, but one that falls primarily on special education teachers when students have disabilities. Each member of the team works together to ensure the paraeducator has the appropriate supervision and support relevant to the paraeducator and their support of students. While team members have distinct roles related to paraeducator supervision, the combined support they provide in supervising paraeducators lead to improved paraeducator support and ultimately better outcomes for students with disabilities. Yet, to do this well there must be established team guidelines and regular meetings. Team members—including special education teachers, general education teachers, administrators, and related service providers—must gain the competencies outlined in this chapter to ensure high-quality supervision of paraeducators. Additionally, they should include and recognize paraeducators as valuable members of the educational team and recognize the important support they provide for students with disabilities. The quality of supervision responsibilities provided to paraeducators ultimately impacts the support provided to students. High-quality supervision leads to high-quality outcomes for children with disabilities.

Chapter Review

1. How do supervision roles related to paraeducators vary among team members? Who holds primary and secondary roles? How does student placement influence the paraeducator supervision decisions?
2. What is the process for formal evaluation of paraeducators? How often should it occur, and who holds primary responsibilities in the process?
3. Why is delegation so important for teachers who work with paraeducators? List five reasons why teachers should delegate tasks to paraeducators.
4. What are the components that should be included in paraeducator job descriptions? Why is it important to have job descriptions?
5. How might supervision of paraeducators differ based on individual student needs? Provide examples and details of the differences.

Resources

Paraeducator Orientation Topics

Calendars and Schedules

- District calendar and school calendar (e.g., professional development days, special events)
- Paraeducator daily schedules—arrival and dismissal times, lunch, breaks
- School building schedules

District Policies and Procedures

- Administrative hierarchy and direct supervisor (e.g., chain of command)
- Attendance at faculty meetings and social events
- Discipline policies (e.g., use of restraint, playground and cafeteria policies)
- Emergency procedures (e.g., tornado drill, earthquake drill, fire drill, lockdown)
- Faculty/staff conduct guidelines/handbooks (e.g., dress code, cell phone/internet/email usage)
- Job description
- List of personnel and positions
- Map of the building (e.g., classrooms)
- Performance expectations and evaluation process
- Salary, fringe benefits, insurance options, and pay schedule
- Sick leave and how to report off for illness
- Student handbook (e.g., dress requirements, discipline policy, cheating policy)
- Training requirements (e.g., after school compensation, training opportunities)

Classroom Practices

- Arrival time and daily schedule (e.g., time, activities, paraeducator responsibilities)
- Classroom rules, code of conduct, expectations, and routines
- Communication (e.g., lesson plans, emails, written notes, meetings)
- Differentiation between roles/responsibilities of paraeducator and professionals (e.g., teachers, related service personnel)

- Equipment and resources (e.g., assistive and instructional technology, printer/copier usage)
- Expectations for team members and philosophy of the classroom teacher
- Storage of personal items
- Work styles inventory

Student Needs

- Activity plans
- Student profiles (e.g., goals, strengths, successes, challenges, accommodations; see Figure 4-1)

Supervision Resources for Specific Team Members

- Causton, J., & Tracy-Bronson, C. (2013). *The occupational therapist's handbook for inclusive school practices.* Brookes Publishing.
- Causton, J., & Theoharis, G. (2014). *The principal's handbook for leading inclusive schools.* Brookes Publishing.
- Causton, J., & Tracy-Bronson, C. (2014). *The speech-language pathologist's handbook for inclusive school practices.* Brookes Publishing.
- Causton, J., & Tracy-Bronson, C. (2015). *The educator's handbook for inclusive school practices.* Brookes Publishing.
- Iowa Department of Education. (2007). *Guide to effective paraeducator practices edition II.* Author.
- Iowa Department of Education. (2013). *Appropriate paraeducator services matrix.* https://educateiowa.gov/sites/default/files/documents/Appropriate%20Paraeducator%20Duties.pdf
- Lieberman, L. (2007). *Paraeducators in physical education: A training guide to roles and responsibilities.* Human Kinetics.
- State Education Resource Center. (2007). *Assessment checklist for paraprofessionals: Preschool-grade 12.* https://portal.ct.gov/SDE/Paraeducator/Paraeducator-Information-and-Resources/Documents
- Steers, A., & Buchinsky, A. (2014). *Communicators: A paraprofessional training program.* Communication and Learning Consultants.

REFERENCES

American Speech-Language-Hearing Association. (2022). *Speech-language pathology assistant scope of practice.* www.asha.org/policy

Ashbaker, B. Y., & Morgan, J. (2012). Team players and team managers: Special educators working with paraeducators to support inclusive classrooms. *Creative Education, 3*(3), 322-327. http://dx.doi.org/10.4236/ce.2012.33051

Berlinghoff, D., & McLaughlin, V. L. (Eds.). (2022). *Practice-based standards for the preparation of special educators.* Council for Exceptional Children.

Biggs, E. E., Gilson, C. B., & Carter, E. W. (2016). Accomplishing more together: Influences to the quality of professional relationships between special educators and paraprofessionals. *Research and Practice for Persons with Severe Disabilities, 41*(4), 256-272. https://doi.org/10.1177/1540796916665604

Brock, M. E., & Carter, E. W. (2015). Effects of a professional development package to prepare special education paraprofessionals to implement evidence-based practice. *Journal of Special Education, 49,* 39-51. https://doi.org/10.1177/0022466913501882

Brown, T. L., Gatmaitan, M., & Harjusola-Webb, S. M. (2014). Using performance feedback to support paraprofessionals in inclusive preschool classrooms. *Young Exceptional Children, 17*(2), 21-31. https://doi.org/10.1177/1096250613493189

Capizzi, A. M., & Da Fonte, M. A. (2012). Supporting paraeducators through a collaborative classroom support plan. *Focus on Exceptional Children, 44*(6), 1-16.

Chopra, R. V., Sandoval-Lucero, E., & French, N. K. (2011). Effective supervision of paraeducators: Multiple benefits and outcomes. *National Teacher Education Journal, 4*(2), 15-26.

Dillon, A., & Ebmeier, H. (2009). The development and field test of an employment interview instrument for school paraprofessionals. *Journal of Special Education Leadership, 22*(2), 93-104.

Douglas, S. N., Bowles, R., & Kammes, R. (2022a). Elementary principals' views on the policies and practices of paraeducators in special education. *Journal of the American Academy of Special Education Professionals, Winter,* 107-126.

Douglas, S. N., Bowles, R., & Kammes, R. (2022b). Paraeducators: An important member of the educational team for students with disabilities. *Journal of the American Academy of Special Education Professionals, Spring/Summer,* 134-150.

Douglas, S. N., Chapin, S. E., & Nolan, J. F. (2016). Special education teachers' experiences supporting and supervising paraeducators: Implications for special and general education settings. *Teacher Education and Special Education, 39*(1), 60-74. https://doi.org/10.1177/0888406415616443

Douglas, S. N., & Uitto, D. J. (2021). A collaborative approach to paraeducator training. *Beyond Behavior, 30*(1), 4-13. https://doi.org/10.1177/1074295621997177

Every Student Succeeds Act of 2015, 20 U.S.C. § 1177.

French, N. (2003). *Managing paraeducators in your school: How to hire, train, and supervise non-certified staff.* Corwin Press.

Gerlach, K. (2015). *Let's team up! A checklist for teachers, paraeducators and principals.* Dude Publishing.

Giangreco, M. F., Suter, J. C., & Doyle, M. B. (2010). Paraprofessionals in inclusive schools: A review of recent research. *Journal of Educational and Psychological Consultation, 20*(1), 41-57. https://doi.org/10.1080/10474410903535356

Individuals with Disabilities Education Act of 2004, 20 U.S.C. § 1400.

McGrath, M. Z., Johns, B. H., & Mathur, S. R. (2010). Empowered or overpowered? Strategies for working effectively with paraprofessionals. *Beyond Behavior, 19*(2), 2-6.

No Child Left Behind Act of 2002, P.L. 107-110, 20 U.S.C. § 6319.

Stewart, E. M. (2019). Reducing ambiguity: Tools to define and communicate paraprofessional roles and responsibilities. *Intervention in School and Clinic, 55*(1), 52-57. https://doi.org/10.1177/1053451218782431

Vasa, S., Steckelberg, A., & Pickett, A. L. (2003). Paraeducators in educational settings: Administrative issues. In A. L. Pickett & K. Gerlach (Eds.), *Supervising paraeducators in educational settings: A team approach* (pp. 255-288). Pro Ed.

Yates, P. A., Chopra, R. V., Sobeck, E. E., Douglas, S. N., Morano, S., Walker, V. L., & Schulze, R. (2020). Working with paraeducators: Tools and strategies for instructional planning, performance feedback, and evaluation. *Intervention in School and Clinic, 56*(1), 1-8. https://doi.org/10.1177/1053451220910740

Paraeducator Training

INTRODUCTION

Paraeducator training is an essential part of ensuring that paraeducators are equipped with the skills needed to carry out their roles and responsibilities effectively. Chapter 5 discusses the importance of paraeducator training, current training practices being implemented by schools, the legal requirements of training paraeducators, and the best practices for paraeducator training. Adult learning theory and team-level training are also introduced relative to paraeducator training. Finally, one paraeducator training model is reviewed in detail and recommendations for implementation are shared.

CHAPTER OBJECTIVES

- Describe the legal requirements based on federal law related to training and professional development for paraeducators.
- Detail common practices for paraeducator training and professional development.
- Identify and describe best practices for providing training to paraeducators based on adult learning theory.
- Explain the benefits of team-level training, where teachers and paraeducators are provided with training together.
- List and describe the steps for the paraeducator training model.

KEY TERMS

- **Adult Learning Theory:** Also known as andragogy, adult learning theory is a collection of different but interrelated theories and methods that address how adults learn, including accelerated learning, coaching, guided design, and just-in-time training.
- **Council for Exceptional Children (CEC):** An international professional organization that strives to improve the experience of individuals with disabilities and/or gifts and talents through advocacy, professional development, resource sharing, and educational standards.
- **Didactic Instruction:** A style of instruction that incorporated lectures and presentations in which the instructor delivers information and the students, or participants, receive the information.
- **Every Student Succeeds Act (ESSA):** One of the main education laws for public schools in the United States that holds schools accountable for student performance. This law ensures equal opportunities for students from disadvantaged backgrounds and students who qualify for special education services.
- **Individuals with Disabilities Education Act (IDEA):** Established in 1990 and reauthorized in 2004, this federal law details special education and related service programming for students with disabilities.
- **Local Education Agency (LEA):** A term used to describe a public organization (e.g., school district, intermediate unit) that serves students with disabilities and ensures they receive the supports and services they are eligible for under the law (i.e., ESSA, IDEA).
- **Performance Feedback:** Performance feedback is a training method and/or part of a professional learning package in which feedback is provided to paraeducators about the quality of their performance.
- **Team-Level Training:** Training that utilizes teams within a particular field to increase knowledge and proficiency when completing a task.
- **Tier 1 Behavior Management Strategies:** Practices that support all students across all settings by establishing a foundation for proactive support and preventing unwanted behaviors.

CASE STUDY 1

Mr. Baskin is a teacher in a self-contained classroom for 10 students in kindergarten to second grade with emotional and behavioral disorders at Valleyside Elementary School. Although this is his fifth year of teaching and he has worked with paraeducators before, he has two new paraeducators starting in his class this fall. In preparation for this school year his building principal, Ms. Turner, has asked him to identify what training support and resources he will need for his new paraeducators and to come up with a training plan for the year.

1. What steps should Mr. Baskin take to identify the training needs of his new paraeducators?
2. What should be included in the training plan for Mr. Baskin's new paraeducators?
3. Describe the initial training, follow-up training, and coaching that should be provided to Mr. Baskin's paraeducators.
4. Detail how performance should be documented for the paraeducators.

CASE STUDY 2

Ms. Garcia has been assigned to supervise Mr. Backus, a paraeducator supporting Mario, a student with autism, in her seventh-grade social studies class. Mr. Backus recently attended a training related to implementing a visual schedule for Mario to help him complete all of his tasks more independently in the classroom. Ms. Garcia did not attend the training, but her principal has asked that she ensure that the visual schedule is successfully implemented in the classroom by the educational team.

1. In what ways would team-level training be beneficial in this case study? What should Ms. Garcia do to ensure she has the background knowledge needed to support the rest of the educational team? What could be done differently the next time a new intervention needs to be implemented with a student?
2. What considerations should Ms. Garcia make when coaching Mr. Backus in implementing the visual schedule in the classroom for Mario?
3. How will Ms. Garcia know when Mr. Backus no longer needs coaching support?

CASE STUDY 3

Mr. Patel is a director of special education for a school district for which he oversees 20 special education teachers and 42 paraeducators. The district has a new initiative for the upcoming school year in which they would like to see paraeducators implement more Tier 1 level behavior management strategies, such as behavior-specific praise (BSP), High Probability Request Sequences (HPRS), and Pre-correction. Mr. Patel organizes a workshop at the start of the school year for all of the paraeducators and their supervising special education teachers to learn about the strategies. The workshop is a full day of training that includes lecture, role play, video examples, small and large group discussion, scenarios, and a time for questions. Mr. Patel lets the staff know that he and the building principals will be looking for these strategies to be implemented throughout the school year. During the first few months of school, Mr. Patel and the building principals note a small increase in the use of these strategies. They assumed that over time the paraeducators would become even more comfortable with the strategies and they would see them implemented at even higher rates. Much to their disappointment, they observed the opposite happen. Upon the third and fourth month of school, the paraeducators are minimally using the strategies and in many situations are not using them at all.

1. What is happening in this situation? Why do you think the paraeducators are not implementing the strategies as they were taught?
2. What could Mr. Patel have done differently when training the paraeducators on these strategies?
3. What are some ways Mr. Patel could help improve the paraeducators' use of these strategies?
4. What role do the special education teachers hold when it comes to the paraeducators implementing these newly learned strategies?

Training and professional development to paraeducators is critical to ensure they hold the knowledge and skills required for the students they support (Biggs et al., 2016). The importance of paraeducator training is noted with federal law (Every Student Succeeds Act, 2015; Individuals with Disabilities Act, 2004), some state guidelines (e.g., see Connecticut Senate bill 913, 2017; Washington State House bill 1115, 2017), and professional organizations such as the CEC (Council for Exceptional Children, 2015). Despite the importance noted within the literature and paraeducators' own recognition of a need for training (Sobeck & Robertson, 2019), most paraeducators receive little to no training (Brock, 2021). In fact, often there is no requirement that paraeducators must have prior experience or training in special education before supporting students with disabilities (Stewart, 2019).

Administrators and teachers have important roles related to supporting paraeducator training. For example, administrators often coordinate formal training for paraeducators and allocate or advocate for funding and time for teachers and paraeducators to engage in on-the-job training. Supervising teachers often support on-the-job training and provide important coaching and related supervision and feedback for trained skills. Chapter 4 provides additional details of the roles of administrators and teachers in relation to paraeducator supervision. Within this chapter we outline the legal requirements related to paraeducator training, current practices related to paraeducator training, and the challenges that are often associated with the most common training methods. We also discuss best practices related to paraeducator training including the use of adult learning practices, performance feedback, and ongoing supervision.

LEGAL REQUIREMENTS RELATED TO PARAEDUCATOR TRAINING

At the federal level, individuals are not required to hold any specific type of certification or licensure in order to obtain a paraeducator position. However, the ESSA of 2015 gives some guidance related to hiring and staffing paraeducators. According to ESSA, and as discussed in Chapter 3, states and LEA must ensure that the paraeducators they employ have a secondary school diploma or an equivalent, such as a General Educational Development (GED), as well as one of the following: (a) 2 completed years of schooling at an institution of higher education (IHE), (b) an earned associate's degree or higher, or (c) the ability to demonstrate a rigorous standard of quality through a formal assessment at the state or local level relative to instructing, reading, writing, and mathematics (ESSA, 2015). Although 2 completed years of school at an IHE and an associate's degree is straightforward to document, the third option does give schools some autonomy related to what assessments they will use to evaluate "highly qualified" status for their paraeducators. Different states and local agencies offer varying assessments that can be used to fulfill this requirement under ESSA.

In addition to meeting one of these requirements, paraeducators must also complete 20 hours of professional development related to their work each year (ESSA, 2015; IDEA, 2004). This training can occur through the school district or educational agencies or be provided by outside agencies/organizations as approved by the paraeducator's employer. Upon being hired, an administrator and paraeducator should discuss continuing education opportunities, determine what qualifies as professional development, clarify if the school will offer the required 20 hours in-house, or if the paraeducator is required to seek out and complete their own 20 hours of training.

It is important for teachers to be made aware of the educational requirements of paraeducators so that they can have a better understanding of the level of knowledge and experience paraeducators bring into the classroom. This awareness can guide the expectations teachers have for paraeducators, as well as how to best utilize them within the classroom. Knowing the level of training and experience required of paraeducators is especially important as the roles and responsibilities of paraeducators continue to expand. Consideration must be given to each individual's prior experiences, training, and certifications or education level. Matching the paraeducator's skills to the responsibilities they are given is crucial. Concerns within the field of special education have been repeatedly raised about placing the least trained staff with students who often pose the most challenging behavior or who require the most support (Giangreco, 2021; Howley et al., 2017). Although the use of paraeducators to support students in the classroom is often well intentioned, the limited amount of training provided to paraeducators has been shown to negatively impact the progress of the students they support (Sobeck & Robertson, 2019). Therefore, it is essential that both administrators and teachers are aware of the amount of preparation each paraeducator brings into the school and classroom. This information must then be used to inform the roles and responsibilities given to each paraeducator and guide the training they require to support the student(s) to which they are assigned.

CURRENT PRACTICES FOR PARAEDUCATOR TRAINING

Research has consistently revealed that many schools do not provide adequate training for paraeducators. A study conducted by Sobeck and Robertson (2019) concluded that the most prominent reasons schools do not provide sufficient professional development for paraeducators include a lack of money, limited time, lack of high-quality trainers and trainings available, lack of priority within the school structure, and too much diversity within the students' needs to have targeted trainings. Research continues to provide recommendations for school districts that face these challenges (Da Fonte & Capizzi, 2015; Douglas et al., 2019), however there continues to be a research-to-practice gap related to paraeducator training and professional development.

Educational organizations that do provide ongoing training rely on a variety of approaches. Often the approach selected depends on the educational organization's financial capability, scheduling, legal requirements for specific certifications (e.g., first aid, CPR), and the focus of the training. Paraeducators who are offered professional development opportunities are provided with training in one of three ways: pre-service training, in-service professional development, or on-the-job training. In some schools, paraeducators are not afforded an opportunity to participate in broader professional development opportunities offered to educators, while other schools give paraeducators the opportunity to participate in a variety of professional development opportunities.

Pre-Service Training

Pre-service training is often provided for one of two reasons. First, the paraeducator may have gone to school to be a teacher and, therefore, may have completed relevant coursework to their position. Although not common in many schools, in these cases the paraeducator has participated in a significant amount of training and education and may come with relevant knowledge and skills. Another way that the paraeducator may have acquired pre-service training is through a paraeducator certification program or several unrelated training opportunities offered by various service providers. Although pre-service training or a full certification process is not required for a paraeducator to be employed, several schools and outside agencies within some states do offer these types of programs to better prepare paraeducators for their position. Classes and workshops can be in-person or online, and if online, they can be synchronous or asynchronous. For example, the Pennsylvania Department of Education offers an online paraeducator training program through Pennsylvania Training and Technical Assistance Network (PATTAN). Similarly, the state of Washington, in collaboration with a variety of partners, has developed a comprehensive paraeducator training resource where paraeducators can select from a variety of professional development options. The state of Idaho gives paraeducators access to a clearinghouse of online training materials, while Arkansas requires paraeducators to complete three online training modules prior to applying for paraeducator positions. Pre-service paraeducator candidates are encouraged to contact the department of education in their state for information on training resources. School leaders can also reach out to the department of education in their state to learn about the types of professional development opportunities available. Completing coursework or a certification program can help more fully prepare an individual for a paraeducator position, and it can also give paraeducators an opportunity to negotiate a better salary or wage.

In-Service Professional Development

More commonly, paraeducators enter their position with little to no training or experience. In these instances, paraeducators rely on in-service opportunities for training. The most common style of training for in-service paraeducators is didactic instruction (i.e., workshops, presentations, lectures). With this type of training, paraeducators participate in a workshop in which a presenter focuses on a specific topic or theme (e.g., behavior management, first aid, special education services). These training types can range from a few hours to a half day to a full day of professional development. They can be offered through the school in which the paraeducator works or through a local educational agency. University professors, educational agency representatives, peer schools, and school leaders are just a few of the individuals who commonly lead didactic training opportunities. Topics covered during these workshops are typically selected by school leaders to address specific areas of need within their school (e.g., behavior management, CPR certification, reading support strategies). These topics may be selected based on perceived need, information gathered from teachers, or the paraeducators themselves.

Although in-service didactic instruction workshops tend to be the most relied on style of training, research has consistently revealed that they often do not produce long-term effects (Poduska & Kurki, 2014; Sobeck et al., 2020; Yates et al., 2020). In many instances, paraeducators attend a workshop and then are left to implement the newly learned strategies without follow-up or feedback from their supervisor. Additionally, paraeducators often attend such workshops without their supervising teacher, so their supervising teacher may not even be aware of the content they were provided. Due to this lack of follow-up, paraeducators may not implement the skills they were taught within the classroom (Sobeck et al., 2020).

On-the-Job Training

With few paraeducators engaging in pre-service training opportunities and the prevalent-yet-ineffective nature of workshop-style opportunities, a large number of paraeducators and school administrators look to on-the-job training to support paraeducator learning. On-the-job training requires the paraeducator to work with their supervising teacher to obtain guidance and instruction. Using on-the-job training approaches, teachers can provide instruction specific to the paraeducator's current role, model how to implement strategies, verbally direct the paraeducator through procedures, answer questions as the paraeducator works through a situation, and much more. This type of training can help paraeducators learn how to implement the skills required in their position and can help clarify the paraeducator's role.

On-the-job training can be broad in scope or it can be narrow, depending on the reason and need for the training. For example, a special education teacher can offer suggestions for implementing Tier 1 behavior management strategies or tips for assisting students with daily living skills. Alternatively, the special education teacher can demonstrate a step-by-step process for responding to challenging behavior as described in the student's BIP. These examples illustrate how the paraeducator is provided with knowledge and skills through close interactions with the teacher.

Although there are numerous benefits to on-the-job training approaches (i.e., it allows for training that is specific, personalized, and presented in a one-to-one manner), some considerations should be made in order to ensure success. First, schools who rely on on-the-job training approaches should recognize that training is not guaranteed to occur. With the packed schedules of teachers, paraeducators, and students, the teacher cannot always pause instruction to provide the paraeducator with guidance, resulting in missed opportunities for on-the-job instruction. This is true even when a need arises throughout the school day. Furthermore, with the ever-changing ebb and flow of schedules, on-the-job training can be difficult to coordinate or may be rushed, which can set the stage for missed information and a lack of follow-up. Third, on-the-job training is less formal and may lack time dedicated to background knowledge and a conceptual framework for the skills outlined in training, which may impact paraeducator buy-in or their understanding of why the skills are needed. Fourth, supportive materials are not often utilized within this style of on-the-job training, which may limit the educational team's ability to refer back to trained skills in a systematic manner. Lastly, the content of on-the-job training tends to be specific to individual paraeducator needs. While this can be beneficial to that paraeducator's work with a specific student or set of students, it should be noted that often the training cannot be generalized to other students or paraeducator positions. As school leaders and teachers prepare to utilize on-the-job training for paraeducators, it is important for these considerations to be reviewed. Yet, on-the-job training can be effective if carefully planned, systematically implemented, and carried out with fidelity.

Performance Feedback

Crucial to the effectiveness of on-the-job training, paraeducators require performance feedback from their supervising teacher. Performance feedback occurs when a paraeducator is observed implementing a process, behavior, or skill and is offered insight on areas of strength, suggestions, and performance data (i.e., graphical display of performance) from a supervising educator, such as a school leader or teacher (Cornelius & Nagro, 2014). Feedback on the paraeducator's performance can be immediate or delayed, and can be delivered in-person, virtually, or in written form (Table 5-1). Performance feedback fits nicely within an on-the-job training program, as the person providing the training usually observes the paraeducator implement the behavior or skill immediately following the demonstration, which allows for an opportunity for feedback to be offered. Researchers in the field have widely agreed that performance feedback is essential for sustained skill acquisition (Brock & Carter, 2015; Fallon et al., 2015; Sobeck et al., 2020; Walker & Snell, 2017), and there is a wealth of published research that shows performance feedback is an effective training tool (Brown et al., 2014; Cornelius & Nagro, 2014; Fallon et al., 2015; Sobeck et al., 2020). However, in order for it to produce lasting improvements, teachers must implement it with fidelity. Although there are many different elements that teachers can incorporate when delivering performance feedback, researchers have identified several components and steps that must be included.

1. **Professional development.** Prior to giving performance feedback, the paraeducator must be trained on the skill or intervention for which performance feedback will be provided (Brown et al., 2014). This gives the paraeducator the opportunity to learn the background knowledge needed in order to implement the skill or strategy effectively. This can occur through a 1:1 or small group discussion, a formal presentation style workshop, video modules, readings and role play, or demonstrations.

2. **Goal setting.** It is common to incorporate goal setting within the performance feedback sessions (Fallon et al., 2015). Giving the paraeducator a target allows the paraeducator something concrete and quantitative to work toward. The goal should be attainable and individualized to the paraeducator's baseline performance. For example, if focusing on using BSP, the performance feedback goal for a paraeducator who has never used the strategy before might be to use BSP five times during the 40-minute reading lesson. This goal can then continue to change as the paraeducator increases their performance.

3. **Observation and data collection.** To provide the paraeducator with an objective perspective on their performance, data must be taken to accurately measure their growth. Data can be collected through an in-person observation or through a video-recorded session. Depending on the target skill or strategy, data should be taken using frequency, duration, intensity, latency, or accuracy. Once the data has been collected during an observation, the teacher should graph the data accordingly. Representing data visually has been shown to improve performance when learning a new skill or strategy (Hawkins & Heflin, 2011). Therefore, teachers are encouraged to provide paraeducators with a visual representation of their performance during performance feedback sessions. This is most often done by using a line graph; however, in some instances a different graph may be appropriate.

Table 5-1. Sample Performance Feedback Form

Paraeducator: _____
Observer: _____
Date and Time: _____
Location: _____
Subject or Activity: _____
Skill Focus or Goal of the Observation: _____

FIDELITY OF THE STRATEGY

Step	Task or Behavior	Completed/Not Completed
1		
2		
3		
4		
5		
6		
7		
8		

Data Collection:
☐ Duration   ☐ Rate   ☐ Frequency   ☐ Latency   ☐ Intensity
☐ Percentage of Opportunity   ☐ Accuracy   ☐ Real-Time

Graph Provided: ☐ Yes ☐ No

Noted Areas of Strength: _____
Areas for Improvement: _____
Action Steps: _____
Goal for Next Meeting: _____

4. **Time to meet.** Once training has been completed, a target goal is selected and the teacher observes the paraeducator while collecting data, then the teacher and paraeducator should schedule a brief meeting. During this meeting, all the moving parts of performance feedback come together. It is important for this time to be scheduled and organized so that every minute is productive. A sample schedule for a performance feedback session includes the following: sharing two to three observed strengths, reporting out on the collected data, visually showing the graph, discussing two areas for improvement, setting a new target for the next session, and leaving a few minutes for questions (see Table 5-1).

Teachers are encouraged to use a fidelity checklist to help evaluate their implementation of performance feedback. This can help ensure they are incorporating all the important steps with fidelity.

BEST PRACTICES FOR PREPARING PARAEDUCATORS

Best practice for preparing paraeducators and providing them with training draws from many areas of research. Adult learning theory and evidence-based training practices provide a guide for the ways in which paraeducator training should be implemented. Additionally, the literature shows support for coaching methods, a systematic approach to performance feedback, to ensure paraeducators can carry out trained skills in educational settings. To provide consistency in student services and ensure that supervising teachers are prepared to support paraeducators in implementing evidence-based practices, team-level training is often necessary. We discuss key team members in this process and provide a model of paraeducator training.

Adult Learning and Evidence-Based Training Practices

As adult learners, paraeducators have unique training needs. Adult learning theory emphasizes the importance of active learner engagement, performance measures, and application to real-world contexts (Dunst et al., 2010). Paraeducators come with their own knowledge and experiences, which often impacts their learning needs and motivation (Taylor & Hamdy, 2013). As adult learners they benefit from training that is relevant to their needs as well as to their current roles and responsibilities (Martin & Albroz, 2014). Paraeducators also indicate a preference for learning environments that are flexible and require active engagement (Martin & Albroz, 2014). This might include training that is provided at convenient times, broken into small segments, incorporates opportunities to practice, includes frequent checks for understanding, and provides scaffold support and models of skills.

Coaching

Coaching is one approach that can be combined with traditional workshop or on-the-job training to help ensure paraeducators accurately implement newly learned skills in educational settings (Andzik & Cannella-Malone, 2019; Brock & Anderson, 2020). Coaching includes the paraeducator implementing new skills with the student while the supervising teacher observes. After implementation, the paraeducators and teacher meet together and the supervising teacher provides performance feedback to the paraeducator to support them in improving skills (Yates et al., 2020). Self-reflection can also be included in coaching sessions to help paraeducators understand how well they are implementing new skills. It is important that coaching be tailored to each paraeducator based on their individual needs. Some paraeducators will need minimal coaching, while others, such as those who are new to the position, will need extensive coaching. When implementing coaching it is critical that the supervising teacher continues to coach the paraeducator until they implement skills and interventions with high fidelity (Bagawan et al., 2022).

Team-Level Training

As discussed in Chapters 3 and 4, teachers are critical partners for paraeducator training. Teachers must often advocate for paraeducator training and time to carry out follow-up coaching and support (Douglas et al., 2016). Because teachers often serve in a coaching role with paraeducators, it can be advantageous to provide teachers with training alongside paraeducators (Douglas & Uitto, 2021; Sobeck et al., 2020). This helps ensure they are provided with the same knowledge and gives supervising teachers information they need to provide adequate coaching and supervision to paraeducators in educational settings.

Important Individuals in Paraeducator Training

There are many important individuals who may be involved in coordinating and providing paraeducator training. This may include administrators, such as principals and special education directors, district specialists (e.g., autism, behavior, hearing, vision, English as a second language, assistive technology), and related support personnel (e.g., occupational therapist, physical therapist, speech-language pathologist). Each of these individuals often have specific roles related to paraeducator training. The specific roles of these individuals are outlined in Chapter 4.

A Model for Paraeducator Training

Douglas and Uitto (2021) developed a model for paraeducator training that considers federal requirements, current practices, and best practice. Guided by adult learning theory, the model includes four steps (Figure 5-1):

1. Define paraeducator training needs
2. Create paraeducator training plan
3. Provide paraeducator training
4. Document paraeducator performance

Each of these steps is critical to ensuring high-quality training. The first step *(define paraeducator training needs)* includes defining paraeducator roles and responsibilities, as well as paraeducator knowledge/skills needed for responsibilities. The needed knowledge and skills can be identified through a self-assessment of skills by the paraeducator, observation of the paraeducator, or discussion with the paraeducator. This might be done using the paraeducator needs assessment we provide in the chapter resources (see PAR^{2}A Center).

The second step *(create paraeducator training plan)* includes setting a goal for each component of training, determining what activities will occur during training, identifying the personnel who will carry out training and their roles, and determining the location of training and the needed resources. Goals can be guided by professional competencies (CEC, 2022; Appendix D) or state standards (Connecticut State Department of Education, 2012; Iowa Department of Education, 2007). Considerations for adult learners should be made when identifying training activities. Creating a plan will ensure that everything is set up to carry out the training efficiently and effectively.

The third step *(provide paraeducator training)* includes several components. First an initial workshop is conducted where general information is shared with a larger group, content that is relevant to the whole group. Then, paraeducators who require specific intervention knowledge to carry out interventions in the classroom attend an intervention-focused workshop. This is often smaller in scale, one-on-one or a few paraeducators at a time. After the intervention-focused workshop is completed, the paraeducator is provided with coaching and performance feedback. This includes modeling the intervention, observing the paraeducator and collecting performance data, and providing specific feedback to the paraeducator to improve their implementation of the intervention.

The last step *(document paraeducator performance)* is important to ensure that all training activities are noted for the paraeducator. A log should be maintained of all training activities, and evidence should be gathered to show paraeducator growth toward the training goals. You can document performance in several ways, often this is done through some kind of portfolio (see chapter resources for several options). This documentation can be reviewed to ensure each paraeducator meets or exceeds the 20-hour training yearly requirement. The performance documentation can also be used to identify and plan for next training steps for the paraeducator where the model cycle begins again: define new training needs, create the next training plan, provide the next training, and document performance. Using this model, administrators and supervising teachers can ensure that paraeducators are provided with ongoing training to systematically address their needs and roles in the classroom (Table 5-2).

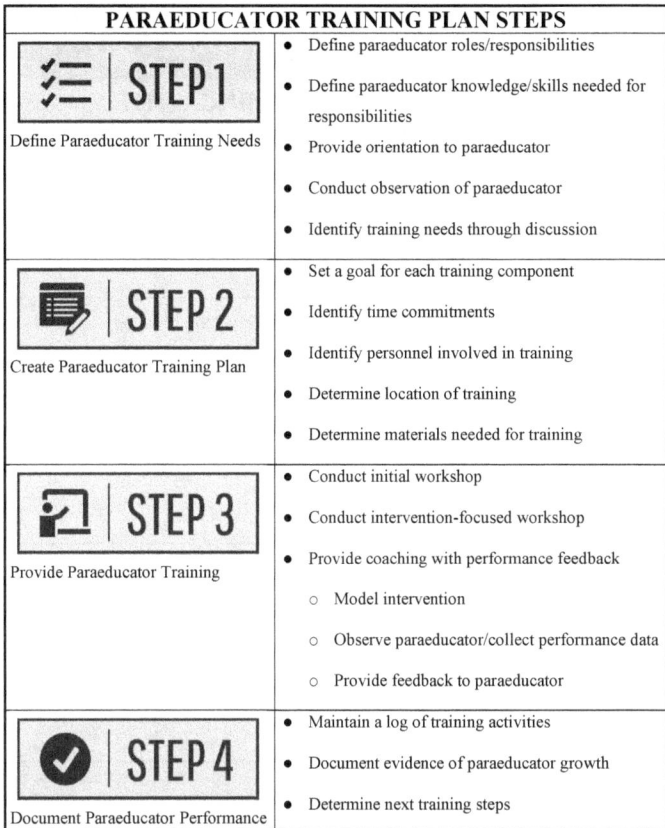

Figure 5-1. Paraeducator training plan steps. (Reproduced with permission from Douglas, S. N., & Uitto, D. J. [2021]. A collaborative approach to paraeducator training. *Beyond Behavior, 30*[1], 4-13. https://doi.org/10.1177/1074295621997177)

Summary

Quality paraeducator training is critical to ensuring paraeducator success. Administrators and teachers hold important roles in ensuring paraeducator training not only occurs, but that it also provides lasting change. It is important that the key personnel involved in paraeducator training be aware of their role and have a plan for training. It is also crucial for school leaders to know which training approaches have been shown to be effective at producing significant improvements and how to implement them with fidelity. With the evolving role of paraeducators, it is of utmost importance that they receive effective and meaningful training. Following the guidelines and using the resources provided in this chapter will help guide schools in providing professional development opportunities that give paraeducators the skills they need to be successful supporting students.

Table 5-2. Paraeducator Training Plan Template

	INITIAL TRAINING WORKSHOP	INTERVENTION-FOCUSED TRAINING	COACHING WITH PERFORMANCE FEEDBACK
Goal	(Refer to paraeducator standards; consider knowledge/skills needed by paraeducators to fulfill responsibilities; be sure goals are specific, observable, and measurable; clearly articulate how goals will be assessed)		
Activities	(Identify the training activities for the acquisition of knowledge and the development of skills such as presentation, case studies, modeling of strategies, role plays, and coaching)		
Personnel	(Consider all personnel who will be involved in the training and explicitly detail their roles and responsibilities)		
Location	(Identify the location for all training activities, ensure the location can accommodate any training activities and has space for planned activities)		
Resources	(Identify the resources to use for materials, costs, and time commitment for each training, such as DVDs, A/V equipment, workbooks, and handouts)		

Reproduced with permission from Douglas, S. N., & Uitto, D. J. (2021). A collaborative approach to paraeducator training. *Beyond Behavior, 30*(1), 4-13. https://doi.org/10.1177/1074295621997177

Chapter Review

1. What federal guidance, if any, is given when it comes to paraeducator training?
2. What are some common challenges related to traditional paraeducator training practices?
3. What is the difference between pre-service training, in-service professional development, and on-the-job training? What are the benefits and shortcomings of these approaches?
4. What considerations should be made when developing and implementing paraeducator training based on adult learning theory?
5. List and describe two benefits to team-level training where paraeducators and teachers are provided with training together.
6. List and describe the four steps in the model of paraeducator training. Detail why each step is important and how it could be implemented in your school.

Resources

Training Resources

- Ashbaker, B. Y., & Morgan, J. (2011). *Assisting with early literacy instruction: A manual for paraprofessionals.* Pearson.
- Ashbaker, B. Y., & Morgan, J. (2013). *Paraprofessionals in the classroom: A survival guide* (2nd ed.). Pearson.
- Ashbaker, B. Y., & Morgan, J. (2015). *The paraprofessional's guide to effective behavioral intervention.* Routledge.
- Balough, W. D. (2014). *The paraeducator's guide to supporting instructional and curricular modifications.* (2nd ed.). The Master Teacher.
- Balough, W. D. (2015). *The personal planner and training guide for the paraprofessional.* The Master Teacher.
- Causton, J., & MacLeod, K. (2021). *Paraprofessional's handbook for effective support in inclusive classrooms* (2nd ed.). Brookes Publishing.
- Center for Parent Information & Resources. (2022). *Categories of disabilities under part B of IDEA.* https://www.parentcenterhub.org/categories/
- Center on PBIS (Positive Behavioral Interventions and Supports). (2023). https://www.pbis.org/
- Children and Adults with Attention-Deficit/Hyperactivity Disorder (CHADD). (2023). https://chadd.org/
- Children and Youth with Special Health Care Needs. (2023). https://cyshcn.waisman.wisc.edu/leadership-about-specific-conditions-disabilities/
- Colorado Department of Education. (2020). *Observation: The heart of authentic assessment.* http://www.cde.state.co.us/resultsmatter/observation
- Connecticut State Department of Education. (2012). *Guidelines for training and support of paraprofessionals: Working with students birth to 21.* https://portal.ct.gov/-/media/SDE/Paraeducator/guidelines_paraprofessionals.pdf
- Connecticut State Department of Education. (2023). *Connecticut paraprofessional guidance briefs and newsletters.* https://portal.ct.gov/SDE/Paraeducator/Paraeducator-Information-and-Resources /Documents
- Council for Exceptional Children. (2023). https://exceptionalchildren.org/
- Doyle, M. B. (2008). *The paraprofessional's guide to the inclusive classroom: Working as a team* (3rd ed.). Brookes Publishing.
- Fitzell, S. G. (2010). *Paraprofessionals and teachers working together: Highly effective strategies for inclusive classrooms* (2nd ed.). Cogent Catalyst Publications.
- Indiana Institute on Disability and Community Indiana Resource Center for Autism. (2023). https://www.iidc.indiana.edu/irca/resources/index.html
- Intervention Central. *Academic interventions.* (n.d.). https://www.interventioncentral.org/
- International Dyslexia Association. (2023). https://dyslexiaida.org/
- Iowa Department of Education. (2007). *Guide to effective paraeducator practices edition II.* Author.
- Iowa Department of Education. (2013). *Appropriate paraeducator services matrix.* https://educateiowa.gov/sites/default/files/documents/Appropriate%20Paraeducator%20Duties.pdf
- Jones, B. H. (2019). *The paraprofessional's guide to managing student behavior* (2nd ed.). LRP Media Group.

- Lasater, M. (2009). *RTI and the paraeducator's roles: Effective teaming.* National Professional Resources.
- Lasater, M., Johnson, M., & Fitzgerald, M. (2019). *The special ed administrator's training toolkit: Professional development for the role and responsibilities of the paraprofessional.* LRP Media Group.
- Lasater, M., Johnson, M., & Fitzgerald, M. (2019). *The special ed administrator's training toolkit: Professional development for paraprofessionals providing special education and related services to students with disabilities.* LRP Media Group.
- Lasater, M., Johnson, M., & Fitzgerald, M. (2019). *The special ed administrator's training toolkit: Professional development for paraprofessionals the IEP process and data collection.* LRP Media Group.
- Lasater, M., Johnson, M., & Fitzgerald, M. (2020). *The special ed administrator's training toolkit: Professional development for paraprofessionals strategies to apply behavior improvement plans and interventions.* LRP Media Group.
- Lasater, M., Johnson, M., & Fitzgerald, M. (2020). *The special ed administrator's training toolkit: Professional development for paraprofessionals applying instructional strategies to develop student independence.* LRP Media Group.
- Lieberman, L. (2007). *Paraeducators in physical education: A training guide to roles and responsibilities.* Human Kinetics.
- NAEYC National Association for the Education of Young Children. (2023). https://www.naeyc.org/
- National Professional Development Center on Autism Spectrum Disorders. (2021). https://autismpdc.fpg.unc.edu/national-professional-development-center-autism-spectrum-disorder
- National Resource Center for Paraeducators. (2023). https://nrcpara.org/
- Paraprofessional Resource and Research Center (PAR²A Center). (2023). *K-12 paraprofessional supervision.* Teachers - PAR²A Center (paracenter.org)
- Russotti, J., & Shaw, R. (2004). *When you have a visually impaired student in your classroom: A guide for paraeducators.* American Foundation for the Blind.
- Sarathy, P. (2012). *Power training for paraeducators: Trainee manual for supporting students with disabilities.* Park Place Publications.
- Smart Kids with Learning Disabilities. (n.d.). https://www.smartkidswithld.org/
- State Education Resource Center. (2007). *Assessment checklist for paraprofessionals: Preschool -grade 12.* https://portal.ct.gov/SDE/Paraeducator/Paraeducator-Information-and-Resources/Documents
- State Education Resource Center. (2007). *Teacher supervisory checklist: Preschool to grade 12.* https://portal.ct.gov/SDE/Paraeducator/Paraeducator-Information-and-Resources/Documents
- Steers, A., & Buchinsky, A. (2014). *Communicators: A paraprofessional training program.* Communication and Learning Consultants.
- The IRIS Center Peabody College Vanderbilt University. (2023). https://iris.peabody.vanderbilt.edu/
- Virginia Commonwealth University Autism Center for Excellence. (2023). *ACE factsheets and briefs.* https://vcuautismcenter.org/resources/factsheets/
- Wallace, T. (2005). *Assisting reading instruction: The paraprofessional's guide.* LRP Media Group.
- Wallace, T. (2007). *The paraprofessional's guide to the IDEA and special education programs.* LRP Media Group.
- William & Mary Training & Technical Assistance Center. (2015). *Paraeducators' tools for supporting the instructional process considerations packet.* https://education.wm.edu/centers/ttac/documents/packets/paraeducatortools.pdf

Paraeducator Online Training Programs

- Arkansas Department of Education Division of Elementary and Secondary Education. (2023). *Paraprofessional training.* https://dese.ade.arkansas.gov/Offices/special-education/paraprofessional-training
- Capitol Region Education Council. (2023). *The compass: Helping paraeducators navigate the profession.* http://www.crec.org/compass/
- Causton, J., & Pretti-Frontczak, K. (n.d.). PD 4 paras. *https://www.inclusiveschooling.com/pd-4-paras/*
- Council for Exceptional Children. (2023). *High-leverage practices for paraeducators.* https://highleveragepractices.org/high-leverage-practices-paraeducators
- LRP Media Group. (2016). *DirectSTEP eCourses.* https://www.lrpdirectstep.com/
- The Master Teacher. (2023). https://www.masterteacher.com/paraeducator-online-training
- National Professional Development Center on Autism. (2021). *Autism focused intervention resources & modules (AFIRM) for paraeducators.* https://afirm.fpg.unc.edu/afirm-modules
- Ohio Center for Autism and Low Incidence Autism Internet Modules. (2020). *ASD strategies in action.* https://autismcertificationcenter.org/
- Ohio Partnership for Excellence in Paraprofessional Preparation. (2023). *OPEPP Professional development modules.* https://www.opepp.org/opepp-professional-development-modules/
- Pennsylvania Training and Technical Assistance Network. (2018). *Online courses for paraprofessionals.* https://www.pattan.net/Supports/Paraprofessionals/Online-Courses

REFERENCES

Andzik, N. R., & Canella-Malone, I. (2019). Practitioner implementation of communication intervention with students with complex communication needs. *American Journal on Intellectual and Developmental Disabilities, 124*(5), 395-410. https://doi.org/10.1352/1944-7558-124.5.395

Bagawan, A., Gerde, H., & Douglas, S. N. (2022). Components of effective supervision and training for paraeducators. *Intervention in School and Clinic, 58*(4), 264-272. https://doi.org/10.1177/10534512221093778

Biggs, E. E., Gilson, C. B., & Carter, E. W. (2016). Accomplishing more together: Influences to the quality of professional relationships between special educators and paraprofessionals. *Research and Practice for Persons With Severe Disabilities, 41*(4), 256-272. https://doi.org/10.1177/1540796916665604

Brock, M. E. (2021). A tiered approach for training paraeducators to use evidence-based practices for students with significant disabilities. *TEACHING Exceptional Children, 54*(3), 224-233.

Brock, M. E., & Anderson, E. J. (2019). Training paraprofessionals who work with students with intellectual and developmental disabilities: What does the research say? *Psychology in the Schools, 58,* 702-722. https://doi.org/10.1002/pits.22386

Brock, M. E., & Carter, E. W. (2015). Effects of a professional development package to prepare special education paraprofessionals to implement evidence-based practice. *Journal of Special Education, 49*(1), 39-51. https://doi.org/10.1177/0022466913501882

Brown, T. L., Gatmaitan, M., & Harjusola-Webb, S. M. (2014). Using performance feedback to support paraprofessionals in inclusive preschool classrooms. *Young Exceptional Children, 17*(2), 21-31. https://doi.org/10.1177/1096250613493189

Connecticut State Department of Education. (2012). *Guidelines for training and support of paraprofessionals working with students birth to 21.* https://docplayer.net/13867300-Guidelines-for-training-support-of-paraprofessionals-working-with-students-birth-to-21.html

Connecticut SB 913. (2017). *An Act Concerning School Paraprofessional Training.* https://www.cga.ct.gov/2017/JFR/s/2017SB-00913-R00ED-JFR.htm

Cornelius, K. E., & Nagro, S. A. (2014). Evaluating the evidence base of performance feedback in preservice special education teacher training. *Teacher Education and Special Education, 37*(2), 133-146. https://doi.org/10.1177/0888406414521837

Council for Exceptional Children. (2015). *What every special educator must know: Professional ethics and standards (*7th ed.*).* Council for Exceptional Children.

Council for Exceptional Children. (2022). *Core competencies for special education paraeducators.* https://exceptionalchildren.org/paraeducators/core-competencies-special-education-paraeducators

Da Fonte, M. A., & Capizzi, A. M. (2015). A module-based approach: training paraeducators on evidence-based practices. *Physical Disabilities: Education and Related Services, 34*(1), 31-54.

Douglas, S. N., Chapin, S. E., & Nolan, J. F. (2016). Special education teachers' experiences supporting and supervising paraeducators: Implications for special and general education settings. *Teacher Education and Special Education, 39*(1), 60-74. https://doi.org/ 10.1177/0888406415616443

Douglas, S. N., & Uitto, D. J. (2021). A collaborative approach to paraeducator training. *Beyond Behavior, 30*(1), 4-13. https://doi.org/10.1177/1074295621997177

Douglas, S. N., Uitto, D. J., Reinfelds, C. L., & D'Agostino, S. (2019). A systematic review of paraprofessional training materials. *Journal of Special Education, 52*(4), 195-207. https://doi.org/10.1177/0022466918771707

Dunst, C. J., Trivette, C. M., & Hamby, D. W. (2010). Meta-analysis of the effectiveness of four adult learning methods and strategies: Supplemental tables and references. *International Journal of Continuing Education and Lifelong Learning, 3*, 91-112.

Every Student Succeeds Act of 2015, 20 U.S.C. § 1177.

Fallon, L. M., Collier-Meek, M. A., Maggin, D. M., Sanetti, L. M. H., & Johnson, A. H. (2015). Is performance feedback for educators an evidence-based practice? A systematic review and evaluation based on single-case research. *Exceptional Children, 81*(2), 227-246. https://doi.org/10.1177/0014402914551738

Giangreco, M. F. (2021). Maslow's hammer: Teacher assistant research and inclusive practices at a crossroads. *European Journal of Special Needs Education, 36*(2), 278-293. https://doi.org/10.1080/08856257.2021.1901377

Hawkins, S. M., & Heflin, L. J. (2011). Increasing secondary teachers' behavior-specific praise using a video self-modeling and visual performance feedback intervention. *Journal of Positive Behavior Interventions, 13*(2), 97-108. https://doi.org/10.1177/1098300709358110

Howley, C., Howley, A., & Telfer, D. (2017). Special education paraprofessionals in district context. *Mid-Western Educational Researcher, 29*(2), 136-165.

Individuals with Disabilities Education Act of 2004, 20 U.S.C. § 1400.

Iowa Department of Education. (2007). *Guide to effective paraeducator practices edition II.* Author.

Martin, T., & Alborz, A. (2014). Supporting the education of pupils with profound intellectual and multiple disabilities: The views of teaching assistants regarding their own learning and development needs. *British Journal of Special Education, 41*(3), 309-327. https://doi.org/10.1111/1467-8578.12070

Poduska, J. M., & Kurki, A. (2014). Guided by theory, informed by practice: Training and support for the good behavior game, a classroom-based behavior management strategy. *Journal of Emotional and Behavioral Disorders, 22*, 83-94.

Sobeck, E. E., & Robertson, R. (2019). Perspectives on current practices and barriers to training for paraeducators of students with autism in inclusive settings. *Journal of the American Academy of Specula Education Professionals*, 131-159.

Sobeck, E. E., Robertson, R., & Smith, J. (2020). The effects of didactic instruction and performance feedback on paraeducator implementation of behavior support strategies in inclusive settings. *Journal of Special Education, 53*(4), 245-255. https://doi.org/10.1177/0022466919858989

Stewart, E. M. (2019). Reducing ambiguity: Tools to define and communicate paraprofessional roles and responsibilities. *Intervention in School and Clinic, 55*(1), 52-57. https://doi.org/10.1177/1053451218782431

Taylor, D., & Hamdy, H. (2013). Adult learning theories: Implications for learning and teaching in medical education: AMEE Guide No. 83. *Medical Teacher, 35*(11), e1561- e1572, https://doi.org/10.3109/0142159X.2013.828153

Walker, V. L., & Snell, M. E. (2017). Teaching paraprofessionals to implement function-based interventions. *Focus on Autism and Other Developmental Disabilities, 32*(2), 114-123.

Washington State HB 1115. (2017). *An act relating to paraeducators.* http://lawfilesext.leg.wa.gov/biennium/2017-18/Pdf/Bills/House%20Passed%20 Legislature/1115-S.PL.pdf

Yates, P. A., Chopra, R. V., Sobeck, E. E., Douglas, S. N., Morano, S., Walker, V. L., & Schulze, R. (2020). Working with paraeducators: Tools and strategies for instructional planning, performance feedback, and evaluation. *Intervention in School and Clinic, 56*(1), 1-8. https://doi.org/10.1177/1053451220910740

Common Challenges and Areas for Growth

INTRODUCTION

Numerous challenges can arise related to the utilization and supervision of paraeducators. Chapter 6 details some of these common challenges and provides suggestions for avoiding or addressing these challenges when they occur. We identify challenges in the areas of professional learning and roles, learner development and individual learning differences, special education and supports in the learning environment, collaboration with team members, and school culture and policies.

CHAPTER OBJECTIVES

→ Identify common challenges facing the field of paraeducators.
→ Discuss current research-based approaches to addressing the challenges facing the field of paraeducators.
→ Identify areas within the field of paraeducators in which growth is needed.
→ Justify why growth is important and needed across the discussed challenges.

KEY TERMS

- **Collaboration:** Occurs when members of a learning team work together to assist students in the classroom or work toward a common goal or purpose.
- **Confidentiality:** The act of protecting all identifiable student data, maintained records, and information regarding the student and family contained within the school district and not discussing it with individuals who do not need to know such information.
- **Council for Exceptional Children (CEC):** An international professional organization that strives to improve the experience of individuals with disabilities and/or gifts and talents through advocacy, professional development, resource sharing, and educational standards.
- **Evaluation:** A systematic process where a student is administered several assessments, academic, behavioral, or social/emotional, to determine the specific domains in which a student needs help and whether the student is eligible for special education services.
- **Family Education Rights and Privacy Act (FERPA):** A federal law that gives parents access to their children's education accounts, the ability to have their child's records amended, and the right to disclose personally identifiable information from the education records. Once a student turns 18 years old, or enters a postsecondary institution at any age, the rights under FERPA apply to the student and no longer the parent.
- **Professionalism:** An individual's actions that follow professional ethical principles, maintain a level of professional competence and integrity, and exercise professional judgment.
- **Supervision:** Roles of educational personnel to provide direction and support to paraeducators.

CASE STUDY 1

Mrs. Mitko is a third-grade special education teacher who has 15 students on her caseload. She also oversees five paraeducators who help support her students with IEPs. At the end of the school day, all the paraeducators in the building are responsible for bus duty and gather at one end of the hallway for this task. Mrs. Mitko's classroom is right next to the paraeducators running bus duty. On several occasions, Mrs. Mitko has overheard the paraeducators discussing the students they support. Their conversations tend to focus on student behavior, parent interactions, academic performance, and various frustrations they experienced throughout the day. Many of the paraeducators refer to their students by name during these conversations. Mrs. Mitko has felt uncomfortable overhearing these conversations and is unsure of how to respond. She manages five of the paraeducators, but not all of them. She is also not their boss, but they are discussing confidential matters about her students. Mrs. Mitko is unsure of her role and responsibility within this situation.

1. Should Mrs. Mitko be concerned about what she is overhearing? Why or why not?
2. What is Mrs. Mitko's responsibility in this situation?
3. How should Mrs. Mitko approach this concern with her paraeducators? With all of the other paraeducators?

CASE STUDY 2

Mr. Park is a seventh-grade paraeducator who primarily supports two students. One of his student's, Zeke, receives special education services under the category of attention deficit hyperactivity disorder (ADHD) and learning disability (LD) in writing (i.e., dysgraphia). During a world cultures lesson, the classroom teacher assigned the students to work with a partner on brainstorming a list of common customs for a specific culture based on a recent reading they were given. As soon as the classroom teacher was finished giving the class directions, Mr. Park told Zeke to move to the table in the back and they would work together creating his list. The classroom teacher approached Mr. Park and shared that he really wanted the students to work with a peer. Mr. Park shared that he did not think Zeke would stay on task or focus if he was mixed in with his peers in the front of the classroom and that he would have a difficult time writing his list accurately without assistance.

1. Should Mr. Park be able to make the decision for Zeke to work in the back of the room with him? Why or why not?
2. How does Mr. Park's decision on moving Zeke to the back table to work with him impact the intentions of inclusion?
3. How should the classroom teacher respond to Mr. Park?
4. How could situations like this be prevented in the future? Give one or two specific examples.

CASE STUDY 3

Ms. Washington is a paraeducator at the 10th-grade level. She supports five students who receive special education services for diagnoses of LD and ADHD. Specifically, the students she supports are identified as having dyslexia and dysgraphia. She spends a significant portion of her workday in Mrs. Patterson's 10th-grade applied English class. She provides support services to these five students across three class periods in Mrs. Patterson's room. In addition to the students with IEPs, each of Mrs. Patterson's applied English classes has an average of six to eight other students who tend to struggle with reading and writing. Several of these students have been identified as at-risk through local assessments and receive Tier 2 supports.

Mrs. Patterson has observed Ms. Washington doing an excellent job supporting the students with IEPs during class. She is attentive to their needs, provides additional guidance, and helps to answer their questions. However, Mrs. Patterson has also noticed that when the students with IEPs do not require assistance from Ms. Washington, she still stays at their side and does not circulate the room to help the other students identified as at-risk. Mrs. Patterson would like for Ms. Washington to help all students who need assistance in the classroom. Ms. Washington feels that her primary responsibility is supporting her assigned five students. She also does not want to interrupt the teacher by moving about the room during lessons to help other students. Ms. Washington thinks she is doing exactly what is expected of her.

1. Is Ms. Washington doing something wrong? Why or why not?
2. Why do you think Ms. Washington was supporting students in this way?
3. How could Mrs. Patterson begin to rectify this situation?
4. What strategies and supports could Mrs. Patterson put in place to prevent this type of scenario?

Over the past decade, much growth has occurred with the utilization of paraeducators. As many can attest, with any type of change, challenges tend to arise. This is true when it comes to paraeducators. Within the field today, schools and paraeducators themselves experience a variety of challenges that often impede the very important work they do. Researchers have consistently documented several specific concerns regarding paraeducators (Chopra & Uitto, 2015; Douglas et al., 2016; Douglas & Uitto, 2021; Frantz et al., 2020; Giangreco, 2010, 2021; Mason et al., 2021; Sobeck & Robertson, 2019; Sobeck et al., 2020). Although some solutions have been found effective, the research to practice gap that many fields face continues to hinder the progress being made within schools. It is important to discuss these concerns and to consider the ways school administrators, teachers, and paraeducators can respond to these challenges. Within this chapter, the most common challenges facing the field of paraeducators are organized through the lens of the *Core Competencies for Special Education Paraeducators,* put forth by the CEC. These competencies represent the knowledge and skills paraeducators need to effectively support students with disabilities within kindergarten thorough 12th-grade classrooms (CEC, 2022). All of the issues discussed within this chapter have been consistently evidenced through peer-reviewed literature. Further, research-based recommendations for addressing these challenges are also provided.

PROFESSIONAL LEARNING AND ROLES

As discussed in Chapter 1, paraeducators hold many responsibilities within the educational setting; however, sometimes the parameters of their roles are unknown, or they end up engaging in tasks that are beyond their position. In both instances, teachers and paraeducators can become frustrated and be unsure of how to move forward. It is important for teachers and paraeducators to be aware of the legal and ethical boundaries specific to paraeducators, as well as strategies that can help support healthy practices.

Research on paraeducators has consistently revealed that clarifying the roles paraeducators hold within various classrooms is often overlooked (Douglas et al., 2016). Paraeducators may find themselves unsure of the specific responsibilities each teacher expects of them, which can lead to confusion and misunderstandings. They may also feel as though they are doing all the tasks the teacher wants them to do and supporting students adequately, while the teacher may feel as though the paraeducator is lacking relative to important responsibilities. This misunderstanding has been commonly reported throughout research, as paraeducators consistently report feeling unsure of their specific roles (Fisher & Pleasants, 2012).

Conflicts stemming from role clarification can often be prevented or addressed by taking time to clarify the expectations for the paraeducator within each classroom or school setting. For example, what are the expectations when the paraeducator is supporting students during reading? When the students are working in small groups, what should the paraeducator be doing? How can the paraeducator best support students during related service sessions like speech-language, occupational therapy, or a social skills group? Teachers should also take time to detail the daily classroom routines and their expectations for the paraeducator during these times. For example, what does the teacher want the paraeducator to do when students are coming into the classroom in the morning? How should the paraeducator support students during restroom breaks or during morning work?

When lesson planning, teachers can also note how the paraeducator should participate within the lesson. Including specific expectations for paraeducators within the lesson plan not only provides the paraeducator with guidance, but it also allows the teacher to think critically through the most effective way to use the paraeducator during the lesson. Within the lesson plan the teacher can also list the accommodations and modifications they want the paraeducator to implement with specific students. Yates and colleagues (2020) offer guidance on effective lesson planning, as well as a lesson plan template that incorporates paraeducators (see Figure 3-3). Giving the paraeducator a copy of the lesson plan the day before or first thing in the morning gives them a little bit of time to review their roles and questions.

There are several common challenges that may arise within professional learning and roles including paraeducators functioning beyond their role, lack of professionalism, confidentiality, and boundaries with families. Let's look a bit closer at each of these common challenges.

Beyond Their Role

At times, paraeducators may find themselves engaging in tasks or participating in activities they feel are outside of their role. For example, this may occur if a paraeducator teaches academic content beyond reviewing material, managing specific challenge behavior in which they do not have the proper training, or being left in a classroom without a certified teacher present. To help prevent some of these instances from occurring, teachers and paraeducators can turn to their district policies, including teacher handbooks and paraeducator handbooks, for guidance. Being familiar with these policies help guide decision making and planning. School administrators can help foster this practice by allocating time at the beginning of the year to review these policies and allow additional time for teacher–paraeducator dyads to discuss the specific policies that pertain to them in more depth. During this meeting time, the teacher can also review expectations and responsibilities for instruction and managing behavior with the paraeducator. If some of these instances still occur, it is important to have an effective process for communication in place, as well as a plan for conflict management (see Chapter 2).

Lack of Professionalism

Teachers may experience a paraeducator working in their classroom who struggles to maintain proper professional practice. This might include issues with cell phone usage, personal use of school equipment, hygiene, dress, or storage of their personal items. These instances can be confusing for the teacher, and teachers may be unsure how to address these situations in a supportive manner since they may not be the official paraeducator supervisor on record.

Issues with professionalism should be reviewed within the district policies, as discussed earlier. Having time to review these policies at the start of the school year allows the teacher an opportunity to further discuss the process they will follow if professionalism becomes a concern. Establishing a process upfront brings clarity to these situations before they arise. The process might include a general reminder to all paraeducators, then a specific verbal reminder to the paraeducator struggling to follow the guidelines, a second reminder in writing to that paraeducator, and then a notification to the building administrator. Discussing this process and having it in writing can be a helpful way for the administrator, teacher, and paraeducator to be aware of the process. It can also be helpful to revisit classroom policies monthly, whether in a meeting or an e-mail exchange, to assist in preventing issues with professionalism.

Confidentiality

Another area that teachers and paraeducators often experience difficulty with is relative to confidentiality. With paraeducators not often formally trained, there may be misunderstandings about confidentiality. Paraeducators may find themselves questioning whether various types of information fall within the category of confidential topics. They may also experience situations in which they are talking to colleagues and feel it is safe to share information because they are a colleague they trust. This can pose some significant challenges for the teacher because they are responsible for ensuring their students' safety and confidentiality.

To help prevent complications involving confidentiality, teachers and administrators can put a few practices in place. All faculty and support staff should be familiar with the information contained within the Family Education Rights and Privacy Act (FERPA). In addition to explaining FERPA in the paraeducator handbook, providing support staff with a handout highlighting important information can be helpful. Designating time to review the FERPA guidelines at the start of each school year can help ensure everyone is made aware of the policies relative to confidentiality. School administrators can also design a specific training for all faculty and support staff regarding who has access to student information and who can share information with others. Teachers can review confidentiality with the paraeducators working specifically in their classrooms at the start of the school year as part of the classroom welcome packet. If desired, classroom teachers may elect to have the paraeducators working in their classroom sign a confidentiality commitment form. Setting aside time on the front end to review FERPA, discuss district and classroom policies, and provide training can help provide clarity on confidentiality. (See the resource from the U.S. Department of Education provided at the end of the chapter.)

Boundaries With Families

Paraeducators often find themselves working with the same student or set of students for consecutive years. This type of consistent interaction can lead the paraeducator into developing a close relationship with the student's family. Although it is beneficial for paraeducators to have a positive and trusting relationship with the student's family, certain boundaries must be established. Maintaining professional boundaries with parents helps keep the student's best interest in the forefront and ensures that confidentiality policies are followed. It also helps alleviate uncomfortable situations in which a paraeducator may be asked questions they do not know the answer to, questions that are outside of their role, or questions they should not be discussing informally.

If a relationship between a paraeducator and a family goes beyond professional boundaries, several challenges can begin to occur. First, confidentiality can quickly become compromised. The paraeducator may find themselves sharing too much information, and the parent can begin to share information beyond the scope of the student's education. Second, the parent may ask the paraeducator to engage in activities outside of the school setting, such as babysitting/respite, birthday parties, and social events. The paraeducator may feel uncomfortable saying no, be unsure of their role within settings outside of the school environment, and experience a blur in their roles within these different settings. Third, while paraeducators should avoid discussing the student's current performance in school, they must also refrain from brainstorming strategies with parents in the absence of the teacher. When paraeducators become too close with families, it can be very easy for the paraeducator to begin to share their ideas on how situations should be handled, which may conflict with the thoughts from other members of the team and result in unwanted team conflicts. Discussing academic or behavioral strategies with parents is the responsibility of the teacher and educational team. If a paraeducator has a suggestion, it should be funneled through the teacher or educational team first. It is the teacher's responsibility to select the strategies to implement with the team, discuss them with the parents, and make any formal changes to the student's educational plan. Ideally one person, usually the teacher, serves as the point of contact with the student's parents to limit confusion and prevent confidentiality from being compromised.

Paraeducators who blur the lines between professional and personal relationships with families can also create challenges for the family and school when a new paraeducator is assigned the following semester or academic year. When the paraeducator and family see themselves as friends, they may not be open to change and may lose sight of what is best for the student. This may also unintentionally hinder the new paraeducator who will be working with the student. Families may expect the new paraeducator to go beyond professional roles as the previous paraeducator may have. While it is important for paraeducators to develop positive working relationships with families, it is crucial that they follow the boundaries set by the school and supervising teacher.

There are several things a teacher can do to help foster a positive working relationship between paraeducators and parents within healthy boundaries. The teacher should review the boundaries with the paraeducator when the paraeducator begins in their classroom. This information can be included in the welcome packet discussed earlier. The teacher should also review the role of the paraeducator with the parents. This can be done at the conclusion of the IEP meeting or through an arranged time to meet. It can be helpful to have a handout prepared that gives examples of the types of things paraeducators are responsible for and are able to discuss. This informs the parents of topics that should be discussed with the teacher and those that the paraeducator can address. Letting both the paraeducator and the parents know the expectations can help prevent boundary blurring.

It can also be helpful to have established consequences if a paraeducator goes beyond the established boundaries. Having established procedures can help alleviate subjective decisions and support a more professional response to the situation.

Learner Development and Individual Learning Differences

There are a number of common challenges that educational teams might encounter in utilizing paraeducators, but also when supporting learner development and individual learning differences. These challenges might include paraeducators acting as a barrier to peer interaction and teacher instruction and language barriers and missteps by the paraeducator. Let's look at each of these challenges and potential solutions.

Acting as a Barrier to Peer Interaction and Teacher Instruction

At times, paraeducators can act as a barrier to natural peer interactions, which decreases social opportunities. This can occur because they are physically separated from their peers or because there is an adult presence nearby the student. The use of paraeducators, especially one-to-one paraeducators, can also reduce teacher engagement with the student and can result in decreased instruction by qualified personnel.

Educational teams can reduce the likelihood that paraeducators will act as a barrier to peer interaction and teacher instruction by implementing these strategies. First, they can clearly define the roles of teachers and paraeducators, including how much support paraeducators should provide to students in various educational activities. This will help reduce the likelihood the paraeducator will hover. Guidance should include when separating the student from classroom activities is appropriate and when it is not. Details about paraeducator and teacher roles are provided in Chapter 1. Next, they can carefully consider where the student should be physically placed within the inclusive setting. Ideally the student is not placed at the periphery, but rather at the center of the room to make the most of social and educational opportunities. The educational team can also identify ways in which the student can be supported by peers rather than an adult (e.g., peer supports). This might require some training to peers by adults in the classroom, but will allow for more natural learning opportunities within the classroom. They can also incorporate other natural supports within the classroom such as self-monitoring, fading of prompts, and visuals.

Language Barriers and Missteps

At times paraeducators may experience language barriers or engage in communication missteps with students. This might include not being able to communicate in the student's or family's native language or use of language that is insensitive, ableist, or can lead to power struggles.

To avoid language barriers and missteps several strategies can be used. First, educational teams can utilize interpreters or ELL strategies for families and students when English is not the primary language of the student or family. This might include school professionals with expertise in ELL such as the ELL teacher, bilingual paraeducator, or home/school liaison. (See Chapter 4 for details about in the roles of these professionals.) Next, educational teams can provide training to paraeducators related to culturally responsive interactions, person-first language, and how to avoid power struggles with students with social, emotional, and behavioral needs. Teams can also provide paraeducators with information about language development, milestones, and what supports can be put into place to help students gain language proficiency.

Special Education and Supports in the Learning Environment

One of the biggest challenges educational teams might encounter when utilizing paraeducators for special education and support in the learning environment is the overreliance on paraeducator support for students with disabilities (Giangreco, 2021). Often one-on-one paraeducator support is requested for students with disabilities, especially in situations where the student requires behavioral, self-care, or medical support. Other times paraeducator supports are provided indefinitely, with no plan for fading support.

Overreliance on Paraeducators

The issue of schools becoming overreliant on paraeducators is not a new concern, especially in the provision of support to students with disabilities (Giangreco et al., 2004). However, overuse of and overreliance on paraeducators can lead to learned helplessness and lack of independence for students (Chopra et al., 2017), which can have a long-term impact.

There are a number of ways educational teams can reduce the overreliance of paraeducators to support students with disabilities and support learning. Here are a few options. First, before allocating paraeducator support, identify where the paraeducator could be the most useful within the school and with which students. We provide several tools to aid in this identification within the resource section of this chapter. Consider alternatives to the use of paraeducators; this might include peer supports, universal design for learning principles, co-teaching with certified teachers, use of assistive technology, and/or teaching students to self-monitor behavior and tasks (see resources at the end of the chapter for tools). When paraeducator support is identified as essential, create a plan for fading paraeducator support utilizing the alternatives listed previously. Be sure to emphasize that the paraeducator's role is to provide support, facilitate learning, and promote student independence—rather than to care for and complete tasks for the student. Provide training to teachers and paraeducators on issues related to student engagement, promoting student independence, and allowing choice making. Be sure to consider how support will look different for each student based on their needs and educational goals. Finally, consider implementing strategies to promote student independence, including providing a consistent schedule, using visuals and checklists to guide tasks in the classroom, breaking down big tasks into smaller chunks (e.g., use of task analysis), use of least to most prompts, and giving the student the chance to problem solve on their own.

Collaboration With Team Members

There are several common challenges that educational teams might have related to paraeducator collaboration with team members. These challenges might include a lack of understanding of team functioning by paraeducators and a lack of sufficient direction from supervising teachers. There are several ways one might address these issues, as detailed next.

Lack of Understanding About Team Functioning

Without proper preparation and training paraeducators can often have misunderstandings about their roles and the roles of other team members (Ashbaker & Morgan, 2012), which can lead to conflicts within the team. There are a number of ways we can address this challenge. First, provide paraeducators with information about the roles and responsibilities of all relevant educational team members. Such guidance will ensure they recognize where their role ends and others' roles begin. Chapter 1 provides various information about these roles that can be consolidated and shared with

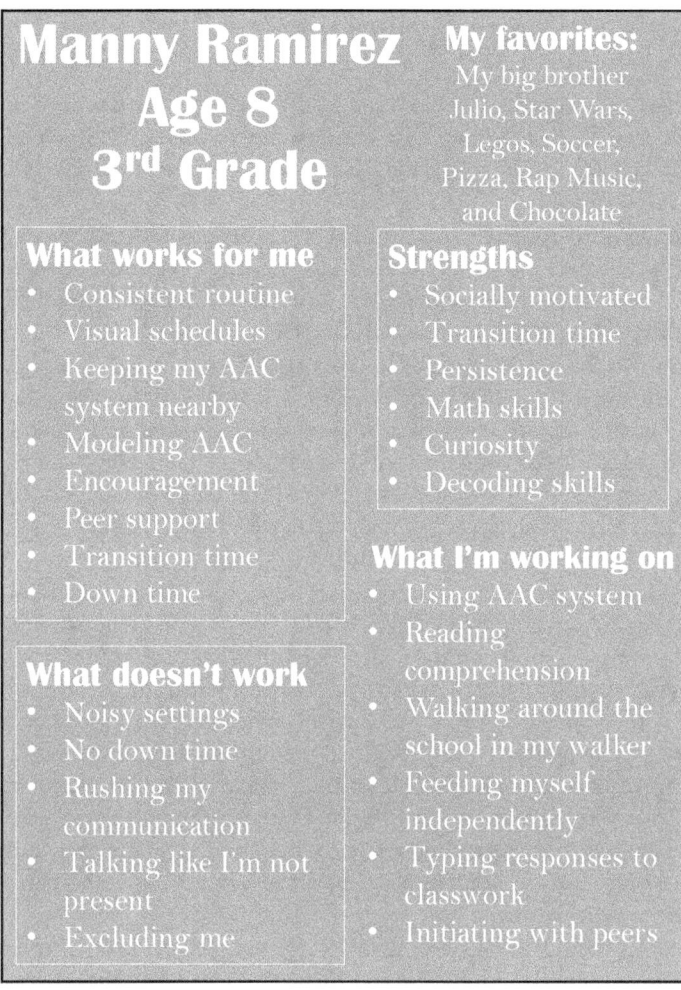

Figure 6-1. Sample of an IEP at a glance.

paraeducators. Next, use active listening strategies when interacting with educational team members. This will help ensure positive communication occurs and will reduce conflicts. Chapter 2 provides details about implementing active listening strategies. You can utilize conflict resolution techniques when active listening strategies with team members are not enough. Chapter 2 provides important strategies to aid conflict resolution.

Lack of Sufficient Direction From Supervising Teachers

At times paraeducators may experience challenges because they lack sufficient direction from teachers. This can be avoided by helping ensure that teachers understand that paraeducator training is important but does not replace high-quality teacher supervision. Supervision is required to ensure fidelity of implementation of trained skills by a paraeducator. Educational organizations can provide teachers with training and support to carry out their supervision duties with paraeducators. Educational organizations should also ensure that teachers utilize effective communication strategies with paraeducators. This should include providing training and support to teachers as they gain and carry out this skill as part of their paraeducator supervision duties. Educational teams should provide paraeducators with clear lesson plans, and written guidance about the accommodations and modifications should be provided to students as well as their educational goals. Chapters 3 and 4 provide several examples of lesson and activity plans, and Figure 6-1 provides an IEP at a glance that can include important information about accommodations, modifications, and individual student goals.

SCHOOL CULTURE AND POLICIES

Although many of the challenges that paraeducators face can be dealt with by the teacher and paraeducator, there are also a number of challenges that school leaders must address. With school administrators taking steps to remediate these difficulties, the teacher and paraeducator are better able to work through many of their challenges.

For teachers and paraeducators to meet routinely to work through problems, discuss student data, ask important questions, and participate in on-the-job training, meeting time must be built into their schedule. School leaders must work closely with teachers to assist them in allocating time for meeting with their paraeducators. As described in detail in Chapter 2, the administrator and teacher should discuss the frequency and the best time of day to schedule this time.

Throughout the school year, paraeducators will inevitably be absent. It is crucial that the paraeducator and teacher be prepared for these absences. In order to assist in this preparation, school leaders should allocate time for paraeducators to compile a substitute folder. Time for this can be given at the beginning of the school year, with shorter increments of time throughout the school year to add, remove, or update specific documents. The teacher should initially assist the paraeducator in creating this folder so they are better able to support the substitute paraeducator as needed.

The building-level school administrator is often most responsible for conducting paraeducator evaluations. However, at times, this can be something that falls under a district-level administrator. In either situation, the school leader must ensure that time is dedicated to observing and interacting with each paraeducator they evaluate. Although they may seek some input from the teacher who manages the paraeducator, it is the administrator's job to formally evaluate the paraeducator. Too often school leaders rely on the managing teacher to provide all the information for the evaluation. This can make the supervising teacher uncomfortable, as it is outside of their duties. School administrators should be aware of this and make every effort to offer paraeducators a helpful and honest evaluation. Just as teachers have a formal evaluation process, school leaders should establish an evaluation process for paraeducators. With a process in place, both the administrator and paraeducator know the expectations' relative evaluations.

Establishing a formal evaluation process is just one of many ways that paraeducators can be shown respect. Research has consistently revealed (Sobeck et al., 2020) that paraeducators are underprioritized and not given the level of respect other school personnel receive; this ranges from not being included in important meetings, to a lack of meaningful training opportunities, to not being given appropriate space in the school (e.g., mailboxes, desk). It is essential that both school leaders and teachers be aware of this discrepancy and actively work toward establishing a strong and supportive working relationship with paraeducators. Arranging for adequate meeting times, establishing a genuine evaluation process, offering meaningful training opportunities, including paraeducators in student meetings, ensuring they have a physical space in the classroom or school for their belongings, and seeking feedback throughout the semester on their needs are just a few ways school leaders can begin to establish a respectful environment for paraeducators.

Finally, school leaders should consider compensation for paraeducators, as well as the supports in place for career advancement. Most paraeducators are underpaid for the responsibilities they hold. These low wages not only deter potentially strong candidates away from the field but also contributes to the low morale among paraeducators and the high turnover rate many schools face (Douglas et al., 2022). Further, when paraeducators earn such low wages, it prevents them from being able to pursue career advancement. Many paraeducators cannot afford to participate in higher education, and career advancement opportunities, such as tuition reimbursement programs, are scarce for paraeducators. Further, many paraeducators themselves take on extra jobs within the school (e.g., bus monitor, after school care provider, summer school) or working a second job outside of the school. Holding additional jobs hinders the time they have to participate in higher education coursework.

School leaders must be aware of how both the lower wages and the lack of career advancement opportunities impact the paraeducators who work in their schools. Ongoing discussion and action should be at the forefront when hiring and supervising paraeducators. Increasing wages and creating career advancement opportunities are essential to hire and retain high-quality paraeducators (Douglas et al., 2022; Yates et al., 2020).

SUMMARY

Educational teams can face numerous challenges when utilizing paraeducators in the areas of professional learning and roles, learner development and individual learning differences, special education and supports in the learning environment, collaboration with team members, and school culture and practices. These challenges can be prevented and remediated through taking the evidence-based steps outlined in this chapter. Although administrators, teachers, and paraeducators may experience some challenges beyond the areas discussed in this chapter, the guidance given throughout the whole text should help school personnel navigate an array of challenges as they occur. Being made aware of common challenges and effective strategies can help every individual take a proactive role in limiting the number of challenges faced. With strong working adult relationships established, preventative strategies in place, and easy-to-follow protocols implemented, then administrators, teachers, and paraeducators are better able to support all students.

CHAPTER REVIEW

1. Name a common challenge that is faced related to professional learning and roles for paraeducators. How can this challenge be remediated?
2. Why can blurred boundaries with families be an issue for paraeducators?
3. Paraeducators can experience a number of challenges related to learner development and individual learning differences. List two common challenges and ways they can be avoided.
4. How can teams avoid an overreliance on paraeducators?
5. Name one challenge related to collaborating with team members and how that challenge can be overcome.
6. What can school administrators do to avoid common challenges related to paraeducators?

RESOURCES

- Connecticut State Department of Education. (2012). *Guidelines for training and support of paraprofessionals: Working with students birth to 21.* https://portal.ct.gov/-/media/SDE/Paraeducator/guidelines_paraprofessionals.pdf
- Council for Exceptional Children. (2023). https://exceptionalchildren.org/
- Gerlach, K. (2015). *Let's team up! A checklist for teachers, paraeducators, and principals.* National Professional Resources/Dude Publishing.
- Iowa Department of Education. (2007). *Guide to effective paraeducator practices edition II.* Author.
- Iowa Department of Education. (2013). *Appropriate paraeducator services matrix.* https://educateiowa.gov/sites/default/files/documents/Appropriate%20Paraeducator%20Duties.pdf

- Kansas State Department of Education. *Paraprofessionals in Kansas public schools.* https://www.ksde.org/Agency/Division-of-Learning-Services/Early-Childhood-Special-Education-and-Title-Services/Title-Services/Federal-Programs/Title-I-Part-A/Paraprofessional
- Nissman, C., & Slater, A. E. (2015). *One-to-one aides for students with autism: A practical and legal guide.* LRP Media Group.
- Northern Lights Special Education Cooperative. (2023). https://www.nlsec.org/resources/pararesources
- Paraprofessional Resource and Research Center (PAR²A Center). (2023). *K-12 paraprofessional supervision.* Teachers - PAR²A Center (paracenter.org)
- State Education Resource Center. (2007). *Assessment checklist for paraprofessionals: Preschool-grade 12.* https://portal.ct.gov/SDE/Paraeducator/Paraeducator-Information-and-Resources/Documents
- State Education Resource Center. (2007). *Teacher supervisory checklist: Preschool to grade 12.* https://portal.ct.gov/SDE/Paraeducator/Paraeducator-Information-and-Resources/Documents
- U.S. Department of Education. (2021). *Family educational rights and privacy act.* https://www2.ed.gov/policy/gen/guid/fpco/ferpa/index.html
- Virginia Department of Education. (2005). *The Virginia paraprofessional guide to supervision and collaboration with paraprofessionals: A partnership.* https://vcuautismcenter.org/resources/paraprofessionals.cfm

References

Ashbaker, B. Y., & Morgan, J. (2012). Team players and team managers: Special educators working with paraeducators to support inclusive classrooms. *Creative Education, 3*(3), 322-327. http://dx.doi.org/10.4236/ce.2012.33051

Chopra, R. V., Carroll, D., & Manjack, S. K. (2017). Utilizing paraeducators: Issues and strategies for supporting students with disabilities in arts education. In J. B. Crockett, & S. M. Malley (Eds.), *Handbook of arts education and special education* (pp. 105-128). Routledge.

Chopra, R. V., & Uitto, D. J. (2015). Programming and planning within a multi-faceted classroom. In D. Chambers (Ed.), *Working with teaching assistants and other support staff for inclusive education* (pp. 175-194). Emerald Publishing.

Council for Exceptional Children. (2022). *Core competencies for special education paraeducators.* https://exceptionalchildren.org/paraeducators/core-competencies-special-education-paraeducators

Douglas, S. N., Bowles, R., & Kammes, R. (2022). Elementary principals' views on the policies and practices of paraeducators in special education. *Journal of the American Academy of Special Education Professionals, Winter,* 107-126.

Douglas, S. N., Chapin, S. E., & Nolan, J. (2016). Special education teachers' experiences supporting and supervising paraeducators: Implications for special and general education settings. *Teacher Education and Special Education, 39*(1), 60-74. https://doi.org/10.1177/0888406415616443

Douglas, S. N., & Uitto, D. J. (2021). A collaborative approach to paraeducator training. *Beyond Behavior, 30*(1), 4-13. https://doi.org/10.1177/1074295621997177

Fisher, M., & Pleasants, S. L. (2012). Roles, responsibilities, and concerns of paraeducators: Findings from a statewide survey. *Remedial and Special Education, 33*(5), 287-297. https://doi.org/10.1177/0741932510397762

Frantz, R., Douglas, S. N., Meadan, H., Sands, M., Bhana, N., & D'Agostino, S. (2020). Exploring the professional development needs of early childhood paraeducators and supervising teachers. *Topics in Early Childhood Special Education, 42*(1). https://doi.org/10.1177/0271121420921237

Giangreco, M. F. (2010). One-to-one paraprofessionals for students with disabilities in inclusive classrooms: Is conventional wisdom wrong? *Intellectual and Developmental Disabilities, 48*(1), 1-13. https://doi.org/10.1352/1934-9556-48.1.1

Giangreco, M. F. (2021). Maslow's hammer: Teacher assistant research and inclusive practices at a crossroads. *European Journal of Special Needs Education, 36*(2), 278-293. https://doi.org/10.1080/08856257.2021.1901377

Giangreco, M. F., Halvorsen, A. T., Doyle, M. B., & Broer, S. M. (2004). Alternatives to overreliance on paraprofessionals in inclusive schools. *Journal of Special Education Leadership, 17*(2), 82-90.

Mason, R. A., Gunersel, A. B., Irvin, D. W., Wills, H. P., Gregori, E., An, Z. G., & Ingram, P. B. (2021). From the frontlines: Perceptions of paraprofessionals' roles and responsibilities. *Teacher Education and Special Education, 44*(2), 97-116. https://doi.org/10.1177/0888406419896627

Sobeck, E. E., Douglas, S. N., Chopra, R., & Morano, S. (2020). Paraeducator supervision in pre-service teacher preparation programs: Results of a notional survey. *Psychology in the Schools, 58*(4), 669-685. https://doi.org/10.1002/pits.22383

Sobeck, E. E., & Robertson, R. (2019). Perspectives on current practices and barriers to training for paraeducators of students with autism in inclusive settings. *Journal of the American Academy of Special Education Professionals,* 131-151.

Yates, P. A., Chopra, R. V., Sobeck, E. E., Douglas, S. N., Morano, S., Walker, V. L., & Schulze, R. (2020). Working with paraeducators: Tools and strategies for instructional planning, performance feedback, and evaluation. *Intervention in School and Clinic, 56*(1), 1-8. https://doi.org/10.1177/1053451220910740

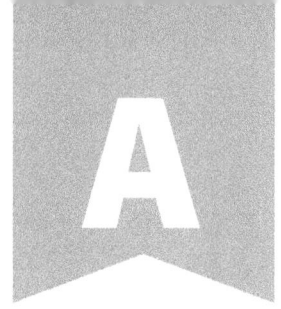

Initial Practice-Based Professional Preparation Standards for Special Educators (K-12)

Reproduced with permission from Berlinghoff, D., & McLaughlin, V. L. (Eds.). (2022). *Practice-based standards for the preparation of special educators*. Council for Exceptional Children.

3100 Clarendon Blvd, Suite 600 | Arlington, VA 22201-5332
(P) + 1.703.620.3660 | (Toll Free) 888.232.7733 | (F) 703.264.9494
exceptionalchildren.org

Field and Clinical Experience Standard

Special education candidates progress through a series of developmentally sequenced field and clinical experiences for the full range of ages, types and levels of abilities, and collaborative opportunities that are appropriate to the license or roles for which they are preparing. These field and clinical experiences are supervised by qualified professionals.

Standard 1: Engaging in Professional Learning and Practice within Ethical Guidelines

Candidates practice within ethical and legal guidelines; advocate for improved outcomes for individuals with exceptionalities and their families while considering their social, cultural, and linguistic diversity; and engage in ongoing self-reflection to design and implement professional learning activities.

Component 1.1: Candidates practice within ethical guidelines and legal policies and procedures.

Component 1.2: Candidates advocate for improved outcomes for individuals with exceptionalities and their families while addressing the unique needs of those with diverse social, cultural, and linguistic backgrounds.

Component 1.3: Candidates design and implement professional learning activities based on ongoing analysis of student learning; self-reflection; and professional standards, research, and contemporary practices.

Standard 2: Understanding and Addressing Each Individual's Developmental and Learning Needs

Candidates use their understanding of human growth and development, the multiple influences on development, individual differences, diversity, including exceptionalities, and families and communities to plan and implement inclusive learning environments and experiences that provide individuals with exceptionalities high quality learning experiences reflective of each individual's strengths and needs.

Component 2.1: Candidates apply understanding of human growth and development to create developmentally appropriate and meaningful learning experiences that address individualized strengths and needs of students with exceptionalities.

Component 2.2: Candidates use their knowledge and understanding of diverse factors that influence development and learning, including differences related to families, languages, cultures, and communities, and individual differences, including exceptionalities, to plan and implement learning experiences and environments.

Standard 3: Demonstrating Subject Matter Content and Specialized Curricular Knowledge

Candidates apply their understanding of the academic subject matter content of the general curriculum and specialized curricula to inform their programmatic and instructional decisions for learners with exceptionalities.

Component 3.1: Candidates apply their understanding of academic subject matter content of the general curriculum to inform their programmatic and instructional decisions for individuals with exceptionalities.

Component 3.2: Candidates augment the general education curriculum to address skills and strategies that students with disabilities need to access the core curriculum and function successfully within a variety of contexts as well as the continuum of placement options to assure specially designed instruction is developed and implemented to achieve mastery of curricular standards and individualized goals and objectives.

Standard 4: Using Assessment to Understand the Learner and the Learning Environment for Data-based Decision Making

Candidates assess students' learning, behavior, and the classroom environment in order to evaluate and support classroom and school-based problem-solving systems of intervention and instruction. Candidates evaluate students to determine their strengths and needs, contribute to students' eligibility determination, communicate students' progress, inform short and long-term instructional planning, and make ongoing adjustments to instruction using technology as appropriate.

Component 4.1: Candidates collaboratively develop, select, administer, analyze, and interpret multiple measures of student learning, behavior, and the classroom environment to evaluate and support classroom and school-based systems of intervention for students with and without exceptionalities.

Component 4.2: Candidates develop, select, administer, and interpret multiple, formal and informal, culturally and linguistically appropriate measures and procedures that are valid and reliable to contribute to eligibility determination for special education services.

Component 4.3: Candidates assess, collaboratively analyze, interpret, and communicate students' progress toward measurable outcomes using technology as appropriate, to inform both short- and long-term planning, and make ongoing adjustments to instruction.

Standard 5: Supporting Learning Using Effective Instruction

Candidates use knowledge of individuals' development, learning needs, and assessment data to inform decisions about effective instruction. Candidates use explicit instructional strategies and employ strategies to promote active engagement and increased motivation to individualize instruction to support each individual. Candidates use whole group instruction, flexible grouping, small group instruction, and individual instruction. Candidates teach individuals to use meta-/cognitive strategies to support and self-regulate learning.

Component 5.1: Candidates use findings from multiple assessments, including student self-assessment, that are responsive to cultural and linguistic diversity and specialized as needed, to identify what students know and are able to do. They then interpret the assessment data to appropriately plan

and guide instruction to meet rigorous academic and non-academic content and goals for each individual.

Component 5.2: Candidates use effective strategies to promote active student engagement, increase student motivation, increase opportunities to respond, and enhance self-regulation of student learning.

Component 5.3: Candidates use explicit, systematic instruction to teach content, strategies, and skills to make clear what a learner needs to do or think about while learning.

Component 5.4: Candidates use flexible grouping to support the use of instruction that is adapted to meet the needs of each individual and group.

Component 5.5: Candidates organize and manage focused, intensive small group instruction to meet the learning needs of each individual.

Component 5.6: Candidates plan and deliver specialized, individualized instruction that is used to meet the learning needs of each individual.

Standard 6: Supporting Social, Emotional, and Behavioral Growth

Candidates create and contribute to safe, respectful, and productive learning environments for individuals with exceptionalities through the use of effective routines and procedures and use a range of preventive and responsive practices to support social, emotional and educational well-being. They follow ethical and legal guidelines and work collaboratively with families and other professionals to conduct behavioral assessments for intervention and program development.

Component 6.1: Candidates use effective routines and procedures to create safe, caring, respectful, and productive learning environments for individuals with exceptionalities.

Component 6.2: Candidates use a range of preventive and responsive practices documented as effective to support individuals' social, emotional, and educational well-being.

Component 6.3: Candidates systematically use data from a variety of sources to identify the purpose or function served by problem behavior to plan, implement, and evaluate behavioral interventions and social skills programs, including generalization to other environments.

Standard 7: Collaborating with Team Members

Candidates apply team processes and communication strategies to collaborate in a culturally responsive manner with families, paraprofessionals, and other professionals within the school, other educational settings, and the community to plan programs and access services for individuals with exceptionalities and their families.

Component 7.1: Candidates utilize communication, group facilitation, and problem–solving strategies in a culturally responsive manner to lead effective meetings and share expertise and knowledge to build team capacity and jointly address students' instructional and behavioral needs.

3100 Clarendon Blvd, Suite 600 | Arlington, VA 22201-5332
(P) + 1.703.620.3660 | (Toll Free) 888.232.7733 | (F) 703.264.9494
exceptionalchildren.org

Component 7.2: Candidates collaborate, communicate, and coordinate with families, paraprofessionals, and other professionals within the educational setting to assess, plan, and implement effective programs and services that promote progress toward measurable outcomes for individuals with and without exceptionalities and their families.

Component 7.3: Candidates collaborate, communicate, and coordinate with professionals and agencies within the community to identify and access services, resources, and supports to meet the identified needs of individuals with exceptionalities and their families.

Component 7.4: Candidates work with and mentor paraprofessionals in the paraprofessionals' role of supporting the education of individuals with exceptionalities and their families.

Initial Practice-Based Professional Preparation Standards for Early Interventionists/ Early Childhood Special Educators

Reproduced with permission from Berlinghoff, D., & McLaughlin, V. L. (Eds.). (2022). *Practice-based standards for the preparation of special educators*. Council for Exceptional Children.

3100 Clarendon Blvd, Suite 600 | Arlington, VA 22201-5332
(P) + 1.703.620.3660 | (Toll Free) 888.232.7733 | (F) 703.264.9494
exceptionalchildren.org

Field and Clinical Experience Standard
Early Interventionist/Early Childhood Special Education candidates progress through a series of planned and developmentally sequenced field experiences for the early childhood age ranges (birth to age 3, 3 through 5 years, 5 through 8 years), range of abilities, and in the variety of collaborative and inclusive early childhood settings that are appropriate to their license and roles. Clinical experiences should take place in the same age ranges covered by the license. If the license covers all three age ranges, the program must provide clinical experiences in at least two of the three age ranges and a field experience in the third age range. These field and clinical experiences are supervised by qualified professionals.

Standard 1: Child Development and Early Learning
Candidates understand the impact of different theories and philosophies of early learning and development on assessment, curriculum, instruction, and intervention decisions. Candidates apply knowledge of normative developmental sequences and variations, individual differences within and across the range of abilities, including developmental delays and disabilities, and other direct and indirect contextual features that support or constrain children's development and learning. These contextual factors as well as social, cultural, and linguistic diversity are considered when facilitating meaningful learning experiences and individualizing intervention and instruction across contexts.
Component 1.1: Candidates demonstrate an understanding of the impact that different theories and philosophies of early learning and development have on assessment, curriculum, intervention, and instruction decisions.
Component 1.2: Candidates apply knowledge of normative sequences of early development, individual differences, and families' social, cultural, and linguistic diversity to support each child's development and learning across contexts.
Component 1.3: Candidates apply knowledge of biological and environmental factors that may support or constrain children's early development and learning as they plan and implement early intervention and instruction.
Component 1.4: Candidates demonstrate an understanding of characteristics, etiologies, and individual differences within and across the range of abilities, including developmental delays and disabilities, their potential impact on children's early development and learning, and implications for assessment, curriculum, instruction, and intervention.

Standard 2: Partnering with Families
Candidates use their knowledge of family-centered practices and family systems theory to develop and maintain reciprocal partnerships with families. They apply family capacity-building practices as they support families to make informed decisions and advocate for their young children. They engage families in opportunities that build on their existing strengths, reflect current goals, and foster family competence and confidence to support their children's development and learning.
Component 2.1: Candidates apply their knowledge of family-centered practices, family systems theory, and the changing needs and priorities in families' lives to develop trusting, respectful, affirming, and culturally responsive partnerships with all families that allow for the mutual exchange of knowledge and information.

Component 2.2: Candidates communicate clear, comprehensive, and objective information about resources and supports that help families to make informed decisions and advocate for access, participation, and equity in natural and inclusive environments.

Component 2.3: Candidates engage families in identifying their strengths, priorities, and concerns; support families to achieve the goals they have for their family and their young child's development and learning; and promote families' competence and confidence during assessment, individualized planning, intervention, instruction, and transition processes.

Standard 3: Collaboration and Teaming

Candidates apply models, skills, and processes of teaming when collaborating and communicating with families and professionals, using culturally and linguistically responsive and affirming practices. In partnership with families and other professionals, candidates develop and implement individualized plans and successful transitions that occur across the age span. Candidates use a variety of collaborative strategies while working with and supporting other adults.

Component 3.1: Candidates apply teaming models, skills, and processes, including appropriate uses of technology, when collaborating and communicating with families; professionals representing multiple disciplines, skills, expertise, and roles; and community partners and agencies.

Component 3.2: Candidates use a variety of collaborative strategies when working with other adults that are evidence-based, appropriate to the task, culturally and linguistically responsive, and take into consideration the environment and service delivery approach.

Component 3.3: Candidates partner with families and other professionals to develop individualized plans and support the various transitions that occur for the young child and their family throughout the birth through 8 age span.

Standard 4: Assessment Processes

Candidates know and understand the purposes of assessment in relation to ethical and legal considerations. Candidates choose developmentally, linguistically, and culturally appropriate tools and methods that are responsive to the characteristics of the young child, family, and program. Using evidence-based practices, candidates develop or select as well as administer informal measures, and select and administer formal measures in partnership with families and other professionals. They analyze, interpret, document, and share assessment information using a strengths-based approach with families and other professionals for eligibility determination, outcome/goal development, planning instruction and intervention, monitoring progress, and reporting.

Component 4.1: Candidates understand the purposes of formal and informal assessment, including ethical and legal considerations, and use this information to choose developmentally, culturally and linguistically appropriate, valid, reliable tools and methods that are responsive to the characteristics of the young child, family, and program.

Component 4.2: Candidates develop and administer informal assessments and/or select and use valid, reliable formal assessments using evidence-based practices, including technology, in partnership with families and other professionals.

Component 4.3: Candidates analyze, interpret, document, and share assessment information using a strengths-based approach with families and other professionals.

Appendix B

Council for Exceptional Children
3100 Clarendon Blvd, Suite 600 | Arlington, VA 22201-5332
(P) + 1.703.620.3620 | (Toll Free) 888.232.7733 | (F) 703.264.9494
exceptionalchildren.org

Component 4.4: Candidates, in collaboration with families and other team members, use assessment data to determine eligibility, develop child and family-based outcomes/goals, plan for interventions and instruction, and monitor progress to determine efficacy of programming.

Standard 5: Application of Curriculum Frameworks in the Planning of Meaningful Learning Experience

Candidates collaborate with families and professionals to use an evidence-based, developmentally appropriate, and culturally responsive early childhood curriculum addressing developmental and content domains. Candidates use curriculum frameworks to create and support universally designed, high quality learning experiences in natural and inclusive environments that provide each child and family with equitable access and opportunities for learning and growth.

Component 5.1: Candidates collaborate with families and other professionals in identifying an evidence-based curriculum addressing developmental and content domains to design and facilitate meaningful and culturally responsive learning experiences that support the unique abilities and needs of all children and families.

Component 5.2: Candidates use their knowledge of early childhood curriculum frameworks, developmental and academic content knowledge, and related pedagogy to plan and ensure equitable access to universally designed, developmentally appropriate, and challenging learning experiences in natural and inclusive environments.

Standard 6: Using Responsive and Reciprocal Interactions, Interventions, and Instruction

Candidates plan and implement intentional, systematic, evidence-based, responsive interactions, interventions, and instruction to support all children's learning and development across all developmental and content domains in partnership with families and other professionals. Candidates facilitate equitable access and participation for all children and families within natural and inclusive environments through culturally responsive and affirming practices and relationships. Candidates use data-based decision-making to plan for, adapt, and improve interactions, interventions, and instruction to ensure fidelity of implementation.

Component 6.1: Candidates, in partnership with families, identify systematic, responsive, and intentional evidence-based practices and use such practices with fidelity to support young children's learning and development across all developmental and academic content domains.

Component 6.2: Candidates engage in reciprocal partnerships with families and other professionals to facilitate responsive adult-child interactions, interventions, and instruction in support of child learning and development.

Component 6.3: Candidates engage in ongoing planning and use flexible and embedded instructional and environmental arrangements and appropriate materials to support the use of interactions, interventions, and instruction addressing developmental and academic content domains, which are adapted to meet the needs of each and every child and their family.

Component 6.4: Candidates promote young children's social and emotional competence and communication, and proactively plan and implement function-based interventions to prevent and address challenging behaviors.

3100 Clarendon Blvd, Suite 600 | Arlington, VA 22201-5332
(P) + 1.703.620.3660 | (Toll Free) 888.232.7733 | (F) 703.264.9494
exceptionalchildren.org

Component 6.5: Candidates identify and create multiple opportunities for young children to develop and learn play skills and engage in meaningful play experiences independently and with others across contexts.

Component 6.6: Candidates use responsive interactions, interventions, and instruction with sufficient intensity and types of support across activities, routines, and environments to promote child learning and development and facilitate access, participation, and engagement in natural environments and inclusive settings.

Component 6.7: Candidates plan for, adapt, and improve approaches to interactions, interventions, and instruction based on multiple sources of data across a range of natural environments and inclusive settings.

Standard 7: Professionalism and Ethical Practice

Candidates identify and engage with the profession of early intervention and early childhood special education (EI/ECSE) by exhibiting skills in reflective practice, advocacy, and leadership while adhering to ethical and legal guidelines. Evidence-based and recommended practices are promoted and used by candidates.

Component 7.1: Candidates engage with the profession of EI/ECSE by participating in local, regional, national, and/or international activities and professional organizations.

Component 7.2: Candidates engage in ongoing reflective practice and access evidence-based information to improve their own practices.

Component 7.3: Candidates exhibit leadership skills in advocating for improved outcomes for young children, families, and the profession, including the promotion of and use of evidence-based practices and decision-making.

Component 7.4: Candidates practice within ethical and legal policies and procedures.

Standards for Professional Practice

Reproduced with permission from Council for Exceptional Children. (2015). *What every special educator must know: Professional ethics and standards* (7th ed.). Council for Exceptional Children.

Standards for Professional Practice

1.0. Teaching and Assessment	
Special education professionals:	
1.1.	Systematically individualize instructional variables to maximize the learning outcomes of individuals with exceptionalities.
1.2.	Identify and use evidence-based practices that are appropriate to their professional preparation and are most effective in meeting the individual needs of individuals with exceptionalities.
1.3.	Use periodic assessments to accurately measure the learning progress of individuals with exceptionalities, and individualize instruction variables in response to assessment results.
1.4.	Create safe, effective, and culturally responsive learning environments which contribute to fulfillment of needs, stimulation of learning, and realization of positive self-concepts.
1.5.	Participate in the selection and use of effective and culturally responsive instructional materials, equipment, supplies, and other resources appropriate to their professional roles.
1.6.	Use culturally and linguistically appropriate assessment procedures that accurately measure what is intended to be measured, and do not discriminate against individuals with exceptional or culturally diverse learning needs.
1.7.	Only use behavior change practices that are evidence based, appropriate to their preparation, and which respect the culture, dignity, and basic human rights of individuals with exceptionalities.
1.8.	Support the use of positive behavior supports and conform to local policies relating to the application of disciplinary methods and behavior change procedures, except when the policies require their participation in corporal punishment.
1.9.	Refrain from using aversive techniques unless the target of the behavior change is vital, repeated trials of more positive and less restrictive methods have failed, and only after appropriate consultation with parents and appropriate agency officials.
1.10.	Do not engage in the corporal punishment of individuals with exceptionalities.
1.11.	Report instances of unprofessional or unethical practice to the appropriate supervisor.
1.12.	Recommend special education services necessary for an individual with an exceptional learning need to receive an appropriate education.

2.0 Professional Credentials and Employment	
Special education professionals:	
2.1.	Represent themselves in an accurate, ethical, and legal manner with regard to their own knowledge and expertise when seeking employment.
2.2.	Ensure that persons who practice or represent themselves as special education teachers, administrators, and providers of related services are qualified by professional credential.
2.3.	Practice within their professional knowledge and skills and seek appropriate external support and consultation whenever needed.
2.4.	Provide notice consistent with local education agency policies and contracts when intending to leave employment.
2.5.	Adhere to the contracts and terms of appointment, or provide the appropriate supervisor notice of professionally untenable conditions and intent to terminate such employment, if necessary.
2.6.	Advocate for appropriate and supportive teaching and learning conditions.
2.7.	Advocate for sufficient personnel resources so that unavailability of substitute teachers or support personnel, including paraeducators, does not result in the denial of special education services.
2.8.	Seek professional assistance in instances where personal problems interfere with job performance.
2.9.	Ensure that public statements made by professionals as individuals are not construed to represent official policy statements of an agency.
2.10.	Objectively document and report inadequacies in resources to their supervisors and/or administrators and suggest appropriate corrective action(s).
2.11.	Respond objectively and nondiscriminatively when evaluating applicants for employment including grievance procedures.
2.12.	Resolve professional problems within the workplace using established procedures.
2.13.	Seek clear written communication of their duties and responsibilities, including those that are prescribed as conditions of employment.
2.14.	Expect that responsibilities will be communicated to and respected by colleagues, and work to ensure this understanding and respect.
2.15.	Promote educational quality and actively participate in the planning, policy development, management, and evaluation of special education programs and the general education program.
2.16.	Expect adequate supervision of and support for special education professionals and programs provided by qualified special education professionals.
2.17.	Expect clear lines of responsibility and accountability in the administration and supervision of special education professionals.

Appendix C

3.0 Professional Development	
Special education professionals:	
3.1.	Maintain a personalized professional development plan designed to advance their knowledge and skills, including cultural competence, systematically in order to maintain a high level of competence.
3.2.	Maintain current knowledge of procedures, policies, and laws relevant to practice.
3.3.	Engage in the objective and systematic evaluation of themselves, colleagues, services, and programs for the purpose of continuous improvement of professional performance.
3.4.	Advocate that the employing agency provide adequate resources for effective schoolwide professional development as well as individual professional development plans.
3.5.	Participate in systematic supervised field experiences for candidates in preparation programs.
3.6.	Participate as mentors to other special educators, as appropriate.

4.0 Professional Colleagues	
Special education professionals:	
4.1.	Recognize and respect the skill and expertise of professional colleagues from other disciplines as well as colleagues from their own disciplines.
4.2.	Strive to develop positive and respectful attitudes among professional colleagues and the public toward persons with exceptional learning needs.
4.3.	Collaborate with colleagues from other agencies to improve services and outcomes for individuals with exceptionalities.
4.4.	Collaborate with both general and special education professional colleagues as well as other personnel serving individuals with exceptionalities to improve outcomes for individuals with exceptionalities.
4.5.	Intervene professionally when a colleague's behavior is illegal, unethical, or detrimental to individuals with exceptionalities.
4.6.	Do not engage in conflicts of interest.

5.0 Paraeducators	
Special education professionals:	
5.1.	Ensure that special education paraeducators have appropriate training for the tasks they are assigned.
5.2.	Assign only tasks for which paraeducators have been appropriately prepared.
5.3.	Provide ongoing information to paraeducators regarding their performance of assigned tasks.
5.4.	Provide timely, supportive, and collegial communications to paraeducators regarding tasks and expectations.
5.5.	Intervene professionally when a paraeducator's behavior is illegal, unethical, or detrimental to individuals with exceptionalities.

6.0 Parents and Families	
Special education professionals:	
6.1.	Use culturally appropriate communication with parents and families that is respectful and accurately understood.
6.2.	Actively seek and use the knowledge of parents and individuals with exceptionalities when planning, conducting, and evaluating special education services and empower them as partners in the educational process.
6.3.	Maintain communication among parents and professionals with appropriate respect for privacy, confidentiality, and cultural diversity.
6.4.	Promote opportunities for parent education using accurate, culturally appropriate information and professional methods.
6.5.	Inform parents of relevant educational rights and safeguards.
6.6.	Recognize and practice in ways that demonstrate respect for the cultural diversity within the school and community.
6.7.	Respect professional relationships with students and parents, neither seeking any personal advantage nor engaging in inappropriate relationships.

7.0 Research	
Special education professionals:	
7.1.	Do not knowingly use research in ways that mislead others.
7.2.	Protect the rights and welfare of participants in research.
7.3.	Interpret and publish research results with accuracy.
7.4.	Monitor unintended consequences of research projects involving individuals with exceptionalities, and discontinue activities that may cause harm in excess of approved levels.
7.5.	Advocate for sufficient resources to support long-term research agendas to improve the practice of special education and the learning outcomes of individuals with exceptionalities.

8.0 Case Management	
Special education professionals:	
8.1.	Maintain accurate student records and ensure that appropriate confidentiality standards are in place and enforced.
8.2.	Follow appropriate procedural safeguards and assist the school in providing due process.
8.3.	Provide accurate student and program data to administrators, colleagues, and parents, based on efficient and objective record-keeping practices.
8.4.	Maintain confidentiality of information except when information is released under specific conditions of written consent that meet confidentiality requirements.
8.5.	Engage in appropriate planning for the transition sequences of individuals with exceptionalities.

9.0 Non-Educational Support	
Special education professionals:	
9.1.	Perform assigned specific non-educational support tasks, such as administering medication, only in accordance with local policies and when written instructions are on file, legal or policy information is provided, and the professional liability for assuming the task is disclosed.
9.2.	Advocate that special education professionals not be expected to accept non-educational support tasks routinely.

Core Competencies for Special Education Paraeducators

Reproduced with permission from Council for Exceptional Children. (2022). *Core competencies for special education paraeducators.* https://exceptionalchildren.org/paraeducators/core-competencies-special-education-paraeducators

Core Competencies for Special Education Paraeducators

Preamble

The Core Competencies for Special Education Paraeducators represent the required knowledge and skills all paraeducators need to safely and effectively support students with disabilities in K-12 settings. Paraeducators work in general education and special education classrooms, non-classroom school settings (e.g., cafeteria, playground), and community-based learning sites supporting an entire classroom of students or individual students with disabilities. Paraeducators provide individualized services to students with disabilities through a range of tasks directed by the instructional team consisting of licensed professionals responsible for planning and implementing specially designed services for students with disabilities. These core competencies address the corresponding role of paraeducators in the four aspects (collaboration, assessment, social/emotional/behavioral, and instruction) of the High Leverage Practices for special educators developed by CEC in collaboration with the Collaboration for Effective Educator Development, Accountability, and Reform (CEEDAR) Center.

Acquisition of these Core Competencies by paraeducators requires support from licensed professionals including administrators, general and special education teachers, and related services personnel who are equipped with knowledge and skills to oversee and direct the work of paraeducators. Licensed professionals provide supervision and guidance to paraeducators, clearly define their roles, direct their work, and determine which practices they implement to support students with disabilities. Licensed professionals can utilize these core competencies to understand the essential knowledge and skills that paraeducators should possess and ensure that they are appropriately prepared for their assigned tasks. It is important to note that in the knowledge and skill statements listed under each competency area, skills supersede the knowledge; in other words, it is understood that paraeducators have acquired the knowledge that is necessary to demonstrate the skill.

Core Competency Area 1: Professional Learning and Ethical Practice

Paraeducators follow district policies, guidelines, and procedures. Paraeducators understand that their practice requires attention to the professional and ethical considerations such as confidentiality, scope and limits of their roles and skill level, and culturally responsive practices. Paraeducators understand that their role is to assist the instructional team and support students under the direction of licensed professionals. As lifelong learners, they participate in professional growth and development, reflect on their professional practices, and use feedback from licensed professionals to improve their skills. **Tasks performed by paraeducators are under the ongoing guidance and direction of the instructional team.**

Knowledge	
K1.1	Principles, standards, and policies that guide ethical practice
K1.2	Personal and cultural biases and differences and how they may influence one's practice
K1.3	Professional growth opportunities for continued learning

Skills	
S1.1	Conduct activities with integrity and in compliance with applicable local, state and federal standards, policies and guidelines
S1.2	Maintain the dignity, privacy, and confidentiality of all students with disabilities, families, and school personnel
S1.3	Follow the chain of command established by the district to address policy questions, system level issues, and personnel practices
S1.4	Report suspected child abuse, suicidal ideation, and dangerous behaviors as required by law, policies, and local procedures
S1.5	Recognize and respect role differences of teachers, paraeducators, and other licensed professionals
S1.6	Recognize the role of the licensed professional as the leader of the instructional team
S1.7	Practice within the limits of the defined paraprofessional role
S1.8	Practice within one's skill limits and request direction, instruction, guidance or additional training for new or unfamiliar tasks
S1.9	Maintain boundaries for relationships and communication with students and their families within the professional and ethical scope of responsibility
S1.10	Refer questions about student progress to appropriate licensed professionals
S1.11	Reflect on one's performance, seek guidance and use feedback from licensed professional to continually improve practice
S1.12	Advocate for participation in ongoing professional growth and development opportunities
S1.13	Demonstrate respect and appreciation for cultural differences in verbal and written interactions with students, families, and school personnel

Core Competency Area 2: Learner Development and Individual Learning Differences

Paraeducators demonstrate understanding of the unique learning needs of individual students. Paraeducators understand the impact of disabilities on development for individual students and their families. They understand and value the diversity and individual differences including the culture, religion, gender, and sexual orientation of individual students, family members, and school personnel. Paraeducators promote the growth of students with disabilities and encourage their independence and self-advocacy skills to assist with transitioning to life after high school. **Tasks performed by paraeducators are under the ongoing guidance and direction of the instructional team.**

Knowledge	
K2.1	Cognitive, physical, social, emotional, and language development which impact milestones of students with disabilities compared to typically developing peers
K2.2	Educational challenges manifested as a result of varying disabilities
K2.3	Effect of disabilities on students, families, and society through the lifespan
K2.4	Family systems and their influence on the educational process
K2.5	Common concerns of families of students with disabilities
K2.6	Effects of cultural and linguistic diversity on the educational process and relationships between school, home, and community
K2.7	Characteristics and implications of one's own culture and use of language, including verbal and nonverbal communication, and how this may differ across cultures
K2.8	Effect of speech and language development on academic and nonacademic learning of students with disabilities
K2.9	Non-verbal modes of communication used by students with disabilities including augmentative and alternative communication

Skills	
S2.1	Support student's independence, self-advocacy, positive sense of identity, self-control, and self-reliance under the guidance of the instructional team
S2.2	Support students with disabilities in their use of self-assessment, problem-solving, and other cognitive strategies under the guidance of the instructional team
S2.3	Recognize and respect individual differences between culture, religion, gender, and sexual orientation of students with disabilities and their families
S2.4	Align communication methods to individual's language proficiency under the guidance of the instructional team

Skills (cont.)

S2.5	Provide opportunities and support for children to understand, acquire, and use verbal and nonverbal means to communicate thoughts and feelings under the guidance of the instructional team
S2.6	Reinforce the use of oral and written communication efforts of students with disabilities under the guidance of the instructional team

Core Competency Area 3: Special Education Services and Supports in the Learning Environment

Paraeducators understand services and supports for students with disabilities is based on the federal law for the inclusion of students with disabilities adhering to the guiding principles of free and appropriate public education (FAPE), least restrictive environment (LRE), and individualized education program (IEP). Paraeducators understand the purpose of special education services and support the instructional, behavioral, social, personal care, safety and medical needs, transitional life-skills and inclusion in school and society. They understand the importance of an organized and inclusive environment and facilitate accommodations, structure, and routines that maximize student's successful access to general educational programming. **Tasks performed by the paraeducators are under the ongoing guidance and direction of the instructional team.**

Knowledge

K3.1	Purposes of supports, services and specially designed instruction which provide access to general education curriculum
K3.2	General knowledge of categories from federal law for students with disabilities
K3.3	General knowledge of principles of inclusive practices for students with disabilities
K3.4	Individual learner characteristics as the primary basis for instructional programming and decision making, rather than disability categories or educational placement
K3.5	District/agency policies and procedures for protecting the safety, health, and well-being of learners and school personnel
K3.6	Rights and responsibilities of students with disabilities and the personnel who serve them
K3.7	Effects of paraeducator's proximity and fading of paraeducator support on student engagement, learning and independence

Skills

S3.1	Access credible and reliable websites and resources to expand understanding of special education services and students with disabilities under the guidance of the instructional team
S3.2	Support a safe and equitable learning environment that honors diversity and inclusion under the guidance of the instructional team
S3.3	Establish and maintain rapport with learners under the guidance of the instructional team

Skills *(cont.)*	
S3.4	Use knowledge of student's strengths and interests to encourage engagement in varied school and community activities under the guidance of the instructional team
S3.5	Prepare and organize materials to support teaching and learning as directed by the instructional team
S3.6	Adapt the physical environment and modify learning materials and activities as directed by the instructional team
S3.7	Support students with disabilities in following established school and classroom expectations and routines under the guidance of the instructional team
S3.8	Use routines and procedures to support effective transitions as determined by the instructional team
S3.9	Use and maintain adaptive equipment/materials and assistive technology for students with disabilities as determined by the instructional team
S3.10	Support students with disabilities in their use of augmentative and alternative communication devices and other assistive technology under the guidance of the instructional team
S3.11	Perform monitoring duties in learning environments as assigned by the instructional team
S3.12	Use universal precautions to assist in maintaining a safe, healthy environment in all settings
S3.13	Understand and articulate common educational and medical terminology used in the school setting
S3.14	Use techniques to address personal care, medical care, and physical assistance to students with disabilities as directed or authorized by a licensed professional

Core Competency Area 4: Assessment

Paraeducators understand the purposes and rationale of various types of assessments, data collection processes and the link between these assessments and individualized instructional planning. Paraeducators play a vital role in assessment practices by collecting multiple types of data during instruction while using tools and assessments designed/provided by the instructional team. Accurate data collection contributes to informed educational decisions that optimize individual plans resulting in enhanced student outcomes. **Tasks performed by paraeducators are under the ongoing guidance and direction of the instructional team.**

Knowledge	
K4.1	Rationale and methods for formative and summative assessment
K4.2	Link between assessment and instruction
K4.3	Accommodations on student IEP and procedures for proctoring accommodated tests

Skills

S4.1	Record objective and accurate data using collection procedures determined by the instructional team
S4.2	Proctor routine classroom and standardized tests following student accommodations as directed by the instructional team

Core Competency Area 5: Instructional Supports and Strategies

Paraeducators understand a range of instructional strategies to facilitate student learning and address IEPs. Under the direction of the instructional team, paraeducators support specially designed instruction for students with disabilities. Paraeducators follow written instructional plans, implement accommodation and modifications, reinforce concepts presented by the instructional team and use effective strategies to facilitate student learning, inclusion, and growth. **Tasks performed by paraeducators are under the ongoing guidance and direction of the instructional team**.

Knowledge

K5.1	Concepts of differentiated instruction, accommodations, modifications, High Leverage Practices, specially designed instruction
K5.2	Instructional strategies and instructional technology to support the individual student's learning

Skills

S5.1	Demonstrate proficiency in academics including oral and written communication, literacy, and mathematical skills appropriate to the job assignment
S5.2	Follow written instructional plans provided by the instructional team, seeking clarification and training as needed
S5.3	Communicate relevant information about the student with disabilities to the instructional team
S5.4	Support the use of effective and culturally responsive instructional strategies in literacy and mathematics as directed by the instructional team
S5.5	Review and reinforce learning activities, essential concepts, and modified content as directed by the instructional team
S5.6	Use instructional time effectively
S5.7	Modify pace of instruction and provide organizational cues under the guidance of the instructional team
S5.8	Make responsive adjustments to instruction under the guidance of the instructional team
S5.9	Provide least intrusive levels of support, fade support, and fade physical proximity from students with disabilities under the guidance of the instructional team

Skills *(cont.)*

S5.10	Provide feedback to students with disabilities regarding their performance under the guidance of the instructional team

Core Competency Area 6: Social, Emotional, and Behavioral Supports

Paraeducators understand state and district policies and procedures as well as ethical and legal practices for the implementation of positive behavioral supports and interventions. Paraeducators facilitate positive social interactions and active engagement by students with disabilities in the learning process. **Tasks performed by paraeducators are under the ongoing guidance and direction of the instructional team.**

Knowledge

K6.1	Basic principles of positive behavior supports to promote social, emotional, and educational well-being of students with disabilities
K6.2	Communicative purpose of behaviors
K6.3	Legal and ethical practices for the use of behavioral interventions
K6.4	State and district policies and procedural safeguards regarding appropriate use of behavioral supports with students with disabilities
K6.5	Importance of the paraeducator serving as a positive model for students with disabilities

Skills

S6.1	Implement positive behavior supports outlined in a behavior support plan as determined by the instructional team
S6.2	Implement individualized reinforcement systems as determined by the instructional team
S6.3	Support the implementation of social-emotional and behavioral interventions as determined by the instructional teams
S6.4	Assist in teaching specific behaviors and procedures to facilitate safety and learning in each school setting as determined by the instructional team
S6.5	Respond to student actions using strategies under the guidance and direction of the instructional team
S6.6	Support development of social skills and facilitate proactive peer interactions for students with disabilities under the guidance of the instructional team
S6.7	Support students with disabilities by modeling and facilitating the use of conflict resolution and collaborative problem solving under the guidance of the instructional team

Core Competency Area 7: Collaboration with Team Members

Paraeducators support the instructional team and collaborate with multiple team members such as general education and special education teachers, related service providers, administrators, families, and community agencies. Paraeducators use effective communication, conflict resolution/management, and problem-solving strategies to function proactively with team members and the broader community. **Tasks performed by paraeducators are under the ongoing guidance and direction of the instructional team.**

Knowledge	
K7.1	Purpose of effective teamwork to improve student outcomes
K7.2	Communication styles and strategies for problem-solving and decision making

Skills	
S7.1	Establish and maintain professional, collegial, and appropriate relationships with school personnel, students, and their families
S7.2	Communicate effectively with school personnel, students and their families as determined by the instructional team
S7.3	Attend meetings and participate with other team members

Glossary

Adult Learning Theory: Also known as andragogy, adult learning theory is a collection of different but interrelated theories and methods that address how adults learn, including accelerated learning, coaching, guided design, and just-in-time training.

Augmentative and Alternative Communication (AAC): Describes multiple temporary or permanent ways to supplement or compensate for the impairment or disability patterns of individuals with a profound expressive communication disorder, such as impairments in speech/language production and/or comprehension.

Behavioral Intervention Plan (BIP): A written plan agreed upon by all team members based on student data and the outcome of the Functional Behavior Assessment (FBA). The FBA identifies the function of the behavior, and the BIP specifies the evidence-based steps and methods to modify or improve the behavior.

CEC Specialty Sets: Knowledge and skills that are used by teacher education programs to develop curriculum and create assessments for their candidates to demonstrate mastery of standards.

Collaboration: Occurs when members of a learning team work together to assist students in the classroom or work toward a common goal or purpose.

Confidentiality: The act of protecting all identifiable student data, maintained records, and information regarding the student and family contained within the school district and not discussing it with individuals who do not need to know such information.

Conflict Resolution: A formal or informal process in which two or more individuals work to find a solution to a disagreement in a respectful manner that satisfies everyone involved.

Contextual Fit Inventory: An inventory tool that examines the extent to which the procedures of the student plan are consistent with the knowledge, beliefs, skills, resources, and supports of the school personnel who are expected to implement the plan.

Core Competencies for Special Education Paraeducators: Refers to the required knowledge and skills all paraeducators must obtain to support students with disabilities safely and in kindergarten through 12th-grade environments.

Council for Exceptional Children (CEC): An international professional organization that strives to improve the experience of individuals with disabilities and/or gifts and talents through advocacy, professional development, resource sharing, and educational standards.

Council for the Accreditation of Educator Preparation: An organization dedicated to evaluating preschool through 12th-grade educator preparation programs through an evidence-based accreditation process that includes continuous improvement, quality assurance, credibility, diversity and equity, innovation, and a strong foundation.

Didactic Instruction: A style of instruction that incorporated lectures and presentations in which the instructor delivers information and the students, or participants, receive the information.

English-Language Learner (ELL): A diverse group of students, with varying language, academic, and social/emotional needs between the ages of 5 through 21 years enrolled in a kindergarten through 12th-grade school and whose native language is not English. These individuals can also be referred to as English learners (EL).

Evaluation: A systematic process where a student is administered several assessments, academic, behavioral, or social/emotional, to determine the specific domains in which a student needs help and whether the student is eligible for special education services.

Every Student Succeeds Act (ESSA): One of the main education laws for public schools in the United States that holds schools accountable for student performance. This law ensures equal opportunities for students from disadvantaged backgrounds and students who qualify for special education services.

Family Education Rights and Privacy Act (FERPA): A federal law that gives parents access to their children's education accounts, the ability to have their child's records amended, and the right to disclose personally identifiable information from the education records. Once a student turns 18 years old, or enters a postsecondary institution at any age, the rights under FERPA apply to the student and no longer the parent.

High-Leverage Practices (HLPs): Recommended practices supported by research that all teachers should implement in their classrooms classified under two aspects of practice, including collaboration, assessment, social/emotional/behavioral, and instruction.

Highly Qualified Teacher: This originated under NCLB (2001-2015). Teachers had to meet three additional qualifications beyond their state teaching certification to be employed by a school. Under the ESSA, any teacher who meets their state's certification qualifications is automatically deemed highly qualified.

Individualized Education Plan (IEP): A formal and legal document that details an individualized school program developed to ensure that an eligible student with a disability who attends a kindergarten through 12th-grade school receives specialized instruction and related services.

Individuals with Disabilities Education Act (IDEA): Established in 1990 and reauthorized in 2004, this federal law details special education and related service programming for students with disabilities.

Individuals with Disabilities Education Improvement Act (IDEIA): A law that was established in 2004 as the reauthorization of IDEA (1990), in which several amendments were added that further detailed special education and related service programming for students with disabilities.

Initial Practice-Based Professional Preparation Standards for Special Educators (K-12): Standards that define what a pre-service teaching candidate must know and be able to demonstrate prior to becoming a teacher.

Interstate New Teacher Assessment and Support Consortium: An association made up of state education agencies, national educational organizations, and institutions of higher education, who strive to reform education, certify teachers, and provide continuous professional development for teachers.

LAFF Method: An active listening strategy that emphasizes four main steps, including listening and demonstrating respect, asking questions, focusing on the main issue, and deciding on the first action step to resolve the situation.

Local Education Agency (LEA): A term used to describe a public organization (e.g., school district, intermediate unit) that serves students with disabilities and ensures they receive the supports and services they are eligible for under the law (i.e., ESSA, IDEA).

No Child Left Behind Act (NCLB): One of the leading laws for kindergarten through 12th-grade general education in the United States from 2002 to 2015 that sought to hold schools accountable for both student and overall school performance.

Occupational Therapist: A hands-on therapist who treats and supports students with physical and/or cognitive disabilities who experience difficulty with fine motor skills (e.g., cutting, printing, grasping).

Performance Feedback: A training method and/or part of a professional learning package in which feedback is provided to paraeducators about the quality of their performance.

Personal Care Support: Hands-on services to assist an individual with daily activities that they cannot perform on their own.

Physical Therapist: A therapist who supports individuals in developing, maintaining, or rehabilitating gross mobility skills, such as ambulating and positioning.

Problem-Solving Approach: Techniques and processes that individuals use to better understand a problem and to develop a solution.

Professionalism: An individual's actions that follow professional ethical principles, maintain a level of professional competence and integrity, and exercise professional judgment.

Specialty Set of Knowledge and Skills for Interveners for Individuals with Deafblindness: Specific competencies for candidates who will serve individuals with deafblindness.

Speech-Language Pathologist: A therapist who supports individuals in developing communication skills including speech sounds, language, social communication, voice, fluency, and augmentative and alternative communication.

Supervision: Roles of educational personnel to provide direction and support to paraeducators.

Team-Level Training: Training that utilizes teams within a particular field to increase knowledge and proficiency when completing a task.

Tier 1 Behavior Management Strategies: Practices that support all students across all settings by establishing a foundation for proactive support and preventing unwanted behaviors.

INDEX

administrator's role within communication, 33
administrators, 61-69, 86
    directing work, 66
    observation/feedback, 67-69
    supportive work environment, 65-67
        hiring, 66-67
        supporting teams, 66
        training, 66
adult learning, 85
adult learning theory, **78**
age of paraeducator, as conflict area in communication, 31
agenda
    meeting, teacher-paraeducator, 21
    teacher-paraeducator meeting, 21
areas of conflict in communication, 31-33
    age of paraeducator, 31
    experience of paraeducator, 31
    lack of follow-through, 31
    lack of involvement in classroom, 33
    parent communication, 31
Arkansas Department of Education Division of Elementary and Secondary Education, 91
    training program, 91
attendance count, plan for, 62
augmentative and alternative communication (AAC), **56**

behavior management strategies inventory, contextual fit, 26
Behavior Skills Training, example, 48
behavior specialist, 71-72
behavioral intervention plan (BIP), **2**
best practices for preparation
    adult learning, 85
    coaching, 85
    evidence-based training practices, 85
    important individuals in training, 86
    team-level training, 85
boundaries with families, 98-99

Capitol Region Education Council, 91
    training program, 91
categories of training, 47
CEC specialty sets, **2, 38**
certification requirements, paraeducator, state-adopted, 40
challenges, 93-105
    collaboration with team members, 100-101
        sufficient direction from supervising teachers, lack of, 101
        understanding about team functioning, lack of, 100-101

learner development/individual learning differences, 99
    barrier to peer interaction/teacher instruction, 99
    language barriers/missteps, 99
learning environment, supports in, 100
professional learning/roles, 96-99
    boundaries with families, 98-99
    confidentiality, 97
    lack of professionalism, 97
    tasks beyond role, 97-98
school culture, 102-103
special education, 100
classroom culture, 27-29
classroom schedule, sample, 44
collaboration, **94**
collaboration with team members, 100-101
    sufficient direction from supervising teachers, lack of, 101
    understanding team functioning, lack of, 100-101
communication issues, 17-35
    administrator's role, 33
    behavior management strategies inventory, contextual fit, 26
    classroom culture, 27-29
    communication, 20-23
        important topics of, 23-27
    conflict areas, 31-33
        lack of follow-through, 31
        lack of involvement in classroom, 33
        paraeducator age and experience, 31
        parent communication, 31
    conflict resolution, 29-30
    contextual fit of behavior management strategies inventory, 26
    flowchart of LAFF active listening strategy, 21
    high-leverage practices, 20
    learning inventory, 25
    philosophy of teaching, 25
    rapport, preference survey to assist teacher in establishing, 28
    teacher-paraeducator meeting agenda, 21
confidentiality, **94**, 97
conflict resolution, **18**
contextual fit inventory, **18**
Core Competencies for Special Education Paraeducators, **2**, 125-133
Council for Exceptional Children, **2, 38, 78, 91, 94**
    standards related to supervision, **2,** 91
    training program, 91
Council for Exceptional Children Paraeducator Competencies, 125-133
Council for the Accreditation of Educator Preparation, **2**

culture of classroom, 27-29
current practices in teaching, 81-84
   in-service development, 82
   on-the-job training, 82-84
      feedback, 83-84
         goal setting, 83
         meeting, timing of, 84
         observation/data collection, 83
         professional development, 83
   pre-service training, 81
cycle of training, sample, 48

defining supervision, 43-51
delegation, 60-61
   rationale, 60
didactic instruction, **78**
directing work, 44-46, 59-63
   feedback, 63
   identifying tasks, 60
   matching task to individual, 62
   observation, 63
   planning development, 60-62
   tasks to delegate, 60-61
   training, 63

English-language learner (ELL), **56**
English-language learner teacher, 72
environments, 13
   inclusive classroom, 13
   inclusive setting, 12-14
   life skills classroom, 13
   special education classroom, 13
   supportive, creating, 43-44
evaluation, **94**
   sample, 68
Every Student Succeeds Act, **38, 78**
evidence-based training practices, 85
experience of paraeducator as conflict area, 31

families, boundaries with, 98-99
Family Education Rights and Privacy Act (FERPA), **94**
feedback, 46-50, 63, 67-69
   form, 84
follow-through, lack of, as conflict area, 31

general education teachers, 63-64
   creating supportive environment, 63-64
   directing work, 64
   feedback, 64
   observation, 64
      feedback, 64
   training, 64
general training cycle, sample, 48
growth areas, 93-105
   collaboration with team members, 100-101
      sufficient direction from supervising teachers, lack of, 101
         understanding about team functioning, lack of, 100-101

   learner development/individual learning differences, 99
      barrier to peer interaction/teacher instruction, 99
      language barriers/missteps, 99
   professional learning/roles, 96-99
      boundaries with families, 98-99
      confidentiality, 97
      lack of professionalism, 97
      tasks beyond role, 97-98
   school culture/policies, 102-103
   special education/supports in learning environment, over reliance, 100
guidelines related to supervision, 40-42

high-leverage practices, **18**, 20
highly qualified teacher, **2**
hiring issues, 66-67
home-school liaison, 72

identifying tasks, 60
importance of supervision, 41
Individualized Education Plan (IEP), **2**
Individuals with Disabilities Education Act (IDEA), **38, 78**
Individuals with Disabilities Education Improvement Act (IDEIA), **38**
Initial Practice-Based Professional Preparation Standards for Special Educators (K-12), **38**, 107-111
Initial Practice-Based Professional Preparation Standards for Early Interventionists/Early Childhood Special Educators, 113-117
Interstate New Teacher Assessment and Support Consortium, **2**
interview protocol, sample, 67
inventory, 25-26
   behavior management strategies, contextual fit, 26
   teaching/learning, philosophy of, 25
involvement in classroom, lack of, as conflict area, 33

job description, sample, 65

lack of follow-through, as conflict area, 31
lack of involvement in classroom, as conflict area, 33
LAFF active listening strategy, flowchart, 21
LAFF method, **18**
language barriers, 99
learner development/individual learning differences, 99
   barrier to peer interaction/teacher instruction, 99
   language barriers/missteps, 99
legal requirements related to training, 80-81
lesson plan, sample, 45
liaison, home-school, 72
local education agency (LEA), **78**
LRP Media Group training program, 91

Master Teacher training program, 91
matching task to individual, 62
material rubric, training, 49-50
meeting agenda, teacher-paraeducator, 21

National Professional Development Center on Autism training program, 91
No Child Left Behind Act (NCLB), **38**
nurses, professional standing, 71

observation, importance of, 46-50, 63, 67-69
occupational therapist, **56**, 71
Ohio Center for Autism and Low Incidence Autism, Internet Module training program, 91
Ohio Partnership for Excellence in Paraprofessional Preparation training program, 91
on-the-job training, 82-84
    feedback, 83-84
    timing of meeting, 84
online training programs, 91
    Arkansas Department of Education Division of Elementary and Secondary Education, 91
    Capitol Region Education Council, 91
    Council for Exceptional Children, 91
    LRP Media Group, 91
    Master Teacher, 91
    National Professional Development Center on Autism, 91
    Ohio Center for Autism and Low Incidence Autism, Internet Module, 91
    Ohio Partnership for Excellence in Paraprofessional Preparation, 91

parent communication, as conflict area, 31
performance feedback, **78**. *See also* feedback
personal care support, **2**
philosophy of teaching/learning inventory, 25
physical therapist, **56**, 71, 137
planning development, 60-62
policies of school, 102-103
preference survey, to assist teacher in establishing rapport, 28
preparation best practices, 85-86
    adult learning, 85
    coaching, 85
    evidence-based training practices, 85
    important individuals in training, 86
    team-level training, 85
principle, important individual in training, 86
problem-solving approach, **18**
professional learning/roles, 96-99
    boundaries with families, 98-99
    confidentiality, 97
    lack of professionalism, 97
    tasks beyond role, 97-98
professionalism, **94**
protocol of interview, 67

rapport, preference survey to assist teacher, 28
rationale, delegation, 60
rehabilitation counselor, 71
related service providers, 69-72
    behavior specialist, 71-72
    English-language learner teacher, 72
    home-school liaison, 72
    nurse, 71
    occupational therapist, 71
    physical therapist, 71

rehabilitation counselor, 71
speech-language pathologist, 69
resolution of conflict, 29-30
roles/responsibilities, team members, 1-16
    environments, 13
        inclusive classroom, 13
        inclusive setting, 12-14
        life skills classroom, 13
        special education classroom, 13
    key team members, 4-12
        general education teachers, 10
        paraeducators, 4-7
        related service providers, 12
        school administrators, 11
        special education teachers, 7-9
    special education setting, 12-14
rubric, training, material, 49-50

sample evaluation, 68
sample interview protocol, 67
sample schedule, classroom, 44
sample teaching performance feedback form, 84
school culture/policies, 102-103
service providers, 69-72
    behavior specialist, 71-72
    English-language learner teacher, 72
    home-school liaison, 72
    nurse, 71
    occupational therapist, 71
    physical therapist, 71
    rehabilitation counselor, 71
    speech-language pathologist, 69
skills needed by supervising teachers, 59
special education director, important individual in training, 86
special education/supports in learning environment, over reliance, 100
special education teachers, 58-63
Specialty Set of Knowledge and Skills for Interviewers for Individuals with Deafblindness, **2**
speech-language pathologist, **56**
Standards for Professional Practice, 119-124
state-adopted paraeducator certification requirements, 40
supervision, 37-54
    Initial Practice-Based Professional Preparation Standards for Special Educators (K-12), **38**, 107-111
    Behavior Skills Training, example, 48
    CEC specialty sets, **38**
    certification requirements, 40
    classroom schedule, sample, 44
    Council for Exceptional Children, **38**
    standards related to supervision, 42
    defining, 43-51
    directing work, 44-46
    Every Student Succeeds Act, **38**
    feedback, 46-50
    general training cycle, sample, 48
    guidelines related to, 40-42
    importance of, 41
    Individuals with Disabilities Education Act (IDEA), **38**

Individuals with Disabilities Education Improvement Act (IDEIA), **38**
lesson plan, sample, 45
No Child Left Behind Act (NCLB), **38**
observation, 46-50
successful, tips for, 43
supportive environment, creating, 43-44
training, 46-47
  categories, 47
  material rubric, 49-50
supportive environment, creating, 43-44, 58-59

tasks to delegate, 60-61
teacher-paraeducator meeting agenda, 21
teaching/learning inventory, philosophy of, 25
team level training, **78**
team members, 1-16, **2**
  behavioral intervention plan (BIP), **2**
  CEC specialty sets, **2**
  Core Competencies for Special Education Paraeducators, **2**, 125-133
  Council for Exceptional Children (CEC), **2**
  Council for the Accreditation of Educator Preparation, **2**
  environments, 13
    inclusive classroom, 13
    inclusive setting, 12-14
    life skills classroom, 13
    special education classroom, 13
  general education teachers, 10
  highly qualified teacher, **2**
  Individualized Education Plan (IEP), **2**
  Interstate New Teacher Assessment and Support Consortium, **2**
  key team members, 4-12
  paraeducators, 4-7
  personal care support, **2**
  related service providers, 12
  responsibilities across environments, 13
    inclusive classroom, 13
    life skills classroom, 13
    special education classroom, 13
  school administrators, 11
  special education teachers, 7-9
  Specialty Set of Knowledge and Skills for Interviewers for Individuals with Deafblindness, **2**

Tier 1 Behavior Management, **78**
topics, conversational, in communication with paraeducators, 23-27

training, 46-47, 63, 77-92
  administrators, 86
  adult learning/evidence-based training practices, 85
  best practices for preparation, 85-87
  categories, 47
  coaching, 85
  current practices, 81-84
  cycle of, sample, 48
  data collection, 83
  district specialists, 86
  feedback, 83-84
    form, 84
  goal setting, 83
  in-service development, 82
  legal requirements related to, 80-81
  material rubric, 49-50
  meeting, timing of, 84
  observation, 83
  on-the-job training, 82-84
  online programs, 91
    Arkansas Department of Education Division of Elementary and Secondary Education, 91
    Capitol Region Education Council, 91
    Council for Exceptional Children, 91
    LRP Media Group, 91
    Master Teacher, 91
    National Professional Development Center on Autism, 91
    Ohio Center for Autism and Low Incidence Autism, Internet Module, 91
    Ohio Partnership for Excellence in Paraprofessional Preparation, 91
  plan, 87-88
    steps, 87
    template, 88
  pre-service training, 81
  professional development, 83
  special education directors, 86
  team-level training, 85

work, directing, 44-46, 59-64, 66
  feedback, 63
  identifying tasks, 60
  matching task to individual, 62
  observation, 63
  planning development, 60-62
  tasks to delegate, 60-61
  training, 63

For Product Safety Concerns and Information please contact our EU representative GPSR@taylorandfrancis.com
Taylor & Francis Verlag GmbH, Kaufingerstraße 24, 80331 München, Germany

www.ingramcontent.com/pod-product-compliance
Lightning Source LLC
Chambersburg PA
CBHW060514300426
44112CB00017B/2664